HATE AND FEAR YOUR NEIGHBORS
for the world outside the commune is ruled by Satan and leads straight to eternal damnation.

DO NOT HONOR YOUR PARENTS
for they are no more or less to you than any other grown-ups in the commune.

LIE, BETRAY AND DESTROY
if your father who has left the commune should try to gain custody of you in court, or if he should try to show you a different way of life.

STIFLE YOUR SEXUAL DESIRES
and if you do not, you should submit to the cruelest disciplines and mortify your own flesh.

SEE NOTHING, HEAR NOTHING, READ NOTHING, THINK NOTHING
but that which the Big Brothers and Big Sisters of the commune think proper.

These are some of the commandments that formed Robert Connor as a child—and almost destroyed him as a man. If you have wondered how a cult gains power over its members and how far it can go in working its will, this book gives you the frighteningly authentic answers.

WALLED IN

Big Bestsellers from SIGNET

- ☐ **THE MANHOOD CEREMONY by Ross Berliner.**
  (#E8509—$2.25)*
- ☐ **THE MAN WITHOUT A NAME by Martin Russell.**
  (#J8515—$1.95)†
- ☐ **NIGHT SHIFT by Stephen King.** (#E8510—$2.50)*
- ☐ **CARRIE by Stephen King.** (#J7280—$1.95)
- ☐ **'SALEM'S LOT by Stephen King.** (#E8000—$2.25)
- ☐ **THE SHINING by Stephen King.** (#E7872—$2.50)
- ☐ **IN COLD BLOOD by Truman Capote.** (#E7863—$2.25)
- ☐ **THE KILLING GIFT by Bari Wood.** (#J7350—$1.95)
- ☐ **TWINS by Bari Wood and Jack Geasland.** (#E8015—$2.50)
- ☐ **.44 by Jimmy Breslin and Dick Schaap.** (#E8459—$2.50)*
- ☐ **HOTEL TRANSYLVANIA by Chelsea Quinn Yarbro.**
  (#J8461—$1.95)*
- ☐ **THE GODFATHER by Mario Puzo.** (#E8508—$2.50)*
- ☐ **COMA by Robin Cook.** (#E8202—$2.50)
- ☐ **FLUKE by James Herbert.** (#J8394—$1.95)*
- ☐ **THE FOG by James Herbert.** (#E8174—$1.75)
- ☐ **THIS IS THE HOUSE by Deborah Hill.** (#J7610—$1.95)

* Price slightly higher in Canada
† Not available in Canada

To order these titles,
please use coupon on the
last page of this book.

WALLED IN

ROBERT CONNOR

A SIGNET BOOK
NEW AMERICAN LIBRARY
TIMES MIRROR

NAL BOOKS ARE ALSO AVAILABLE AT DISCOUNTS IN BULK
QUANTITY FOR INDUSTRIAL OR SALES-PROMOTIONAL USE.
FOR DETAILS, WRITE TO PREMIUM MARKETING DIVISION,
NEW AMERICAN LIBRARY, INC., 1301 AVENUE OF THE
AMERICAS, NEW YORK, NEW YORK 10019.

Copyright © 1979 by Robert Connor

All rights reserved

SIGNET TRADEMARK REG. U.S. PAT. OFF. AND FOREIGN COUNTRIES
REGISTERED TRADEMARK—MARCA REGISTRADA
HECHO EN CHICAGO, U.S.A.

SIGNET, SIGNET CLASSICS, MENTOR, PLUME AND MERIDIAN BOOKS
are published by The New American Library, Inc.,
1301 Avenue of the Americas, New York, New York 10019

First Printing, May, 1979

1 2 3 4 5 6 7 8 9

PRINTED IN THE UNITED STATES OF AMERICA

To the other children raised by Angels

NOTE

What is told in this book really happened. To protect the privacy of certain individuals, many names, including those of the author and his family, have been partly or completely changed.

ACKNOWLEDGMENTS

I am grateful to the close friends who encouraged me to write and publish this very personal story.

My thanks to Lesley Litzenberger for typing, to Arturo Islas, my English professor, to my agent, Julian Bach, and to the editors at The New American Library.

Also, I thank *Time* Magazine for permission to reprint the excerpt from the October 13, 1952, issue.

The manuscript as a I originally wrote it lacked some of the professional quality needed for publication. I am grateful to John Greenya, who edited portions of the book.

Finally, I thank everyone I interviewed, and in particular those who provided the written documents I needed.

A Personal Prologue

Six years ago I left the only community I ever knew and entered the world. Six years. Yet I still find it hard to call my father "Dad." I would like to tell my mother that I love her, but I simply cannot. I want someone to hold me and to whisper, "I love you. I really do." But if someone said that to me, I know I would cry, because it would be the first time I ever heard those words. I am twenty-seven years old.

For years I have felt that I *should* be able to explain all of this to someone; at the same time I fear that no one would ever truly understand. Because I know this conflict is all in my mind, I tell myself that I will change tomorrow. But then I said the same thing yesterday.

My story began when my parents, under the influence of religious enthusiasm, left the world, left me and my four brothers, and, finally, left each other. But I choose to begin the story with the events of a day in late March of 1962, when I was twelve years old. To any normal child, it would have been a very important day.

I was not, strictly speaking, a normal child. Nor, for that matter, were any of the thirty-eight other children with whom I grew up. What made us other than normal (for we were all certainly normal physically and intellectually) was that, on a particular religious feast day in the third or fourth year of our lives, we were taken from our parents.

From that day forward we were raised, and lived, communally. All the children ate together, prayed together, and were schooled together. We never again slept in the same quarters as our parents, but were under the constant supervision of other adults, called Angels. Each night we slept in dormitories, the boys on one floor, the girls on another.

After a few years, although we knew who our parents were, we attached no special significance to the relationship. We were in fact taught not to. Children of the same parents were not any closer because of that blood relationship. But that did not seem odd to us, for no one was supposed to be close to anyone else; all children were forbidden to have what was termed a "particular friendship."

We were part of an outcast and unofficial Roman Catholic religious community established by Father Leonard Feeney, a once-famous and then excommunicated Jesuit priest, and Mrs. Catherine Goddard Clarke, a devout but dictatorial woman. Almost a hundred strong in the late 1940s and early 1950s, we were the true believers who refused to give in to the prevailing liberalism of the day. Our cause became known to Catholics everywhere, and to many non-Catholics as well, as the Boston Heresy Case.

What began as a polite disagreement over the doctrine of no salvation outside the Catholic Church (which we stubbornly held) soon flared into the most bitter of controversies. Eventually violence erupted, and every Sunday when we demonstrated on the Boston Common, there was a need for the Boston mounted police. Then, suddenly, in 1958 the organization turned its back on its enemies. It moved from Cambridge to the small farming community town of Still River, a part of Harvard, Massachusetts. It remains there to this day.

I was born into the community in 1950, and I did not leave on my own until I was twenty-one years old. I was neither the first nor the last of the children to leave. Eventually almost all would leave, but I did stay longer than many others. The depth of my faith was not the reason I stayed as long as I did. I stayed because of guilt feelings reinforced by a regime of fear.

At first, it was a fear of punishment. Physical punishment, at times severe and on occasion brutal, was a fundamental part of the children's lives. Also, we had an extraordinarily strong fear of spiritual punishment. I wonder if very many people today have any real fear of hell. I doubt it, but for us it was so real as to be almost tangible. "Eternal damnation in the fires of Hell" was no mere phrase to us.

Later, I stayed because of guilt before God, disgrace before the rest of our community, and even a slight fear of the outside world. We had been raised, purposely, with little or no knowledge of the "corrupt world" outside our doors—no newspapers, radio, or TV—and the thought of joining it was at times as upsetting as it was attractive.

I had lived my life under strict discipline for those first twenty-one years, and when I finally left, that self-discipline helped me to make the adjustment. The habits of hard work and single-mindedness enabled me to graduate from MIT, complete a master's degree at Stanford (in electrical engineering), and land a job with a large electronics corporation.

Some of the other children have not been so fortunate. Of the original thirty-nine, five women and one man are still in the order. Several of those who left have had serious problems with alcohol and drugs. Some have had trouble with authorities of various types. One had a breakdown.

My relations with the opposite sex have at times been nerve-racking and even frightening. Several of the other children have admitted to similar problems.

The religious order into which I was born was an outgrowth of the St. Benedict Center of Cambridge (and then Still River), Massachusetts, and its members were called Slaves of the Immaculate Heart of Mary. With each new year, I can see more clearly just how extensive that slavery was for the children. I am beginning to see not just how much was kept from me, but also how much was taken away.

I have remained in contact with many of the other former Center children, and when I told them I might write a book about our upbringing, their reactions were strong but mixed. They were determined to express their own feelings freely, yet some feared to criticize or—even worse—to embarrass their lifelong superiors. I knew that same dichotomy of feeling.

We children were the by-products of a religious fanaticism that had run rampant, and that in doing so had seriously hurt many people. However, I believe that telling *my* own story may help others whose lives were also affected by the Center to come to grips with *their* own problems. Also it may save someone else from the effects of similarly misguided "goodness." And, perhaps, by telling my story, I can begin to open up as a person, to more easily express my emotions.

My story begins in the late winter of 1962, just weeks after my twelfth birthday. It was a day on which something very important happened to me. However, as was always the way of life at the Center, it would be years and years before I fully understood the event or felt its significance.

Chapter One

I raced down the hill and across the lawn. The warm spring weather made me feel very athletic. I wore a dark-blue sweater and the "uniform" of all the Little Brothers: white shirt, blue trousers, and black shoes. I scrambled into the apple tree at the foot of the lawn beside St. Anne's House, where we and the Big Sisters and the Little Sisters lived, and in ten seconds was clutching the highest branch. I thought I was the most agile of all the nineteen of the Little Brothers, and I looked around to see if there were any grown-ups who might have seen me climb so skillfully.

From the top of the tree, some fifteen feet up, I could almost see into the long corridor, directly above ours, where the twenty Little Sisters had their cubicles. I didn't try to look into the cubicles, because that would have been a terrible sin against holy purity. I turned my gaze from St. Anne's House toward the barn. I could see the silo and the cows in the pasture outside St. Marcian's Barn, where the Big Brothers stacked the hay.

A crow flew out from Our Lady's Hills. It went over the barns, across the pasture, the chicken coop, and St. Therese's Field, and disappeared among the pines in the woods. I tried to see if the flooding from the river at the foot of our property had spread any farther, but it was too far away.

All the other Little Brothers were playing on the lawn or in the branches below me. Looking up the hill, I could see St. Therese's, and waited, hoping one of the grown-ups would cross the yard and see me at the very top of the tree. No one did.

A short time later we were called from our fun by two long blasts of the Angel's whistle. We hurried up the lawn to find Sister Mary Judith waiting for us. When I saw who it was, I felt my stomach begin its familiar tightening; Sister Mary Judith gave out most of the harsh punishments. She dismissed all but five of us—Michael, Benedict, Matthew, Paul, and me. My name was Luke. (I had been baptized Robert, but four years later my name was changed to Luke.)

Fortunately, Sister Mary Judith did not seem angry. In fact, even though her tone was serious, she seemed to be trying to be pleasant. As we walked across the wide, carefully tended yard, she told us that Sister Catherine wanted to see us in the Office.

"The Office," I repeated silently, "she wants to see us in the Office." I gripped the rosary beads in my trouser pocket and promised Our Lady a rosary "if I get out of this somehow." I tried to think of what we might have done wrong.

Matthew was always in trouble and Michael and Paul sometimes, so I felt uncomfortable being grouped with them. Besides that, I was one of the Five, the five oldest. Michael was one of the Nine, Paul one of the Seven, and both Matthew and Benedict were among the ten youngest children. It seemed strange being called to the Office with younger Little Brothers from the Nine, Seven, and Ten. They were not at my table* and I rarely associated with them in my activities. I simply could not understand how we could all be in trouble together.

Although I knew I could be punished, I didn't think Sister Catherine would give me the B.P., or Big Punisher, anymore. She now sent the oldest boys to Brother Isidore, and I was twelve. I had been sent to him several months before, and he had spanked me and Michael with a plank of wood, a two-by-four. Everyone in the house, I was certain, had heard our screams. For days I had faced no one; I was so ashamed.

Sister Catherine had punished me only once with the B.P. The details were still vivid in my mind. All the other Little Brothers had been called out of the corridor, and I, as ordered, had waited in my cubicle. She had come down with the B.P. in the black bag. I had begged for one more chance, but the punishment was inevitable. With all my clothes off except my underpants, I was told to lean across the bed. The black bag had opened, and a long, black rubber hose had come out.

My hands clutched the mattress and I stared at a knot of wood on the wall. I waited. I sensed the swing of her arm, and then I screamed as the hose slapped across my back and

*The children were organized in groups called tables because we sat at the same tables at meals.

stung my stomach with its tip. I jumped around, cringing on the bed, and turned my face up to her. She looked away with what I thought was horror. She had seen the pain and the panic in my face. Desperately, I pleaded with her to stop, but she had thrust me over the bed. I had to take my medicine like every other Little Brother. I thought the blows had gone on forever, often landing in the same spot, but it was actually only ten lashes. I had been lucky.

I remembered the pain and also the shame. That night, when my Angel, Sister Julia, had come in during my bath to give me Dr. Truth's medicine, I had not wanted to stand up out of the suds of the bathwater. But I had to, and she saw the purpled hose tracks across my body.

We entered St. Therese's House. I could see the fear in Matthew's eyes as he walked as close to Paul as he could get.

When we arrived at the Office, Sister Mary Judith tapped on the door. No one answered. I could hear talking.

I knew what the Office looked like inside. There was Sister Catherine's desk over at the window, Father's big red cushion chair and footrest, a telephone by the other window, Father's closet and the cubicle where we confessed our sins every Saturday night. On the wall opposite the windows hung a large plaque of the Last Supper. I wondered if all the Angels were in there waiting for us. My knees felt weak and I wanted to sit down.

At the very moment I am writing this, fifteen years later, I am going through a smaller version of the gut-wrenching fear that gripped me on that special day.

Our entire life as children was lived in the service of two clear goals: honoring God and avoiding trouble. The former was frightening in a long-range sense, but the prospect of physical punishment was so real to almost everyone of us that it replaced, it transcended, any spiritual concerns.

Being called to the Office—Sister Catherine and Father Feeney's office—was an unusual happening, a rare event. I could not remember it happening to me in a long time, and certainly not in the company of those particular four boys, all of them younger than I.

I would eventually remember that those four Little Brothers were also my own little brothers in a blood relationship. I was twelve years old, but that distinction meant nothing to me. All I can remember, in recalling the fear that coursed through me that day, was worrying about myself.

Sister Mary Judith knocked again, and Sister Catherine asked us to come in. She was sitting in her chair across the room by her desk. She inclined her head to one side and looked at us lovingly. Could it be? Had we done something good? Her eyes made me feel that she understood each of us so well. I knew by her smile that she wanted us to feel at ease; yet, even when she was smiling, there was something fearful about her. It was the same face, the same eyes and teeth, the same deep furrows below the cheeks that I had so often seen in her anger, and that were always the first sign of frightening punishments to follow. As usual, she called us "darlings," and asked us to sit down on the bench against the wall. I started to cross my legs, but luckily remembered it was against the Rule.

There were Angels there: Sister Susanna, Matthew and Paul's Angel; Sister Julia, my Angel; and, of course, Sister Mary Judith, Angel for Michael and Benedict. But I hardly took note of them because someone else was there—Sister Mary Agnes. I wondered why. All she did for us was to make and mend our clothes. (Had we torn or soiled some of them? I had ripped my parka last week climbing up to my tree house.)

Sister Catherine did not look at us now, but at the floor, as though something serious was on her mind. Her smile left her face. All the Angels were trying to be pleasant, though obviously quite concerned. It was useless trying to guess, and I was afraid, so I waited. I knew that whatever followed had been well-planned by them, and this added to the suspense.

Sister Catherine looked up and glanced at the empty chair between me and Sister Mary Agnes, who was seated right beside her. Nodding at the chair and then suddenly looking at me, she asked if we noticed that someone was missing. That chair was usually left empty for Christ the King, as Sister Catherine had often told us in her loving way, so I really did not expect to see anybody there. I looked at Sister Mary Agnes and then at the five of us, and suddenly someone came to mind.

I looked at everyone again, and puzzled by what this could mean, yet also wondering whether I should suggest it, I asked hesitantly if they were thinking of Brother Mark. Sister

Catherine seemed a bit surprised at my response, but she slowly nodded yes.

Her nod fired my imagination. What was wrong? He couldn't have died. Maybe he was very sick? Sister Mary Agnes seemed sad, and by looking closer I saw that her eyes were red. Her hands were clasped together in her lap, and her lips were quivering as she turned her head away and looked down.

She and Brother Mark were part of my own family. I knew that much. They were my parents. She was my mother and Brother Mark was my father. All five of us—myself, Michael, Paul, Matthew, and Benedict—were their children. That was why, when we had a community meeting on four or five of the big feast days of the year, we always went to talk to them before we wandered about the living room visiting other groups like ours. *That* was why they had called the five of us into the Office.

I could not remember the last time I had seen Brother Mark. I tried to think if I had seen him going to Holy Communion that morning or the day before or any time that week. Then I realized that I had not noticed him around for some time.

Looking at Sister Mary Agnes, Sister Catherine told us that Brother Mark had left and had gone into the world. At this, Sister Mary Agnes started sobbing, but she quickly tried to suppress it as she repeated what Sister Catherine had said. Never before had I seen one of the grown-ups (the Angels, or Sisters, or Brothers) cry, and I felt that something really tragic had happened. Shocked and confused, I asked why he had left. Had they sent him away? They said that he had left because he did not want to live here anymore. It seemed strange to me that he would want to leave our community and go out into the world, which was so wicked.

I remembered others who had suddenly left: Sister Jane Frances and Sister Mary Ignatius. One had come back for a few months and then left again, and the other had come back as Sister Petronilla, who was still with us.

Certainly Brother Mark would change his mind. I asked if he would ever come back. Sister Catherine said that he had gone for good and that she did not think he would ever be back. Seeing everyone so sad—and Sister Mary Agnes tearfully looking at us as each of us spoke out at once between periods of dead silence—made me feel like crying. But I did not want the Angels or the other Little Brothers to see me with tears in my eyes. It would be too embarrassing. I was strong and I did not let myself feel sad.

Sister Catherine tried to explain that Brother Mark had forsaken Our Lady and had decided that he wanted to live in the world. But all this made no sense. We were having such a good time. We had two donkeys and a pony to ride, and Sister Catherine said we might get some more ponies. Also I looked forward to the fun of planting my own vegetable garden in the summer and building hermitages in the woods like the saints did. Why would anyone want to live in the world? Surely he would change his mind. It was too bad that I could not have talked to him before he left. I would have convinced him to stay.

I was terrified by the idea that he would lose his soul because he had left us. Sister Mary Agnes tried to encourage us by telling us to pray that we remain good and always do Our Lady's will. Sister Catherine reminded us that the devil is out to get souls, and so we always have to be obedient and continually beg Our Blessed Mother for her protection.

It was hard to imagine how one of the grown-ups could go bad. They were always good, but then the stories of the saints and martyrs proved that even the best can sell their souls to the devil.

I was even more confused as I listened to the conversation change. Sister Mary Agnes became happy when Benedict, the youngest, told her how he always said his rosary, and Michael piped in to say the devil would never get him because he said five rosaries every day. The tone of the gathering had switched to a happier mood; everyone was talking at once. One of the Angels assured Sister Catherine that indeed Matthew had been very good the last two days. Matthew beamed with satisfaction as Sister Catherine told him how pleased she was to hear that. Sister Mary Agnes listened with great interest as Paul told her about his plan to become a missionary when he grew up.

I didn't try to join the conversation. It seemed so empty. I felt sad, confused, and sorry for myself. We had just been given special attention, not for doing something wrong, but in order to be informed that one of the Big Brothers had left. We were just children and what the Big Brothers did was none of our business. I realized then that he must have been someone very special to the five of us. Was he gone forever?

Sister Catherine turned to me and asked how my tree house was coming along. I had told her about it the previous night, just before the meeting of Our Lady's Army. She had warned me to be very careful, because she knew a little boy who had broken his arm when he fell out of a tree house just like mine. I had convinced her that it was safe because I was always very careful. Last night, I had wanted to ask her for special permission to use some tar paper that had been used on the new chicken coop, but I had decided to wait for another opportunity. Too many children were listening, and I thought that they might also ask for some. I knew the tar paper was too expensive to be used on children's projects, but I hoped an exception would be made for me. Now seemed the perfect time. She was being so kind to everyone. I told Sister Catherine that my house could be completed as soon as I found some tar paper, "just a little for the walls and roof." She was very concerned, and when I told her that there was some tar paper left over from the chicken coop, she gave me special permission to take it. She called Sister Julia over and told her that I had special permission to use the tar paper if Sister Sylvia did not want it. Sister Julia assured us that she would take care of it, and that she was quite sure that the tar paper was a leftover. Sister Catherine asked Sister Mary Agnes if she had heard about the ingenious tree house I had built all by myself. I forgot all about Brother Mark and became very excited as I described my plans.

The excitement I felt was not increased by the fact that Sister Mary Agnes had taken a sudden interest. The fact that anyone took a special interest was the point.

If a passing Big Brother had stopped and admired my tree house, I might well have poured my heart out to him—as long as I was sure no one could see me and there was no possible way that I could be caught.

We had spent nearly an hour in the Office when Sister Catherine mentioned that it was very late and that she had another appointment. She told us not to talk about Brother Mark to the other Little Brothers. As we left the Office I told Michael that only we were supposed to know about Brother Mark's leaving, and that it was no one else's business. I was proud that we were somehow special. I liked the idea that we were the only Little Brothers who knew.

After lunch I went to the chapel beside the dining room. We were supposed to pay a visit to Our Lord in the tabernacle after each meal. As I knelt there, I heard a car horn. At first it was a few short honks, but then it sounded like the horn got stuck. Then I remembered. It was just Father Feeney, waiting for Sister Catherine. Father always did that when she did not come out right away. Sister Catherine never minded. "Isn't that sweet of him?" she would say. "He is so concerned that I'll be late."

As I walked across the yard I saw two of our black cars parked in the driveway. Father, Sister Catherine, and Brother Alphonsus Maria, the driver, were in one, and Brother Leonard Mary in the other. Sister Catherine always left the Center Saturday afternoon and came back early Sunday morning. I was very familiar with her schedule. She also had to be away the latter half of Sunday and Wednesday, and she would reappear late in the morning the following day. I knew I would see her the next day just before the sermon started at First Breakfast (our code word for Mass). Brother Basil was smiling as he stood by the car chatting with Sister Catherine in his appreciative way. As I walked by, I saw them watching me, watching my behavior now that I knew what had happened. Sister Catherine saw me and smiled. I returned the smile, waved, and hurried along as they resumed their conversation. I felt like just any other Little Brother.

The afternoon passed according to the Saturday schedule. After our nap at 2:30 we all went down to Slaves' Field. The Little Sisters played in the Little Children's Field, where my tree house was, so I did not get to work on it.

At 4:45 each table, accompanied by the assigned Angel, walked across the yard from St. Anne's to St. Therese's House, making the usual salute, the Sign of the Cross, and throwing a kiss to the statue of Our Lady. Entering the chapel, we took great care to be quiet so we would not disturb the Big Brothers and Big Sisters at prayer. (Sister Catherine would tell us to be "as quiet as Indians.") It was not my turn to serve as altar boy, so I went to my bench on the right side of the altar. When the whole community had collected for Tea (our word for Benediction) and Rosary, I tried to look back among the grown-ups to see if I noticed anyone else missing. I could not see several Big Sisters. I knew that they could be in the kitchen preparing supper or off the property on a bookselling trip. I waited for the prayers at the end of Tea, when Father usually would say a "Memorare for the booksellers." That evening he said one for the sisters on the road, so I postponed my head-counting until the next morning, Sunday, when everyone would be home.

We left chapel when Tea was over, and we went to our places at table. We stood in silence until the Angelus bell rang and Father led the prayers. As we started eating, the Roman martyrology was read. It commemorated the death of the saint or saints whose feast day we would celebrate the next day. That night I paid close attention to the stories of the heroic saints being tortured, eaten by wild animals, burned alive, beheaded, or whatever fate earned them the right to be crowned in heaven.

I always listened closely to these accounts, for I was frightened by the idea that someday I might be called upon to lay down my life for the Faith. I could not imagine myself siding with the devil and turning away from Our Lady as Brother Mark had done. Though I was sure it would be hard for me to have the courage to face a painful death, I knew that somehow I would be able to do it because the alternative of spending an eternity in everlasting flames was much worse. I could not understand how Brother Mark had chosen hell. He certainly was not forced into it by the threat of martyrdom. He chose the wicked world on his own, and that just did not make sense to me.

Sister Julia brought in our table's dessert at the end of supper. She said, *"Deo gratias,"* and we answered, *"Semper Deo gratias et Maria,"* which meant the silence was over and we could talk until grace was said and dish-washing started. I did not have much to say, so I listened to the conversation at the table.

Louis Mary and James Mary were arguing over who won the war that afternoon. Apparently they had been playing army and navy. I did not enjoy playing group games where someone else decided on the rules. My favorite game was cowboys and Indians. Like a real Indian, I could climb trees or hide wherever my imagination led me. But my own projects were beginning to take more of my time. I enjoyed them more because I could plan them myself. I had carved a crucifix, painted a holy card, started a vegetable garden, and dug a cave in the side of a hill. Now my tree house was well under way. Sister Julia had forgotten to ask about the tar paper I needed, so I reminded her before we said grace.

It was confession night. After supper our table went to the beginning of the line because it was Sister Julia's turn for D.N. As I entered the little room in the Office, I tried to make up my mind whether I should use the words "many," "several," or "a few," for each of my usual sins. I knelt down and hoped Father had forgotten my last week's confession.

"Bless me, Father, for I have sinned. I was distracted during First Breakfast and Tea and Rosary many times. I broke the Rule a few times. I was disobedient a few times." I had decided to say "many times" for the first one, even though I felt it was probably just "several times." I always liked to be on the safe side.

Father continued reading his breviary. He wasn't paying attention, so I knew that he wouldn't scold me for what I had confessed.

"That's all," I said.

Father looked up and, blessing me, said, "For your penance say six Our Fathers and six Hail Marys." I prayed the act of contrition, was absolved from my sins, and left.

As I entered the front room, I saw Brother Leonard Mary kissing the relics of the saints on the wall. I knelt down before the statue of the Infant of Prague to say my penance.

I thought it was ridiculous that my penance was twice as long as last week's, even though I had broken the Rule only "a few times" instead of "many times." Suddenly, I became distracted. I thought about Brother Mark. I remained kneeling. Then I saw that Brother Leonard Mary was already over in the corner, blessing himself with the flesh and bones of the Popes. I didn't want him to think I had been very bad, that Father had given me many prayers to say. I blessed myself and rose, pretending I had finished my penance. I threw a kiss to Our Lady's picture and returned to help with the dishes.

None of us enjoyed doing dishes, so we tried to do them as quickly as possible. Our table was done before the others. We had a head start because Sister Julia had to take D.N. She received Father's permission to take the Blessed Sacrament from St. Therese's House to St. Anne's, where we lived. As I was folding the dishrag, I suddenly thought of our many top secrets: D.N. for Dominus Noster, which was Latin for Our Lord; First Breakfast for Mass; Tea for Benediction; and several others. I wondered if Brother Mark would reveal these to our enemies in the world.

Today, when I think back on our mania for secrecy I cannot easily dismiss it as wrongheaded or foolish. The adult members of the Center were convinced that they were under siege from the outside world, the world of nonbelievers, and they passed that belief on to us, the children. We had no cause or reason to question the validity of those adult convictions.

Believing as we did, we understood the need to give secret names to a wide variety of what should have been harmless, even insignificant objects, people, and events.

St. Benedict Center had to succeed. It was the last repository of truth, and thus secrecy and subterfuge were not wrong. They were justified because they were necessary.

I had to believe that the Center was sincere in all that it did and said.

While we were making our usual visit to Our Lord in the chapel after dishes, Sister Julia came in and checked to make sure all the blinds were drawn. Each of the chapel windows had a special wooden border to prevent people in the world from looking in or, we were told, from trying to shoot at Father. Father Feeney went up and took a pix, which contained the hosts, from the tabernacle. As he walked down the aisle, he quickly handed it to Sister Julia, who was kneeling down in the benches alongside. She waited until Father left, and then, when she arose, we also got up. We rang the bell hanging by the door as we left the chapel to warn everyone that we were coming. As we passed through the dining rooms, everyone whispered, "D.N.," and they dropped to their knees, bowing their heads.

I always felt embarrassed when I accompanied the Angel with D.N. I wondered if some would think that I enjoyed seeing everyone kneeling in the traditional position of adoration as I walked through. I wished that there were some outward way I could show that I too was adoring Our Lord.

At the seven-o'clock bell for silence I quickly got ready for bed and waited in my cubicle for Sister Julia to take us upstairs to the chapel to say our night prayers. It was dark in the chapel and the flame in the sanctuary lamp made the shadows of the statues dance noiselessly on the walls. The nose of Saint Anne was huge as it darted in and out of the corner. Sister Julia said an extra prayer to Our Lady for special protection against the devil, and I knew what she was thinking of. The devil had won over Brother Mark.

I looked into the dark corner. I thought of the time the devil had broken the stove pipe in Cambridge. It was at night and I had been in the kitchen when Philip Mary came screaming out of his room. He screamed and he screamed. His mouth, eyes, and hands, I could still see them wide open with terror. Then I had started screaming until the Brother in charge had come downstairs. The devil had knocked the crucifix off the wall and it had fallen and broken the stove.

Sister Julia prayed for our own special intentions. I quietly asked Our Lady to send Brother Mark back, since she was all powerful and could do it if she wanted to.

I was very tired that night, but for many hours I was not able to sleep. A lot had happened, and as I lay in bed looking up at the pattern of holes in the tiled ceiling and waited for the corridor lights to be switched off, I started thinking of all I remembered of Brother Mark. I was very sad, and yet in a way I could feel but not explain there was a kind of sweetness about that day.

Until that day, I had not fully realized that one of the Big Brothers had somehow belonged especially to me. Sister Catherine and the Angels had thought that I should be told personally about his leaving. But why? I wondered if he liked me a lot, more than all the other Little Brothers. If he did, then why did he leave?

As soon as the lights went out, I no longer tried to suppress my tears, as I thought over and over again that someone who could perhaps have been very close to me had gone forever. I turned my face into the pillow, trying to smother my sobs so that none of the Little Brothers in the cubicles near mine would hear me.

I loved crying; it made me feel good.

I stopped crying when I heard Sister Mary Judith at the end of the corridor. She was pulling the bench across the fire door so Michael would not be able to walk upstairs in his sleep and into the Little Sisters' cubicles. Then I could hear her coming down the corridor to turn on the night-light. I wiped my eyes. I did not want anyone to know I had been crying.

Sister Mary Judith always made me feel nervous because of her severity. Just this morning she had punished Jerome Mary (J.M.) because he wet his bed again. This time she used the strap. Because J.M. was very stubborn, the Angels and Sister Judith had tried everything—the strap, the Big Punisher, bread and water for days, hot water, matches, everything. Nothing worked. J.M.'s screams always made my stomach go tense, but I knew it was all for his own good. Nobody wanted him to spend all of eternity in the fires of hell.

Anyone who reads this today and thinks I am exaggerating the nature and the extent of the punishment is wrong.

I am continually aware, as I write, of the ease with which I could leave reality and slip into sensationalism. But that is not the way I want to tell the story of my life. There is no need for embellishment. The truth is harsh enough.

"Middle-sized crimes" meant you got the B.P. or Big Punisher, a piece of tough rubber hose. The disobedient Little Brother or Little Sister would receive many hard strokes on the naked back, legs, and buttocks. Those children (few in number) who repeated their transgressions often got the same punishment, but this time their arms and legs were tied to their bedposts.

As we grew older the punishments were no less physical, but often a psychological element was introduced. When that aspect failed, as it did with only the most stubborn and difficult of the children, the Center reverted to simple brute force. A boy would be turned over to a man who would beat him with his fists, a belt, or a two-by-four. On rare occasions, for instructional purposes, an audience would be required.

We never missed the point of the lesson. It was not at all subtle. All we knew was that it worked.

When I thought about punishments, the two faces that always came to my mind were those of Sister Mary Judith (her lips pinched as tight, in anger, as the bun of black-and-gray hair rolled up against the back of her head) and Sister Catherine (she also wore her hair in a bun like all the Big Sisters, but her color was a golden red. She smiled a lot, but her eyes through the plain glasses showed her determination to make us obey). I was always very careful to do what I was supposed to do.

Each morning after I made my bed and placed my crucifix on the pillow, I carefully mopped under my bed and dusted my bureau and windowsill. Whenever we had army inspection, my cubicle always passed. And when I got dressed each morning, I made sure to pull the curtain across the doorway of my cubicle and catch it between the bed and the plywood wall. That way none of the other Little Brothers could see me getting dressed—and no one could accuse me of trying to see them. Anthony's curtain was usually open, but I never looked in.

It would be a mortal sin if I saw him when he had taken off his pajamas, and I was afraid to tell such sins in confession. Father Feeney would get very mad.

Every morning during First Breakfast (Mass) I would get distracted, and then immediately I would start to worry about the punishments I would receive after death for not thinking about the prayers. I knew about the heavenly angel standing among us taking down all the names of the Little Brothers and Little Sisters who were allowing themselves to be distracted. Someday I would be holy like the Big Brothers and Big Sisters, even as holy as Brother Giles, whom I considered the holiest, and I could make up for my sinfulness and selfishness.

Whenever Father Feeney warned in a sermon, angrily rubbing his hands together, that God would punish those who had selfish interests, I paid strict attention. It seemed as though he were looking straight at me. I would feel so guilty. I would not turn my eyes or bow my head, because then it would be obvious that I was culpable and he would get even angrier. And then I would of course feel other eyes on me, which would make my face grow red with shame, and I would want to scream and run out of the chapel. So I would return Father's stare until he grew calm again.

I never wanted to be punished. Even just being made to stay in one's cubicle was embarrassing. This morning Thomas Mary had to stay in his because of a show of disobedience; two days ago, in Slaves' Field, he had not responded immediately when the Angel blew her whistle, which was probably why he lost his Obedience badge.

Every week, the Angels sent reports to Sister Catherine concerning our behavior. On Friday mornings, each Angel turned in a list of the badges that the children at their table had earned or lost. That evening when we went to Tea at 5:00 P.M., we all had to file into the chapel wearing pink sashes on which were glued the badges we had earned for our good performance the previous week.

This week I had received all my badges, which of course I knew I deserved. I wore the pin of the Order of the Most Precious Blood, which was only for the best children. As I genuflected before the altar on my way to the Little Brothers' benches, I had taken great pride in letting the Big Brothers and Big Sisters see that I had not lost any of the six badges. I had received my Devotion, Obedience, Humility, General Manners, Table Manners, and Curiosity badges. Thomas Mary, I remembered, had lost his Curiosity, which was usual because he was always paying attention to things that were none of his business. He had also lost his Obedience and that was more serious than losing one's Devotion. So it was no surprise to me that he was being kept in his cubicle for the morning. At least he was lucky that he did not get the strap.

I did not like thinking about badges. The week had been bad. No table had won the flag, there was no table at which everyone had received all of his or her badges. Friday evening after supper Sister Catherine had read the list of badges that each person had lost. She had told us how displeased she was, and that she wanted to see an immediate improvement. Only one Little Brother, J.M., had lost his sash, which meant that he had lost all his badges, as he often did. He was the worst of the Little Brothers, and an example of sheer bad will.

He was so wicked that he had even taken off his pajamas one night in the middle of the corridor when the Angel was gone. We thought he was possessed and had collected some prayers from our books, *Mary Speaks* and *Mary My Hope*, to drive the devil out. But one of the Angels found out and told us that only Father could exorcise him. We could not understand why he was deliberately and continually disobedient to all the Angels. No matter how often or how hard he got the strap or the B.P., he never stopped wetting his bed. Matthew was the next worst, but he had not lost his sash for several weeks.

When I heard Sister Mary Judith leave our corridor, I relaxed, and my thoughts returned to Brother Mark. I recalled that I never really liked Brother Mark any more than anyone else. He had chatted with us on only a few occasions a year, at community meetings, and I always spent most of my time visiting others, like Brother Giles (whose holiness fascinated me). I also remembered I had told Brother Fabian nearly a year ago that I liked him the best and that if he wanted to leave the Center secretly I would go with him. He had asked me if I would miss anyone here, and I said no. When he mentioned Brother Mark, I told him that he, Brother Fabian, was my favorite person.

I enjoyed my special relationship with Brother Fabian. It had started about three years before, when he was the sacristan for that week and therefore in charge of the altar boys. He took me downstairs to the cellar to spank me for not folding my hands during First Breakfast. However, he changed his mind and told me that he would forgive me and that he liked me the most of all the Little Brothers. I was very grateful for his show of mercy that day and I was deeply touched by his interest in me.

From then on, I returned his friendship as best I could, by winks and smiles when no one was looking.

I knew it was wrong to have particular friendships. Sister Catherine often reminded us that no particular friendships were allowed. However, she was referring to relationships among the children, because the only contact between the children and the grown-ups was through the Angels and the two or three Big Brothers who were in charge of the altar boys. I thought my friendship with Brother Fabian was safe. No one would ever guess that my best friend was one of the Big Brothers.

Brother Fabian had told me many secrets that no other children knew. He told me about the time Brother Henry Maria ran away one night from the Center by stealing one of our cars and leaving it in a garage in Boston. But I was puzzled by why he should want to run away.

Brother Fabian was always truthful to me. When I asked him if Baby Jesus really gave us our Christmas presents, he admitted that the Angels bought them for us. He told me that the baby lambs were born in the barn (Sister Catherine had announced that the Center had bought them). For a time, I began to doubt almost everything I was taught. He became my special informant and I used him to help me get at the real truth of what we were being told by the Angels. But I did not consider the Angels wrong. I knew they told us these things to protect us. It was for our own good.

There were certain facts that I believed I should not know. When he offered to explain how babies were born, I said that it was dangerous for me to learn about it. I was very aware of the great troubles Sister Catherine was taking to protect us from such things. However, I wanted to be able to see the whole picture, and I appreciated his information. He trusted me and I liked him for that.

Our friendship grew until I gradually realized that maybe he was not so holy himself, even though he was a Big Brother. On several occasions he had done things that worried me, because I thought they might be sins against holy purity. I decided to ease off on our friendship a little, though I did not want to end it. Then after Christmas he disappeared, and I knew that he had left. I was surprised that he had not even indicated to me that he was planning to leave.

He was my favorite person. I liked him better than Brother Mark, and he had left me, I feared, forever.

Brother Mark, I began to realize as I lay in bed, was someone I should have liked more. Though I knew it was wrong to have particular friendships, even those based on family ties, maybe I should have at least showed him more interest by staying longer with his group during community meetings. I usually left because he was kind of boring. Other Big Brothers were much more interesting. Brother Mark always acted as though he were reluctantly content with everything, and he did not seem like the type who would have the nerve to leave. Because he would look out the window while in chapel instead of being absorbed in prayer like the others, I never thought he was very holy.

My tears had dried up and I started to recall my earliest memories, in the hope of finding some explanation of why Brother Mark had been unhappy.

Before we had moved out to Still River in the country, we had lived in the city of Cambridge in a group of houses surrounded by a big red fence. The fence had been built to protect us from the corrupt and evil world outside. Brother Mark, Sister Mary Agnes, and each of their five sons, as we came along, had lived in a small red house called St. John's. It was at one end of the cluster of houses where the twelve families in the community lived. My family lived upstairs and Brother Isidore's family downstairs. I could only remember a few distinct episodes at St. John's. I remembered asking Sister Mary Agnes if she would get us a baby girl instead of another boy.

I remembered the time Michael and I were walking down the stairs at night toward the front door, tripping in our pajamas as we trailed a blanket behind us. Our venture was interrupted when Sister Mary Agnes and Brother Mark walked in the door and caught us out of bed. I recalled the time Sister Mary Agnes showed me such kindness when I was sick. She did not make me eat a bowl of soup she had just prepared. When not eating with her, I always had to eat my whole dinner. I could still see myself sitting at the table by a window with the orange alphabet soup before me.

I remembered the day I had peeked out of my window and had ridiculed some boys in the parking lot below. Their response was a brick through my window. I had enjoyed the long line of people who had come to see the broken glass that evening.

I recalled another episode, when I was coughing into a sink, with Sister Mary Agnes bending me over as she realized that I had swallowed the mercury end of my thermometer. This was the only close call that I actually remembered, though I had heard that it was only one of several. Oddly, I was pleased to learn that while still a baby I had drunk a cup of Clorox and had kissed a hot iron.

Those memories triggered others. I remembered the time I had asked Sister Mary Agnes, "Aren't you afraid of being eaten by a big lion?"

"Oh, yes, that would be very frightening; I would be scared to death to be eaten by a lion."

"Then would you give up the Faith so you wouldn't be fed to the lions?"

"Oh, that is different. God would give us the strength if we were to be martyred."

I was not happy with that answer. My problem remained. I did not want to be martyred and I did not want to go to hell either.

There is no way of exaggerating the role fear and guilt played in my early years.

"Eternal damnation in the fires of Hell"—it was not just a phrase as it is to most Catholics today. It was a real and a dreadful fear, one that was intensified by the sermons of Father Feeney and the vivid impromptu "lectures" of Sister Catherine.

Depending on my own evaluation of my own religious behavior, I was facing either the distinct possibility of eternal hellfire or its strong probability. However, martyrs were never sent to hell, we were told.

The awareness that I was not suffering, not being martyred, not being punished as I thought I deserved, somehow made me feel perpetually guilty.

Those extremes—the fear-plus-guilt problem—are still with me today, as an adult. No matter how simple and harmless the stimulus that triggers them, I have to deal with them.

As each of us had reached the age of three we had been transferred from our own houses to St. Francis Xavier's House, where all the boys were taken care of by a few Big Brothers on one floor and the girls by some Big Sisters on another. I knew that I met with my family at community meetings on Sunday nights after supper for several years afterward. But, try as I might, I could not recall memories of Brother Mark.

New people had come into my life. Brother Isidore and Brother Christopher had been put in charge of all the boys who were old enough to be away from their families. I remembered the time I had tried to avoid a spanking from Brother Christopher. I had told him that I would be good only if he would not punish me. He had ignored my promise, and so when the spanking was over I insisted that I would be bad again. After a second spanking I had given in.

I remembered seeing Brother Mark with a bandage around his head one day. He had received a bad wound when he had been hit on the head with a lead pipe by someone who disliked the sign he was carrying. He was just one of many Big Brothers and Big Sisters who were then protesting the plan to keep the Blessed Sacrament in an interfaith chapel complex at Brandeis University.

This episode reminded me that he had fought like all the other grown-ups in defending Our Lady against her enemies. He had gone to Boston Common with all the others every Sunday for years and years to denounce the wicked world. He had been just as brave as everyone else. I remembered how much I had feared that the Big Brothers and Big Sisters would someday be martyred while they were defending the Faith on the Common. Late on Sunday afternoons they would come back and tell us about the excitement of standing up on their boxes, above the angry crowds screaming at them. But they had assured us that the Boston police were on their side. I had always wished that I could watch the brave policemen defending us as they drove the crowds back with their big brown horses.

I remembered hearing that Brother Mark was the one who had built the burglar alarms to protect the Center buildings from the wicked people in Cambridge. They had smashed the big glass windows and had broken the statues that stood outside across the street from Adams House and the other Harvard buildings. Brother Mark was very smart, and he had known how to prevent the bad people from destroying our property. When anyone crossed onto our walkway, the alarm would go off and the police would rush down to see if they could catch them. I could not understand why he had left after all the years of trouble he had helped us get through.

I heard water rushing and the radiator pipes creaked and cracked. The noises moved down the corridor. I rolled over in my bed and searched my memory for more recent recollections of Brother Mark's activities.

We had moved up to the country four years ago in order to be far away from our enemies. All the Big Brothers had moved into St. Therese's above the chapel and the Big Sisters and children had moved into St. Anne's. We lived in one wing (the Little Sisters upstairs and we downstairs) and the Big Sisters in another wing. Brother Mark came over every once in a while to fix something. He was in charge of the electricity. I often saw him working on the lights and the electric wires in the walls of the house.

I remembered that I had spoken to him one day when I was dumping the rubbish barrels in back of St. Anne's. They were kept by the boiler room, and that day I saw him working there. No one was around, and I had a question I wanted to ask him.

"Do you remember the squirrels that you and Sister Mary Agnes kept in a cage? What did you feed them?"

"Squirrels in a cage? We never kept any squirrels," he replied.

"You know, the cute squirrels she told me about at the community meeting," I continued. "She said that she had some pet squirrels when she was a little girl."

"Oh! That was long before I met her. I don't know what she fed them. She never told me."

"Do you mean you didn't grow up together?" I inquired, very surprised.

"Of course not," he said. "Do you think I am her *brother*?"

He seemed annoyed at my question, and I realized that I did not know as much about his early life as he had expected. Maybe he had left the Center because he thought I was not interested in his childhood. I had never asked him about it. We had been told not to talk about P.L., which stood for Past Life.

I recalled another episode that made me feel that Sister Mary Agnes had known, before Brother Mark left, that he was not entirely good. I had been given a yo-yo as a dishwashing prize. At one of the community meetings I gave it to Brother Mark to teach me some tricks. While he was spinning it, the yo-yo flew up and almost knocked Sister Mary Agnes' glasses off. When he apologized, she looked at him the way the Angels do when we children have done something bad. I did not know what to think, but I remembered the incident clearly.

I wondered if it was too late to get Brother Mark to come back. Convinced that something could be done, I started thinking what I could say to Sister Catherine. She thought that I loved Brother Mark.

I had gone to her office more than a year before, when I had overheard that he had been in bed for several days. I told Sister Catherine that I had noticed that he was not around and that I wondered about him. I was afraid that she would be angry with me for not minding my own business. But she smiled and said that he was okay. He had sprained his ankle severely and had to wear a cast on his foot that had to be kept off the floor for several days.

I was relieved at this news, and I was pleased by her kindly response. But I felt that I should express my honest reaction, and thus I began to cry. I tried to explain that I feared he might have been very sick.

Sister Catherine called Father Feeney in from the library and told him how much I loved Brother Mark and how sweet it was for me to be concerned. The way she said it made me feel that it was a brand-new realization for her. That was why I knew that Sister Catherine would understand—and would not get mad—if I came back to her and talked about Brother Mark.

That idea, that plan, seemed to quiet my mind, and soon afterward I fell asleep.

For several days after that, I tried to see Sister Catherine. I made appointment after appointment. I tried to find out the *real* reasons why Brother Mark had left. And I tried to get her to agree that he would probably come back. I sometimes cried as I told her how I wished he would return.

I had one consoling thought: If he were truly sorry for what he had done, and wanted to be a Big Brother again, the Center would forgive him. It would be up to him, and Our Lady would grant him the grace if he deserved it.

As the days passed and summer came to St. Benedict's, I thought of Brother Mark less and less.

Chapter Two

"I Preach Hatred"

There were 50 of them, almost all under 35, the men dressed in black suits and black ties, the women in black dresses and short-visored caps. As a small crowd of spectators watched, they set up a portable platform with a painting of the Madonna and a crowned figure of the Infant Jesus. . . .

Father Feeney, a flashing-eyed man of 55, took over the platform. "Archbishop Cushing is a heretic," he began. A heckler interrupted. Shouted Feeney, "I came here to preach the love of the Blessed Virgin Mary, and I found nothing but filthy adulterous faces, who attacked her." He pointed to a newspaperman making notes in the crowd. One of the girl slaves turned, scowling, and sprinkled some holy water in the reporter's direction. "I preach hatred of those who hate Jesus. . . ."

His speech over, Father Feeney and his young followers concluded the meeting with some prayers and a Latin blessing. Then the Slaves of the Immaculate Heart of Mary lined up and marched off the [Boston] Common. As they passed the reporter, the scowling girl held up a bottle and shook more holy water at him.

Time
October 13, 1952

The young woman who sprinkled holy water on the reporter that particular Sunday afternoon on Boston Common was probably not my mother. She never scowls, but has a pleasant though determined expression when she feels she's fighting for God. However, she is certainly capable of that kind of boldness in defense of what she believes.

I doubt that my father made much show of his feelings when he was on the Common. He probably marched along quietly. But if things had gotten out of hand (as they did quite often during the 1950s, when Father Feeney's preaching of hatred turned specific and vicious), he would have soon been in the middle of things. He was "a good man in a pinch." But although no one would have pushed him around, he would have preferred to remain in the background until needed, for the simple reason that he has always been a shy person.

I have a great deal of that same shyness myself (though for quite different reasons), and I have always wondered how my father ever got up the nerve to introduce himself to the woman who would become my mother. But that is just what he did, one hot summer night in 1948 in Cambridge, Massachusetts. He was twenty-two years old and a student at the College of the Holy Cross, and she was twenty-seven and worked as a teller in a Boston bank. With jet-black hair and large expressive eyes, she was strikingly attractive. The place was St. Benedict Center, and they were both there to hear a lecture by the Center's dynamic chaplain, the famous Jesuit, Father Leonard Feeney.

From that moment on, the story of Robert Connor and Loretta Cleary must be set in the context of St. Benedict Center, and thus some history of that unique and controversial organization is in order.

Almost all written accounts of the Center credit its rise to prominence and its eventual fame to Father Feeney. And those accounts are in large part true, but the real force behind St. Benedict Center from the very beginning was a remarkable woman by the name of Catherine Goddard Clarke. (I and all the other Center children of course knew her only as Sister Catherine.) And when I say "remarkable," I do not mean it in a totally complimentary sense. Sister Catherine had a true genius for organization, but she also had an uncanny ability to manipulate people.

In the late 1930s and the early 1940s, the Boston area was one of the nation's most active Roman Catholic centers. Some people considered it the most Catholic city in the United States. In addition, with the troubles in Europe as a nagging reminder of the fragility of the human condition, many people were turning to (or returning to) religion, and there was widespread interest in theological matters. One of the barometers of that interest was a bookstore near Harvard Square, the St. Thomas More Bookshop. Its proprietor was Mrs. Catherine Goddard Clarke, a forthright, devout, and ambitious person of middle age.

Mrs. Clarke was a busy woman. She had two children and a husband to take care of, yet she was away from home much of the time. Prior to the bookstore she had worked in the dean's office at Wellesley, the prestigious secular college for women. She herself had taken courses at various colleges, though she had never received a degree.

(I found it interesting, years later, to learn that Mrs. Clarke had never actually spent enough time in college to complete a degree, though she had given the impression to the students and faculty who came to her for advice that she had been in intellectual circles all her life.)

In 1940, noting the increased interest in all things that pertained to Catholicism, and knowing that the Catholic students at Harvard, Radcliffe, Wellesley, and other secular colleges and universities in the Boston area had no central gathering place, Mrs. Clarke and two others founded St. Benedict Center in a onetime furniture store at 23 Arrow Street (right across from Harvard's Adams House). She eventually left the St. Thomas More Bookshop and devoted her full time to the Center in the newly leased store.

Two other people aided in founding the Center. The best-known, then and now, is Avery Dulles, the son of John Foster Dulles. In 1940, Dulles was a recent convert to Catholicism and a student at the Harvard Law School. Today he is a Jesuit priest and teacher. But, as he left soon after the Center was formed, he did not play a role in its later growth—or problems.

Within a very short time, St. Benedict Center became so popular a meeting and discussion place for bright young Catholics that its fame came to the attention of Father Feeney. Father was then teaching at Weston College, a Jesuit seminary, and when he visited St. Benedict's, he took an immediate liking to it. The students and the Center's staff took an equally hard-and-fast liking to the dynamic Jesuit who was soon giving regular Thursday-night lectures.

One of the many gifts of this highly talented man was his ability to explain thorny theological issues in a manner that the young could understand, and that did not insult their obvious intelligence. Within months the Thursday-night lectures were so popular that the line of those who wanted to get seats—or standing room—stretched out into Harvard Square.

In 1944, the Pope sent a message of congratulations and a blessing to St. Benedict Center. Such recognition of a new organization was so rare as to be almost unique.

Many of the former students from the Boston-area colleges and universities who had attended the Center's functions had become servicemen (and servicewomen) and praised the Center and its work to anyone who would listen. Soon the Center was getting mail from interested Catholics, and potential Catholics, who had never set foot in Boston. When the war ended, the young people flocked back to the Center, and once again the crowds trying to hear Father Feeney's lectures overflowed into the streets.

Many of these young veterans returned with a zeal that had not been apparent before the war. As Sister Catherine would later write, "They had looked death in the face."

In 1945, the Jesuit authorities had given in to the inevitable and had assigned Father Leonard Feeney to the Center full-time. St. Benedict's finally had its own priest. The flock had its shepherd. Standing slightly in the background, but mightily pleased, was the Center's president, Catherine Goddard Clarke.

The importance of this unusual reassignment should not be missed. Father Feeney was an enormously popular and well-known figure, not just within Jesuit or religious circles but even to the world at large. As far back as 1937 he had been pictured and written about in *Time* and other national magazines for a sermon he gave at St. Patrick's Cathedral in New York City. In that sermon he called for America to produce its *own* saints. (St. Barbara of the Bronx, for example.) For four years he was an editor with *America,* the Jesuits' influential weekly magazine.

Describing Father Feeney at the time he was assigned to the Center, John Deedy, a religious writer, recently wrote,

> Leonard Feeney was then in his mid-40's and as genuine a religious celebrity as one could find. He had a dozen books to his credit, including *In Towns and Little Towns,* which had gone through eleven printings between 1927 and 1930 alone, and *Fish on Friday,* a best seller after its appearance in 1934. Sheed & Ward was readying for the presses a *Leonard Feeney Omnibus,*

and organizations across the country were vying for his presence. The past was a succession of glorious moments. . . . For Feeney the future seemed unlimited. It was a wonderful world for this son of Irish immigrants, the oldest of the three Feeney priest-brothers from Lynn, Mass. Leonard Feeney enjoyed his fame immensely.

Father's literary reputation, coupled with his flair as a dynamic speaker, made the Center a popular place within the student city of Cambridge. As Father Feeney attracted others to assist in the teaching and lecturing, the Center expanded into a full-fledged school. It offered classes in Latin, Greek, philosophy, Church history, and the classics.

His converts to Catholicism and his recruits to religious orders began to explode in numbers: 200 converts, 100 young people studying to become priests or nuns, and 250 students studying at the Center itself.

Less than a year after Father Feeney was assigned to the Center, the organization started its own quarterly publication, *From the Housetops*. Through its pages the Center people planned to thunder from the housetops the truths of the Catholic Church. They planned to wake up a half-dead world, and they did not worry about giving offense. They began as proud and open, but eventually they were simply bold. They attacked what they considered the anti-Catholic teachings of Harvard University, and they berated those Catholics who sat calmly listening to atheistic lectures and lecturers. There were several Jesuits attending Harvard at that time, and Father Feeney forbade them to come to the Center.

Students began to leave Harvard and join the Center school. My father left Harvard in October 1947 and transferred to the College of the Holy Cross which was run by the Jesuits. Another student, Temple Morgan, who had converted to the Church earlier that year, resigned from Harvard just weeks before he was to receive his degree. He had been a member of the exclusive Harvard Porcellian Club, and his grandfather, E. D. Morgan, cousin to J. P. Morgan, had donated one of the gates at Harvard. His family became furious, but he ignored them and enrolled at St. Benedict Center.

As students continued to resign from Harvard and Radcliffe, startled and angry parents began to put pressure on the archdiocesan authorities to check the Center's "undesirable influence" on their children.

In the face of this pressure, the Center grew even more dogmatic. They had detected the cause of the liberalism that they thought was corrupting the Church: Catholics no longer believed in the infallibly defined doctrine that there is no salvation outside the Church. Tension mounted as the doctrine was argued by Center students and outside theologians in their respective publications. The Center considered ridiculous any interpretation of the dogma that concluded that "*no* salvation outside the Church" really meant "*some* salvation outside the Church." Ecclesiastical authorities preferred to avoid a theological confrontation over what was, in the modern age, an embarrassing dogma of the early Church, and thus took steps to quiet St. Benedict Center.

The struggle that ensued turned Center members into a fiercely militant group. The hard-core community numbered about eighty. They were single and married men and women. There was an army lieutenant from California, a physicist from Connecticut, a professor from Lebanon, and a geologist from Spain, but most were former students from the local universities and colleges. The things they had in common, which held them together, were an interest in the Catholic Faith, undaunted courage, a spirit of independence, and the unbounded enthusiasm of youth. As far as they were concerned, there was nothing planned or manipulative about the formation of their organization. It evolved under the spontaneity of a crisis, and they made the sacrifices that God required of them. According to their consciences, they could not have done otherwise.

In August 1948 Father Feeney's assignment to St. Benedict Center was revoked and his Jesuit superior ordered him to the College of the Holy Cross. He refused to go, saying that his conscience obliged him to take care of the Center students who had planned to attend his lectures. He contended that it would appear that his teachings on "no salvation" were erroneous if he, the main spokesman, were removed. For a Jesuit, such resistance was unheard of.

Five months later Church authorities ordered the Center to desist publication, but it would not. Nor would Father Feeney report to Holy Cross. Instead, certain students and teachers at the Center banded together and formed a secret order called the Slaves of the Immaculate Heart of Mary.

They took vows of obedience to Father Feeney, whom they promised to obey in their "crusade" for the preservation of a doctrine of the Church.

In April 1949 four teachers, members of the Center, were fired from Boston College. They had refused to retract their charges of heresy against Boston College's Jesuit theologians, whom they accused in a letter to Father Janssens, General of the Society of Jesus in Rome.

The news splashed across the papers of the country. The *New York Times* front-page caption ran, "BOSTON COLLEGE OUSTS 4 TEACHERS AS INTOLERANT: *They charge 'Heresy.'*" *Time* called it "Heresy in Boston." *Newsweek* referred to it as "The age-old controversy about salvation"; and *Life* explained that they were fired "for promoting 'intolerance' and 'bigotry.'" But the Boston Heresy Case, as it came to be known, was really launched when Father Feeney came out in support of the four fired teachers and commended them on their fearless defense of the Faith.

Richard Cushing, Archbishop of Boston, retaliated by silencing Father Feeney and forbidding Catholics to have any association with St. Benedict's.

But the Center members believed that no Catholic could be validly punished by the Church for teaching what he or she considered to be the true Faith. With renewed vigor they struck back, exploiting every opportunity to bring to the public's attention the "heretical" reasons why they were being "persecuted." The ecclesiastical authorities avoided the theological issues by forcing it into a case of disobedience. They increased the severity of the canonical punishments. In October of that year Father Feeney was dismissed from the Jesuit order, and three years later, in February 1953, he was excommunicated by the Holy See.

For the members of St. Benedict Center the situation became dire, as one after another lost his job in the thoroughly Catholic city of Boston. The state took away their school's accreditation, thereby wiping out its funding from the G.I. Bill. Their longtime benefactors forsook them. The Slaves of the Immaculate Heart of Mary pooled their resources, bought some houses in the Cambridge slums, surrounded them with an eight-foot-high wall, which they painted bright red, and crowded in with their families. The world, they thought, was against them because of their beliefs. They were being persecuted for their faith as had happened to saints for centuries.

They were even ready to lay down their lives as the holy martyrs of the Church had done.

A new source of income was desperately needed. They started writing and publishing their own books, which they sold door-to-door in the business districts of cities throughout the eastern part of the United States. Through their books, they explained the traditional Catholic Faith as they understood it.

When at home, they continued their studies and listened attentively to the daily lectures. They saw Father Feeney as a heroic saint who had given up his literary career and his millions of admiring readers to stand up for the Faith regardless of the price he had to pay. He preached to them the horror of damnation and the importance of following the will of God, not part way, but all the way to perfection, to the sanctity of the saints.

Eventually, these comparisons with the saints were taken more and more seriously. They listened often to the story of Joachim and Anne, offering Mary, their three-year-old daughter, to God by giving her up to the care of the holy women in the Temple. "Joachim and Anne became saints," Father Feeney would preach, "because of the sacrifice of surrendering their child to God."

Not long after that the families decided to give up their *own* children to God. On each November 21, the annual feast day commemorating the presentation of Mary in the Temple, the parents would send their three-year-old children away from their house to be brought up under the careful religious training of certain members assigned to the task.

Father Feeney's lectures continued. "Imagine a boy making love to anything so frail as a girl, and not being able to offer her the Christian securities that God puts at his disposal. And then imagine death striking this young girl swiftly, and leaving her loved one never to know in his heart what her ultimate destiny has been!" And, extolling the exemplary purity of St. Joseph, he would say, "And imagine a man so beautiful in purity that the Holy Spirit can make fruitful the virginal bride he has taken to his heart—whom he will never outrage, never dim, never overshadow in all the singularity of her virginal and maternal beauty."

Many young couples at first refused to "volunteer" to take the more perfect path, but eventually all gave in and took vows of celibacy for the rest of their lives. The husbands would never "outrage" their wives again. By mid-1955 all the couples were on the road to sanctity. Two years later, when the couples were required to separate and live in different houses, only one couple remained "selfishly attached" and was promptly dismissed from the order.

If there were any second thoughts, there was not much time for them amid all the excitement. Every Sunday for seven and a half years, the members of the Center (feeling "terrible as an army set in array") marched down to Boston Common and berated the milling mobs of unbelievers. As Mrs. Clarke put it, "Better to speak out now, in the hope of reaching some souls somewhere, than to wait until another war is upon us and an atom bomb blasts millions into hell."

But the people of Boston did not notice their benevolent interest in the salvation of souls; rather they saw them as Father Feeney once depicted a London preacher in Hyde Park: "It was the voice of a wild evangelical, with hatred in his very teeth, clutching a Bible and spitting insult into the face of the most innocent of his listeners!"

Time called Father the "hate-priest" and his followers "Feeneyites." *Life* magazine, with its vivid pictorial displays of a wild Father Feeney and his followers marching "four abreast, their eyes fixed stonily ahead," labeled their weekly performance "a peculiar and frightening demonstration."

Fellow priests and Jesuits who knew Father Feeney for his charm and wit were confused by his transformation. They wondered if under the heat of the controversy he had gone mad. His own loyal followers saw him as an angry defender of the Faith who was hated and maligned by the enemies of the Church. Father Feeney, no doubt, understood what was happening. Years earlier he had written, "I am not good at suffering for the Faith. I thrive on affection and can never cope with a smoldering enemy. When I am disliked I lose all powers of social intercourse. Interruptions occur in my digestion. I become rigid, cautious, frightened, ungrammatical."

The crowds saw just such a person and they reacted with vehemence. Father Feeney probably was not surprised. He wrote about that shared nationality that dominated the Boston scene: "The Irish are intense, positive, assertive with an infinite capacity for hatred." And so it must have appeared to the Boston mounted police who struggled to keep the inflamed crowds under control on those weekend afternoons on the Common.

Sunday was not the only day for excitement. During the week the members of the Center had to "battle" with the P.F.s (Pious Frauds) who tried to thwart the selling of their books in the cities throughout the country. Most of the booksellers had their turn behind bars. Gradually, however, their constitutional rights to disseminate their religious teachings were respected and trouble subsided. But to an outsider reading the papers, it was hard to believe that they wanted to avoid trouble.

There was the time that "25 YOUTHS DEMONSTRATE IN THE VATICAN DELEGATE'S HOME" in Washington, D.C. Or the incident in Chicago when "6 BELIEVERS IN EX-PRIEST INVADE OFFICE OF CARDINAL STRITCH." For that one they were sent to jail after refusing to pay the ten-dollar fines assessed against them in court. Newspaper photos showed them with bowed heads praying the rosary behind bars. The last major confrontation took place in September 1955. As the *New York Times* reported it, "The police broke up a disturbance today on Boston Common between a religious group and bystanders who objected to a placard message." Father Feeney was quoted as telling reporters that the pulled-down placard had read: "Catholics of Boston, stop the Jews from dishonoring and desecrating the Blessed Sacrament at Brandeis University."

In January 1958 the demonstrations on the Common suddenly ceased. The people of Boston had not listened to the Slaves, so they "shook the dust from their feet," and went forth out of Boston, remembering what Scripture had said concerning such obstinacy to the Truth: "It shall be more tolerable for the land of Sodom and Gomorrah in the day of judgment, than for that city."

The order moved to the quiet country town of Still River, a part of Harvard, Massachusetts—some thirty miles inland, to the west of the "other Harvard"—and settled their community on a hillside overlooking a beautiful wooded valley and facing Mount Wachusett in the distance.

The "love story" of Loretta Cleary and Robert Connor was subsumed in the larger story of what happened to the followers of Father Feeney and Mrs. Catherine Clarke. What follows is a brief account of the most salient facts, as best I have been able to reconstruct them from conversations—years later—with both of my parents.

In 1948, my father was a twenty-two-year-old war veteran torn by a number of forces. He truly believed that Father Feeney and Sister Catherine represented the Truth, and that belief conflicted with what he was hearing in his own college classes, first at Harvard and then later even at the Catholic Holy Cross. At the same time he was deeply in love with Loretta, a woman whose faith and trust in the leaders of St. Benedict's made my father's seem pale in comparison.

Several years later, Mrs. Clarke wrote of what happened, and how happy she was, when my father finally "saw the light."

> In 1947–1948, Philip Gammans, Robert Connor, Charles Forgeron resigned from Harvard. . . . Philip Gammans and Charles Forgeron entered the Center School, and Robert Connor transferred to Holy Cross College, since he wished to go on with his pre-medical studies. There he discovered, much to his chagrin, that secular standardization, combined with Catholic Liberalism, had made for the same materialism at Holy Cross which he had found at Harvard. His friends at St. Benedict Center were more and more under siege for holding to their beliefs, and he knew that it had to be the whole way, for him, or nothing.

What Mrs. Clarke did not see fit to include in her account of my father's joining the new and secret order was that my mother had broken their engagement—not once but three times—over his refusal (or reluctance) to join. Mrs. Clarke may have been able to arrange her own domestic situation so that she could be in the order while her husband and family remained on the outside, but my father had no such choice. My mother was one of the most loyal and devout of the followers, and there was no way by which she would marry my father if he intended to remain a part of the "wicked world" outside the Center and the Slaves of the Immaculate Heart of Mary.

He decided to go "the whole way or nothing." They were married in April 1949, first by Father Feeney, and then some months later by a justice of peace in New Hampshire (because the Center was worried that the state might not recognize the validity of marriages performed by Father, as he was then in trouble with the Church).

My father, who by this time had dropped out of school, took a job with a large insurance company. Also, using his own G.I. Bill and the Center's six hundred dollars for a down payment, he bought a house in a run-down area of Cambridge. The Center made the payments, and my parents used only part of the house; the rest was occupied by two other Center families. Bit by bit, the Center was moving its wagons into a circle. When a few other houses had been purchased, the red fence went up around the community.

Those members who did not have outside employment continued to work and to study at the Center. When I was born in February 1950, there were nine children within the little community.

It was not an easy time. Above and beyond the question of finances, the members of the new order found themselves in the midst of a doctrinal battle that American Catholicism had never before witnessed. From all accounts, life was a swirl of events, from one crisis to another.

If either of my parents ever wondered just what it was they had gotten themselves into, I doubt very much if they would have had the time to reflect upon it.

Their sacrifices seemed small compared to the awesome punishments God would inflict on those who deserted Him in this time of crisis. Mrs. Clarke wrote: "Now, the time was growing short. The Mother of God had said so, at Fatima, in Portugal. She had said that God's punishments are very close. The people must be prepared." She reminded her "children" of the vision of the recent Pope Leo XIII, who had seen Lucifer and his devils. "He saw their fearful triumphs in all the countries of the world in the days soon to come. He beheld their evil glee and unholy mockery as they ravished the Mystical Body of Christ, stilled heavenly espousals in the hearts of maidens, muted the voices of priests and bishops, imprisoned the Popes and silenced the song of monks and nuns in monasteries and convents grown empty of vocations."

The Slaves of the Immaculate Heart of Mary were reminded of what Our Lord had said in the Bible, "I am come to cast fire on the earth" (Luke 12:49). "For I came to set a man at variance with his father, and the daughter against mother. . . . The brother also shall deliver up the brother to death, and the father the son. . . . And a man's enemies shall be they of his own household. . . . And he that taketh not up his cross and followeth Me, is not worthy of Me"

(Matthew 10:35, 21, 36, 38). These last scriptural admonitions were not taken lightly.

The once-dutiful sons and daughters now shifted their earthly allegiance from their own fathers and mothers to the leadership of the Center, Father Feeney and Mrs. Clarke. Bit by brutal bit, all communications with parents and other family members were cut off. The more the members were urged to leave the Center, the more completely they cut their family ties.

My mother's mother had been dead for years, but her father, a fireman, was no longer able to reach his daughter. Both my father's parents were living, but he soon stopped all communication with them.

My grandfather Connor, who happened to be a judge in Ohio, stood it for as long as he could. He knew that his son had married and that he and his wife were members of a dissident, highly controversial Catholic sect. Beyond that he did not know a great deal, which put him on a par with all the other parents, brothers, sisters, and other relatives. In March 1950 (at a time when he did not know that I, his first grandchild, had even been born) he wrote to the pastor of St. Paul's Church in Harvard Square, the church that had original jurisdiction, so to speak, over the Center.

But events had moved most quickly, and St. Paul's no longer exercised any force whatsoever over the Center or the Slaves.

My grandfather phrased his concern rather conservatively, not knowing what kind of reception his letter would receive, but he made it quite clear he was seriously worried about his son and his son's health. And he asked that his letter be kept secret.

> Dear Father,
>
> It is with considerable hesitancy that I approach you for information concerning my son Bob who left Holy Cross College a year ago last February to join Father Feeney and his St. Benedict Center. Owing to the strong disapproval that we have expressed about the activities of the Center, Bob has presumably become resentful of us and has neglected to write. We have heard nothing from him since January 12th. His letters contained nothing that would suggest that any members of this group intended to submit to the orders of their superiors. Bob's

letters contained so much emotional reasoning that I have wondered if he was in fact well. You will appreciate our concern and distress over this situation, I trust.

Would you be so kind as to write me whether this group of persons is continuing with its original work. Particularly, can you give me any information about Bob. I thought that you or your Assistants might know him. I am quite sure that he has been living at 23 Arrow Street.

Please do not make known to him that I have written to you. I would be most grateful for your answer.

                        Sincerely,
                        /s/ Stephen C. Connor

The pastor replied that he had no comforting information to give, and ended his short letter saying that the situation was painful in the extreme, that it was incredible that intelligent young people would continue to follow a leadership that was obviously mentally deranged. He sympathized with my grandfather and wished he could be more helpful.

My grandfather responded almost by return mail, for he had just received a letter from my father that disturbed him and my grandmother deeply. He told the pastor of St. Paul's:

We received a letter from Bob on Tuesday. He appears to be attached to the Center with fanaticism in the extreme. He writes that he intends to live the life of a Saint, that he is interested in spiritual values alone while we are absorbed in material things, and that it will be necessary for him to go along without us. I would conclude that he is mentally ill if all those other persons were not likewise afflicted. The behavior of the Center people is something that I cannot understand. Until Bob became attached to Father Feeney he was most considerate of us in all that he did. Now, we scarcely know that he exists. Certainly the Center's leadership must be mentally deranged. It seems so incredible.

Indeed, it must have seemed incredible to anyone on the outside. To those on the inside, however, they were following the Will of God—as made clear to them by Father Feeney and Sister Catherine.

By the mid-1950s, the Center's main source of income was revenue from the sales of books written by Father Feeney or Sister Catherine and published by the Center itself (often without specifying authorship, so as not to offend Catholics who might have heard of Father Feeney and the Boston Heresy Case). Each week teams of booksellers would fan out to different areas of the United States, where they would sell these religious volumes on street corners and business offices for "only a dollar." They were *very* successful.

Their methods were not always aboveboard. The arrest of Feeneyites were reported in city after city, and occasionally my grandparents would find their son listed among the peddlers who had been jailed for selling without a license.

I do not know if my grandfather was directly responsible or not, but Akron, Ohio (where Judge Connor had his court), was one of the few cities in the country that took active measures to prevent the Center's bookselling efforts. (Other cities waited until complaints were lodged.) Certainly he was furious that my father had cut off all communications with his own family.

As the 1950s turned into the 1960s, my grandparents renewed their efforts to reach their only son. They wrote to a number of priests, trying for news of him, and were finally put in touch with a priest who was known as "the Father who contacts the gentleman who writes to the families of those in Father Feeney's group." The go-between told them that the last time he had seen their son he had looked well, and he mentioned that he himself had a daughter in the group, which was the reason he had kept track of it. He said that all the parents had gone through the same experience— even severe sickness had not brought them together, which he considered to be diabolical and not in accordance with God's commandments.

After a decade of silence, my grandparents took it upon themselves to get in their car and drive east to visit the Center unannounced. They did so, and were permitted to see their son for a brief visit. But they had to return home without so much as a glimpse at their five grandchildren—all of whom they had never even seen. Angry, depressed, and bitter, my grandparents had about given up hope.

Then, little by little, as if in answer to their constant prayers, their son—my father—began to wonder if he had made the right choice after all.

As the years wore on, my father began to feel strongly discontented with his way of life. It was hard to believe that it was God who demanded such a sacrifice. He no longer had a family. He saw his wife as a devout nun, and his five boys as inevitably becoming monks and booksellers serving Father Feeney and Sister Catherine.

To him, the two leaders appeared more like proud selfish rulers than holy religious superiors. During the day Sister Catherine would send Father Feeney away so she could run the Center's business unencumbered. One of the brothers would be assigned each day as Father's chauffeur, and would drive him around to buy holy pictures and ornate relic cases that he used to decorate the walls of the houses. Greed seemed to be corrupting Father Feeney and Sister Catherine, whom my father once overheard questioning the need of hospitalization costs for a brother who was already terminally ill.

My father worried and worried about what he should do. Torn with indecision, he became ill. The doctor said it was ulcers. He was no longer able to go bookselling, and he could eat only certain foods. As he continued to do his chores about the Center, he began to question the very purpose of the Center's existence. He felt guilty listening to Father Feeney's tirades against the Pope and other Church leaders. Bookselling seemed fraudulent, as he recalled instances of poor people donating their last dollar to what they thought were "Catholic Brothers." (Only Father Feeney's title was considered valid by the Church; all the others, including "Sister" Catherine, were self-proclaimed Brothers and Sisters.)

Of greatest importance, however, was that the Center's interpretation of the doctrine of "no salvation" came under his close scrutiny. After reviewing the decrees of the Holy Office and the Pope, he became convinced that Father Feeney was in error and therefore properly outside the Catholic Church himself. He realized, as he would tell me years later, that he had wasted thirteen years of his life on a fanatical movement. He had sacrificed his family life, his children, his education, and his career for a cause that now seemed repugnant in the eyes of God.

He was not sure what to do. If he left, he feared that he might lose his wife and children forever. He needed support and advice, so he devised a plan. He got the confidence of an electrical-supplies salesman who came to the Center. Through him he sent a letter to the Bishop of Worcester, and two weeks later, after reading the bishop's reply (also secretly delivered), he resolved to leave. He tore up the draft of his letter as well as the reply and buried them in a trash can.

The next morning, March 24, 1962, he made a bold move and went across the yard to the Big Sisters' house. He informed Sister Mary Agnes, his wife, that he no longer believed in the Center's interpretation of the doctrine on salvation. She was shocked and refused to go or let him take any of the children. After a dramatic series of events, he escaped from the company of two Center Brothers and made his way to Father Bernard Flanagan, Bishop of Worcester. Through the bishop's help, he was put in a monastery for a week so he could pull himself together before returning to his parents in Akron, Ohio.

Back at the Center, one of the Brothers found a part of his letter to the bishop in a rubbish barrel. The Brothers searched his desk, his bed, his wastepaper basket, everything—looking for more clues. They found notes on his careful analysis of the doctrinal issue.

A group of Brothers rushed to the town dump, located and searched through the Center's trash. By the end of the day the Center had assembled two letters. The first was an initial draft of my father's letter to the bishop; the second was the reply.

My father's letter was long and emotional, but he stuck to his promise (in an early paragraph) to tell his story "in a fair light without exaggerating or minimizing any portion of the story." He gave his personal and religious history, told of how he left Harvard, and gave a brief history of the Center prior to the formation of the Slaves of the Immaculate Heart of Mary.

As to why he joined, he explained, in part, "I was told quite plainly that if I did not resign from Holy Cross and join the Center immediately, I would be excluded forever. My fiancee said that she believed Fr. Feeney completely and would follow him no matter what happened, with or without me. Foolishly and over the protests of my parents I resigned from Holy Cross and became an active member of Saint Benedict Center."

He then traced the subsequent history of the Center, including the turning over of the children, the vows of continence, the bookselling, and the move to Still River. He explained to the bishop that he no longer held the Center's view on the doctrine of no salvation outside the Catholic Church, said that his conscience bothered him about the deception involved in the bookselling operation, and that he hated to hear the Pope and other church leaders ridiculed.

He asked the bishop's help in his predicament and told him how he could communicate with him secretly. ("Fr. Feeney reads all mail and monitors all telephone calls. Any direct contact either by mail or phone would naturally have the immediate result of immediate expulsion.")

Bishop Flanagan's reply, which the Center authorities read with particular interest, said that he would help all he could, agreed that secrecy was necessary, and contained a phrase that must have startled Father Feeney and Sister Catherine. In reference to us, his children, and our status should he leave the Center, the bishop wrote that outside, my father might be able to find some legal means of helping us.

The Center became very anxious. A delegation was sent to visit Bishop Flanagan and confront him with the letters, hoping to get his promise that he would do nothing to help Robert Connor find the "legal means" to get his children out of the Center. The bishop told them flatly that it was too early to worry about such a possibility. They left the bishop with the assurance that whatever happened they would fight back. That statement was hardly necessary, for Bishop Flanagan knew all about Father Feeney and his followers. He had no doubts whatsoever that they would fight.

The Center contacted the salesman who had smuggled the letters in and out. They threatened him with economic reprisals, and he quickly told them everything he knew about the correspondence, and his conversations with Robert Connor.

My father had left on March 24, 1962. One week later he was met at the bus station in Akron, Ohio, by his parents. Overjoyed, they pledged to help him in any and every way that they could. He settled into their comfortable home and tried to plan the next stage of his life.

First, he wrote Bishop Flanagan and thanked him for all of his help. That same day he also wrote another letter, one he felt would never be answered and might never be read by the person to whom it was addressed—my mother. After stating, "I love you as much as I always have. Without you here with me life no longer seems the same," he asked her to come to Akron with us, their children, to start a new life.

There was no answer. Three weeks later he wrote again, pleading for word of the children. No reply. In midsummer (while he was studying at John Carroll University to make up courses so that he could get back into Holy Cross in the fall and at least be near us geographically while he prepared for law school) he tried one more time.

One paragraph struck me, when I read the letters for the first time years later.

> Do the children ever ask about me? I wonder if they will remember their father after a time. I don't suppose you do anything to remind them of me. They haven't even a picture of me nor do I have any of them.

As my father had expected, there was no reply to this letter either.

While my father was attempting to plead with my mother, my grandfather was taking a different tack. He began to look for legal advice. An old friend and Harvard Law School classmate who practiced in Massachusetts advised him that the ground for taking the children would have to be carefully surveyed and the plan of action considered. He said that the effort to be successful would contend against opposition that was almost diabolical. He did, however, find a lawyer to handle the case, in the event that one became necessary. The choice, who was recommended by Bishop Flanagan of Worcester, was Mr. Walter J. Griffin of that same city. My grandfather wrote to Mr. Griffin in August, asking for an appointment in September, when he and my grandmother would be driving my father out to Holy Cross.

My grandfather also mentioned that there would be an attempt, at that time, to visit the Center and see the children. He had no way of knowing just how dramatic a scene that would turn out to be.

On Monday, September 10, my father and his parents pulled into Worcester in my grandfather's big green Buick. After visiting both the bishop and Mr. Griffin, they headed out for Still River.

When they got to the Center, my father went up to the door, leaving his parents in the car on the road in front of the main building. Shortly after he knocked, my grandparents were attracted by the noise of a commotion on the porch. They heard shouting and looked to see their son arguing with Father Feeney.

Moments later, my father came back to the car. His glasses were broken and there were slight cuts and some blood near one eye. "He hit me, Father Feeney hit me," said my father in apparent disbelief.

With Father Feeney in the lead, a group of Sisters and Brothers had gathered around the car. In angry voices, they were yelling at my father and calling him "Traitor! Traitor!"

Then someone ran to the house and called my mother, whom my father had been asking to see. When she joined the group, my father called her by her first name and told her that he still loved her. His use of her "name in the world" infuriated her, for she screamed, "Don't call me Loretta," and with that she began to swing at him through the open back window of the car.

My grandfather got out of the car and walked to the other side, but several of the men and Father Feeney put their hands on him. He began to get angry too, and in firm tones told them to let him go, which they did.

Father Feeney kept shouting that my grandparents had never liked my mother, that they had always "hated her." And then a woman who my grandfather thought was Sister Catherine said, "If you cause us any trouble, or do anything to us, we will ruin you back in Akron."

At that, everyone turned and went back into the house. My father and his parents left. Again, no one had seen the children.

There was no communication of any sort for two and a half months, until November 28, when my father wrote a long and tender letter to my mother. This time, instead of addressing her as Sister Mary Agnes, which she preferred, he called her simply Loretta. He poured out his love for her and reiterated his desire to see his children. Again, there was no answer, nor did he really have any way of knowing if the letter had actually reached her. For all he knew, it never got past Father Feeney and Sister Catherine.

On the last day of 1962, my grandfather wrote to Mr. Griffin, the lawyer. It was a long letter, detailing his own research into the laws of the Commonwealth of Massachusetts in regard to child-custody cases and those that governed an organization's legal responsibility to children within its care.

The letter ended with a short and rather ominous paragraph: "I dislike the idea of getting involved in a legal controversy. However, the children's welfare presents a matter of duty that must be met. So let's get down to business."

Chapter Three

Even under normal circumstances, a lawsuit in which one party to a marriage seeks the custody of the children takes a great deal of time. The first half of 1963 was almost gone by the time the legal machinery got around to the question of my father's right to visit his own children.

I was thirteen by then, and a bright, devious youth. No one at the Center prepared me or any of my brothers for the ordeal that we were to face, until the very last minute. Unschooled as we were in the ways of the world, we nonetheless accepted our role with an awful glee.

What we did to our own father, in the name of goodness, is something that has haunted me for a long time.

I sat and stared at my eggs, applesauce, toast, and milk. My head was still filled with the horrible dreams of the night before. It was hard to remember where the dream had ended and my thinking began. What had been actual terror during the night—visions of beheadings and crucifixions on the lawn of the Center—had given way to the normal routine of the early morning. First Breakfast, or Mass, went by in a fog.

Second Breakfast was almost over. Sister Julia scolded James Mary for washing down his food with his milk. Sister Susanna stood over Matthew and threatened to punish him if he dared to throw up. His cheeks were bulging beneath his wide blue eyes and his little hands were pressed against his mouth. He swallowed. He knew he would get the strap if he didn't finish his breakfast.

It was Tuesday, June 11, 1963. Only ten days until the end of school. The birds' chirping reminded me of previous summers—nests, robins' eggs, the swamp, redwing blackbirds, my garden, picking beans, the sweat, and the heat. Through the window blinds I could see sparrows quarreling over a hole in the drainpipe on the roof behind the purple and white lilacs. But the summer images were still a little faint.

I had sensed that there was trouble ahead. On Sunday I had smelled guests in the front room. Monday night, Sister Catherine had said things that made me feel a crisis of some sort was developing.

A blue car had been spotted spying on us. We were to get the license numbers of any cars seen parked by the white fence where we waved good-bye to the booksellers.

Sister Catherine had talked of martyrdom. Even death, she hoped, would never separate any of us.

"It would be beautiful if we all died together," she had said, "the whole community standing in line on the lawn sent to heaven by one sweep of a machine gun." She had swung her arm in a wide circle over our tables, exclaiming how glorious it would be. But I didn't think so. I was different. Afraid to be killed, I was a coward.

Sister Julia saw something. She was staring out of the window. Her eyes got bigger. "Oh, Mother of God," she said. "Close the blinds! Thomas Mary! Quick! Pull the thing!" She jumped up from her seat and pulled the blinds shut. The doorbell rang. The Angels looked at each other as though what they dreaded was about to happen. They seemed scared. I wished I had seen what was out there, but it happened too fast. Angels bumped between tables and chairs, closing blinds while others scattered away. The room became dark and I felt cold. They all knew something. It seemed rehearsed, as they moved in speechless panic.

Sister Catherine entered. "Children are not to make a sound," she commanded. I felt I had been bad. She was gone. Brothers rushed through—Brother Simon, Brother Isidore, Brother Giles, and Brother Boniface, who ran right into Sister Catherine coming back in. "Everyone upstairs, right this minute!"

I assured myself that the Big Brothers and Big Sisters were very brave. But I had never seen them running about so excitedly. I wasn't sure we would be safe.

There was a burst of loud shouting outside. I heard Brother Isidore's powerful voice. Sister Julia pushed us upstairs, where we had never been before. We went into one of the Big Brothers' rooms and sat on the beds and floor. There was silence. We held our breath and listened for what would happen next. Just then I thought of Brother Mark. More than

49

a year had gone by since he left, and he had never been mentioned again. I was always hoping that he would come back someday. Perhaps he was frightened to death, all alone out there in the world, and our superiors wouldn't forgive him and let him return. I remembered about the cars spying on us, and martyrdom. It must be our enemies out there, I thought, not Brother Mark. He was too nice to cause all this trouble.

It was quiet. I felt weak all over. I wrapped my arms around my knees as I sat on the floor. Whispering started, and I listened.

Thomas Mary said he saw a policeman outside. Alexander had never seen Brother Giles so angry. John thought that classes would be called off, and Joseph wondered who would feed the pigs. Sister Mary Judith, who was in the room with us, said that one of the Big Brothers like Brother Leo would take care of the animals. I thought Brother Isidore should do it. He was the strongest and could fight any of our enemies.

At lunchtime we went downstairs. All the blinds were open again. The sunshine I'd noticed on the lilacs had gone, and now it was sprinkling lightly. The door to the hallway near the front porch was still closed. I sipped my soup, but I wasn't hungry. The Angels were being very nice. Things were not normal.

Our spoons went down and the dishes became quiet. Sister Catherine's voice was coming through the kitchen. It stopped. There was whispering. She came in. "Luke, Michael, Paul, Matthew, and Benedict." I stared at her and waited. She looked around the room and spotted each of us. "Would you please come to the Office." She glanced down at Matthew's soup. "Drink it up, dear." Sister Mary Judith stepped forward. She would take care of it, and would have us ready immediately. The phone rang, and Sister Catherine was gone.

"Finish your milk." "Wipe your mouth and hands." "Straighten your collar." "That's right." The Angels moved us down to the Office.

"We're on our way." Sister Catherine hung up the phone. "Come in, darlings." She watched us for a moment, then looked into my eyes. "D'you remember Brother Mark?"

I held my breath and nodded.

"He is trying to take you away from us," Sister Catherine said.

He hadn't forgotten us, I thought. So that was what caused

the commotion. I said nothing, and shivered. She told us that Brother Mark's lawyer had threatened to break down our doors. The court, the sheriff, and the police had tried to get us, but the Big Brothers wouldn't let them in. Now special arrangements had been made. We would not be taken into the court, but would see a judge in private.

I was bewildered. Brother Mark was out there trying to take us away. He must have changed, I thought. What was he like now? He must be mean and wicked. Fears went through my mind. The five of us living all by ourselves in the world with no Angels around? Would Brother Mark give us to strangers? They would torture us until we renounced our Faith. Then we would go to hell. I felt weak. Why did it happen to me? I wasn't ready.

Sister Catherine asked us if we wanted to live at the Center or in the world. It didn't make sense. She was our superior and we were just children. Why would she ask us what *we* wanted? Brother Mark must be forcing her into it. Maybe he had a right to us because we were his children? I felt guilty that I was one of them.

She told us that the judge would let us stay at home if we said that we didn't want to leave. She smiled at me and said that I was the oldest and she trusted me. I felt proud of her confidence and said I would tell the judge that we hated the world and wanted to live at home.

"Now, the judge has to live in the world," she said, "so don't say you hate it. Just say, 'I want to live at the Center because Sister Mary Agnes is here, and she is my mother.' The judge knows that children want to live where their mother is. Okay?"

I was confused by her words. Why did children want to live where their mothers were? But, as she explained it, I began to realize that the judge would pay more attention to the people who were our parents than to our superiors. That must be the way they do it in the world, I thought.

"I want to be at the Center with my mother." We repeated it several times. It sounded so worldly. Sister Catherine put me in charge of the other Little Brothers, who promised to be good soldiers. We should be polite and always call the judge "your Honor."

We said a prayer in the car like Father Feeney always did when he took us out to see firemen or soldiers at Fort Devens. Brother Canisius drove us to the courthouse in Worcester. I recognized other Center cars there. The buildings looked powerful with their huge gray walls of stone. I could see the black figures of the Brothers and Sisters all over the place. They seemed so brave. Brother Mark would never let them be martyred, I hoped. Brother Simon ran out and whispered to Sister Catherine and Sister Sylvia, who had followed us in another car. Brother Canisius made Benedict stop pointing at a fierce old man who was growling at us. We entered a building. There were so many people. I kept watching for Brother Mark. I was planning to convince him to return to the Center.

First, the Big Brothers took us to the bathroom. It was a large room and it smelled like grapes. None of the Big Sisters came along. We had to wait because all the doors were closed. I noticed that the Big Brothers were "excusing" themselves up against the wall into white things that looked like tall narrow sinks. Matthew asked Brother Canisius what they were doing. I was embarrassed and told him that the white things were another type of toilet. He kept quiet when he caught on. Other men came in and did it also. It was frightening. We were already in the midst of the wickedness of the world. We waited until we could use the normal toilets, which were enclosed like the ones at home.

Sister Catherine and Sister Sylvia sat beside us outside the courtroom. People walked by and stared at us. A lady with tall skinny heels on her shoes stopped and talked to us. She smelled like the lilies of the valley that grew near St. Joseph's Hills. She said we were so cute all dressed up in blue and white. We kept silent. I knew she was trying to flatter us so we would go with the people in the world. As she left, Benedict asked why she had such long thin heels. "They wear crazy shoes to be worldly," I said.

We got up. Sister Catherine reminded us to be good soldiers and to say "your Honor" to the judge. Sister Mary Agnes came out of the courtroom. She smoothed out our shirt collars and smiled at each of us. I could see worry in her eyes.

As we walked down the hall, I saw Brother Mark talking with a man. I knew it was Brother Mark because I recognized his face, though his head had become smaller. He wore colored clothes like the people in the world. His hair was redder than it used to be. He didn't seem angry or mean. I wondered if he was plotting with one of our enemies.

Suddenly, we were abandoned with strangers in a room. I was afraid. Brother Mark came in and smiled. "This is Luke, and Michael, and Paul, and Matthew, and Benedict." He introduced each of us to a man he called Judge Wahlstrom, and to an older man and woman. He said they were his parents. The man was Judge Connor and the woman was Mrs. Connor.

Brother Mark sat down and crossed his legs. "Now at last you have met my parents," he said. He had a wristwatch and his socks were brown. He acted like he enjoyed living in the world. I wasn't afraid of him. His glasses had dark frames, which made him look different. But he spoke and smiled just the way I remembered him at our community meetings. He was so at ease. He would never hurt us. I felt I could talk him into coming back when we were alone, and the strangers had gone.

"We have longed for this day for many, many years," Judge Connor said. He was bald, with some white hair on the back of his head. It seemed strange that he was Brother Mark's father. I wondered if he was in charge of Brother Mark.

Mrs. Connor spoke up. "We have had such a hard time trying to see you. Are you taken care of very well?"

"Oh, yes," I answered, and the other Little Brothers agreed.

"You boys are the first interest of the court," Judge Wahlstrom began.

"Yes, your Honor," I said. He smiled because I knew what to call him. He was older than Brother Mark, because his hair was white and he was partly bald. I wondered if he was a good Catholic and wanted to protect us. I decided I should not trust him.

"This is a very happy day for your grandparents," he said, "they are the sweetest people in the world."

Everyone was very kind. They treated us as though we were important and had never been bad in our whole lives. I realized that they didn't know anything about us. They asked our ages and where we got our freckles. I was thirteen, and Benedict, the youngest, was eight. They were so concerned about what we wanted. But I knew it was all a trick to get us to leave the Center.

Judge Wahlstrom asked us if we went out of the place to see things. I told him that Father Feeney took us out sometimes. Brother Mark asked if we had ever seen a TV or a circus, and we said that we hadn't. They talked about college and said that I should be thinking of the future. But I didn't know what our Angels had planned for us.

Judge Wahlstrom turned to Paul. "Your father is a wonderful man. A father is a blessing to a son, and the son is a blessing to the father." Then he looked at us. "Would you like to visit your father? It would be for a few hours each time. He can take you to the circus or the park or wherever you want to go."

I looked at Brother Mark. He was smiling and his eyes were so hopeful. I just knew that if we visited him I could talk him into coming back, and then all the trouble would be over. But I remembered that Sister Catherine had told us that they really wanted to take us away for good. "No," I said, "we don't want to go out and visit."

"How about you, Matthew?" Judge Wahlstrom leaned toward him. "What would you like? Do you want to see monkeys and lions in the zoo?"

Matthew hesitated, then looked at me.

"Well, I don't want to leave home," I said. "Everything is so interesting at home; we'd never think of going anywhere else."

"I see that only Luke doesn't want to go. How about the rest of you boys? You could have so much fun."

I glanced angrily at the other Little Brothers, and they replied that none of them wanted to go. Judge Wahlstrom winked at Judge Connor. "I guess we asked that one too soon." He cleared his throat. "I want you to go out on visits with your father just for a few hours each time. Get acquainted. Be friendly. That's the way I feel. Okay?"

We nodded.

"Do you have any questions?" he asked.

"If we go for visits, can he take us away?" Paul asked.

"Oh, no, he cannot do that."

"Will our superiors know about it?" asked Michael.

"We'll work it out."

Judge Wahlstrom left the room after telling us to visit with our father and grandparents for a while. They showed us pictures of their house, and Brother Mark's sister's children. As we were leaving, Brother Mark said, "Good-bye now. Say a prayer for me, Matthew." I thought that he must be faking, because he still wanted to be wicked.

Back at home, Sister Catherine said that they were only pretending to be nice to us. Benedict told Sister Mary Agnes that he loathed Judge Connor's face, and mentioned that his thumb was cut off. Sister Catherine praised me for seeing through Brother Mark's tricks. She put me in charge of the others when we were with him. Sister Mary Agnes explained how wicked Brother Mark was. He had been with our enemies at the College of the Holy Cross for a whole year to get a degree, and he had told the court that we were in the hands of strangers. His lawyer wanted to put the Brothers in jail for contempt of court, and take us away. When Father Feeney came in, Sister Catherine said that they really wanted to destroy "our dear" Father. He gave us his blessing and, rubbing his hands in anger, said that God would punish Brother Mark, a traitor to Our Lady. Sister Catherine quieted him down by saying how wonderful I had been. He agreed that I was very holy, which he sensed when he gave me Holy Communion every morning. I felt embarrassed. I didn't need any praise. I knew I was very clever and could not be fooled by anyone.

During the week Mr. Anderson came to visit us. He was to be "our" lawyer. He was a tall older man, and he didn't speak much. We were told to perform our very best and to show our happiness by always smiling. He saw our swimming pool, the gardens, the ponies, donkeys, and chickens. We galloped our horses across the fields, paraded in the uniforms of Our Lady's Army with our military marches echoing through the hillsides. That evening we recited prayers in ten different languages and sang songs with very difficult harmonies.

The sun set across Mount Wachusett, fifteen miles to the west, and the red glow of the clouds colored the white table linen in the front room. Mr. Anderson had finished the homemade ice cream and apple pie. He sat back, listening to the last strains of our choir. As we bowed to leave, he turned to Sister Catherine. "Never in my whole life have I seen such innocent, happy children. The peace and beauty here—this really is a paradise." I saw Sister Catherine was pleased with our performance.

On Saturday, Judge Gould, whom the court had appointed as our legal guardian until the case was over, came out to the Center for his first visit. He was a stocky man with a deep voice and piercing eyes. Unlike Mr. Anderson, he seemed unimpressed by what he saw. He told us bluntly that visitations with our father would be on Mondays and Fridays from 1:00 until 5:30. We would meet Brother Mark at the judge's office in Clinton, only ten miles away. Sister Catherine couldn't persuade the judge to have the visitations at the Center. He must hate us because he is a Jew, I thought. He talked just like Father Feeney's imitations. (It was no secret around the Center that Father Feeney did not like Jews. He was often making fun of them and mocking the way they talked, even in some of his sermons. And the Center's publications, especially a magazine called the *Point*, contained many articles against Jews.)

Our lunch was served early on Monday, June 17, the day of the first visitation. We were given some coins and shown how to call home collect if we got in trouble. Michael and I tried to explain the values of the coins to the others who hadn't had it in class yet. We promised to be miserable.

As we waved good-bye, I saw that Sister Mary Agnes had tears in her eyes. She was worried that I might cooperate with Brother Mark, I thought. During our meetings, when they attacked him I had just kept quiet. Sister Catherine had asked me several times if I understood what to do, and I had nodded yes. I intended to obey. I didn't want Sister Mary Agnes to be sad, yet I felt I could decide what should be done. Also I didn't hate Brother Mark. I thought he might still come back.

Brother Giles drove us to Judge Gould's office. Brother Mark got up and greeted us. He showed us to two young ladies sitting at desks. One with blond hair asked our names. She had red fingernails and kept banging her cigarette on the edge of a brown dish. It smelled awful, just like the front room at the Center after guests had passed through. I noticed there was music coming out of the ceiling. They were trying to impress us, but I was disgusted.

Brother Mark made us meet his companion Dr. Pax, a professor at Holy Cross. Then, he drove us in his car to Whalom Park, where Father Feeney had taken us before.

Brother Mark was smiling a lot. I guess he thought that we couldn't resist having a good time in an amusement park. We had a surprise in store for him.

"Now, who's for a roller-coaster ride?" Brother Mark said. "I bet you wouldn't dare. You have to be very brave."

We all refused at once.

"How about the rocket ship?"

"We don't want to go on a rocket ship," I told him. "We don't like this. We're miserable."

People stared at us as we stood there in our blue and white uniforms looking down at the ground. I didn't like to be so mean to Brother Mark, but I realized that the court would take us away if we were happy in the world.

"You're going to make up your minds to like these things," Brother Mark said. "Normal children like them."

He finally got us to go on the merry-go-round. Father Feeney had taken us on this ride before, so I thought it would be all right, but right away Matthew started to wave his arms as if he were having fun. I looked angrily at him, and he stopped at once. I resolved to tell on him.

"Look at those bicycles. Wouldn't you like to have your own bicycle?" asked Brother Mark. I had seen bikes before and wanted very much to try one.

"We have horses at home," I replied.

When he bought sodas for us, we refused to drink them, but ate our own "goldsticks," the oganic candy bars we had brought from home. (We found out that Brother Mark didn't even know that the food in the world was inorganic and had poison in it.)

Dr. Pax, Brother Mark's companion, got more and more upset as the afternoon wore on. At first, he seemed about to cry when we refused to call Brother Mark "Dad." He thought we had a "rebellious attitude." I hated Dr. Pax. He was a sissy. I wished he hadn't come along, so I could talk to Brother Mark alone.

At 5:30, Brother Mark left us at Judge Gould's office. I called after him, "Remember to tell Judge Wahlstrom that we didn't like it."

I realized that Brother Mark could be scheming too, because he said, loud enough to make sure Brother Giles could hear it, "You seemed to be having lots of fun."

At home, we made our report, and Sister Catherine and Sister Mary Agnes said that they were proud of our courage to resist enjoying ourselves. Sister Mary Agnes was so happy. We agreed that Brother Mark was no longer a Brother and that we should call him Robert Connor, or R.C. for short. Sister Catherine scolded Matthew for waving. He promised never to be happy again. We talked about some new ways to make the visits annoying to R.C.

When one of the Little Brothers asked if Father Feeney

could take them on the roller coaster sometime, Sister Catherine told us they were planning the best summer we had ever had. We might even go to the ocean. But, she warned, that was a secret just for us. We promised not to talk about our visit to any of the other Little Brothers.

On the second visit, R.C. came alone. He brought us to Holy Cross, where many of our enemies lived. When we protested, he forced us to leave the car and go to his apartment, where he kept his bat and ball. While we were in the same room, he changed into older clothes. I was horrified. I realized then how sinful he had become.

That afternoon we tried to misbehave. We dented his bat by hitting stones and other hard objects with it, hurled the ball at him, and even destroyed his slides of our grandparents. We again refused any cookies or soda. Paul wrote on his desk, "You are wicked."

"When you force us to eat and drink even though we hate it, you treat us as slaves," Paul said defiantly.

R.C. got very angry. "I'm trying to get you away from that life where they make you do things. You've never had any choice. You do what they *make* you do." We didn't even bother to answer that one.

He tried to offer us money. "Luke, I will give you an allowance, and also Paul and Michael, if you clean the car."

"We are not interested in having money," Michael said.

"Oh, yes. Soon you will love money and what it can get you." I felt that he was determined to make us become like everyone else in the world.

On the way back, Michael opened the car door while it was going. R.C. hit him and threatened to tell Judge Gould. Then he turned on the radio with its crazy music, again trying to make us worldly. People on the radio kept telling us how wonderful everything was: beer, potato chips, cars. Sister Catherine had forbidden us to listen to such things, so I started talking and made him turn it off.

I tried to find out why he wasn't afraid of the punishments he would get in hell. He said that what he was doing was Our Lady's will. I wondered how he could have changed his mind so completely.

"You used to be one of us," I said. "You believed in everything we did."

He didn't answer right away, and then he said, "We didn't have a family life. Well, for three short years we lived in St.

John's House, and then you were taken away. I want you to have a normal family life. You won't think it now, but someday you will look back at what I've done and be grateful to me."

"But didn't you consent to do it the other way, when the families went to live the way they are now?" I asked.

He nodded his head. "I did it reluctantly, and now I see what a big mistake that was. I left because I knew those people didn't know what was best for you. You really aren't being smart by continually saying that you are miserable. Why don't you just try to cooperate? Otherwise, you'll have to leave right away. I don't want to do that because I love you. I'm trying to do it gradually, so it won't be a shock to you."

LOVED us? LOVED us? What could he possibly mean?

I laughed at him. "If you loved us, you wouldn't make us so miserable."

"You don't understand," he said. He was twitching his eyebrows as he talked. There were freckles beneath the hair on his arm. I had never noticed them before.

"When I was your age, I thought I knew a lot too, but now when I look back, I see I knew very little." He went on and on about how he knew what was best for us. What he said made little impression on me. I felt he had sold his soul to the devil. It was frightening. I wanted him to admit that he no longer believed in the doctrine of no salvation outside the Catholic Church. Then I would know that he was a heretic. But I was afraid to mention it. Sister Catherine said he would use it against us in court.

"You're never going to get us to like these visits no matter how hard you try." I loved being stubborn when it wasn't a sin. I could finally show grown-ups that they could not make me do something unless *I* chose to do it. I wanted to show R.C. and the Big Brothers and Sisters what a strong will I had.

At Judge Gould's office the tall lady with the dark hair tried to make us look happy. "Is that the way you are going to behave? You must practice a lot to keep a sad face like that. Smile. You are so fortunate to have a father."

"We are miserable on these visits," I explained.

"Don't you see," she said, "that when your father goes home all alone at night he is the saddest man in the whole world if he hasn't made his boys happy?"

"If he wants to make us happy, then he should leave us alone," Michael said.

Brother Giles came in and we left. Now, I thought, I could prove to Sister Catherine that we had made it clear to everyone that we wanted to be at the Center, for even the secretaries noticed how miserable we were.

"We're home," we shouted as we pulled up in front of the Center one afternoon.

"This is a wonderful place," Fred said in surprise, looking at the view of the hills and mountains miles away. Fred was R.C.'s companion for the day.

"I admit it is a beautiful place," R.C. said, "but it isn't good to stay here all the time."

"But we go out very often. All the things you have shown us up till now we have seen many times," I said. (That wasn't quite true, but I did not worry about lying to R.C., who wanted to take us away. I never even mentioned it in confession.)

"You ought to go out," R.C. replied. He was looking up at the windows in St. Therese's.

"We do! Why don't you let the people in charge take care of it?" I said, hoping someone inside would hear me.

"People out in the world can decide better than Brothers and Sisters and Father and Mrs. Clarke," R.C. said.

"You should call her by her right name. She is Sister Catherine," Michael said angrily.

We went under the apple trees and sat in the white garden chairs. Brother Boniface brought out some cold ginger ale and cookies. It was a treat for us, so we drank it up immediately.

R.C. sent me inside to see how far within the Center we could go. Sister Catherine, who told me they were watching every move he made, said we could go to the barn, the horses, and the swimming pool.

As we walked through the pear orchard, one of the Little Brothers brushed R.C.'s hand with poison ivy. We had been told that he was very allergic to it, that his face would swell up and he would be forced to stay in bed for weeks. R.C. never noticed it, though, and continued toward the cow pasture. The barn phone rang.

"They're giving the emergency signal," R.C. joked. "The Brothers will have to escape from the barn on foot before we get there." Just then Brother Gregory sauntered out of the barn. R.C. burst out laughing and turned to Fred. "That's John Conant. They call him Brother Gregory. His father is a Harvard professor. Look at him walk. Nothing ever bothers him, even an emergency like this visit."

R.C. showed Fred the wiring he had done in the barn. When we went to the pool, he pointed out the Angel escorting the children up the hill. "They're always accompanied by one of the women. The children are never alone, even at play." I didn't understand why he made such a point of that.

Back at Judge Gould's office we told everyone what a good time we had at the Center. They laughed at us. But we went home giddy—at the thought of R.C. with his poison ivy.

He never got it. As he took us across the street on the next visit, I looked at his hands. They looked normal. The devil, I thought, must have protected him so he could continue his wicked plans. Nothing would stop him.

He led us down the street and then pointed. I was horrified. R.C. was going to do the one thing that Sister Catherine had strictly forbidden. I felt all the energy drain from me. This was an emergency and I remembered our plan. This visit, R.C. was with a man he called Lee, and I thought they would probably use force. It may be difficult, I thought. We got nearer and nearer.

"We don't want to go," I shouted.

"No, none of us want to go!" The Little Brothers pleaded as he moved us closer to the building.

"It's only a movie. Children love it," R.C. explained as we stopped outside the Strand Theater.

The word "Tarzan" stood red and terrifying on the white board. I *had* to act now. R.C. was determined to have his way. I dreaded the embarrassment of screaming to get out of it, with all the people staring at us. They wouldn't understand. I gave the signal to Michael, and at the same moment the five of us ran off in several different directions.

I took off with Benedict and Matthew. We ran down the street for more than a hundred yards, then stopped and walked along casually. We glanced into the store windows to make it look natural. I heard R.C. shout, but I didn't dare look back. Michael and Paul, I hoped, had gone in the other direction. We were all by ourselves and people walked by as though nothing were wrong.

"Come on." Lee grabbed Matthew's arm. "We're down

here. You probably lost your way." We stopped. He had caught us. Now I could tell Sister Catherine that we ran away, but they caught us and forced us into the movie anyway. I saw R.C. running after Michael at the other end of the street. He would be furious, I thought.

"You are purposely disobeying me, aren't you?" he said sternly as we reassembled. He was out of breath.

"They must have lost track of where they were," Lee said calmly.

"Don't you want to go to the movies?" R.C. must have been pretending he didn't know how wicked movies were.

"No! You know we don't," I answered.

"That isn't the way to tell me, by running down the street." R.C. was gritting his teeth and talking low so people around wouldn't notice. "Is it?"

"We have told you before," I said in a loud and deliberate tone.

Now he knew that I was capable of causing a lot of trouble. He better not try to force us to go in, I thought, or I'll cause a big scene in front of everyone. I could see that he would hate that. He gave up and took us to Judge Gould's office.

"Why are you boys back so soon?" asked the secretary.

"These boys don't seem to understand they are supposed to obey me," R.C. said. "When I started to take them to the movies, they suddenly dispersed. Some went down the street, some went the other way. When I caught Michael, he tried to hit me."

"I did not," Michael said. "I was guarding myself in case you tried to slap my face."

"You boys don't seem to have any discipline," the secretary said. "If I disobeyed my father—*zing!*"

They were going to use punishments to force us into sin, I thought. We would be just like the saints. I was scared.

R.C. drove us to Greenhill Park in Worcester to see the animals. He had a camera and tried to take pictures of us, but we wouldn't smile. We knew he would use the pictures in court to prove we were happy in the world.

"You are a handsome boy," Lee said to me. "Don't you want your picture taken? There are so many people in Worcester that know you it isn't funny." I knew I was very handsome. Father Feeney had told me several times that I reminded him of the Kennedy brothers. I really wanted a picture of myself, even though I wasn't important. But I remained sullen.

Lee turned to Benedict. "Don't you want everyone to see your picture?"

"No! I'm just a little boy," he said.

Throughout the afternoon, R.C.'s friend Lee kept trying to prove that we were not normal. "Do you know what a balloon is or a motorcycle? Do you think lights are sometimes bright?" he would ask. "Of course," we would say. And then he imitated us, "Of course, of course, of course."

Near the end of the visit we were taken to Holy Cross. A priest came out wearing a wristwatch. I was scandalized. He told us that some movies are very good. I realized how wicked priests in the world had become. Father Feeney and Sister Catherine were right.

Back at Judge Gould's office he called us into his room. He smoked a big cigar and leaned back in his chair.

"Did you have a good time?" he asked.

"We had a very happy time last time when we went home. That was the only happy time we have had," I said.

"I know, you went to the Center," Judge Gould said. "But what about today? You remember, last time, I told you to be soldiers and obey? You should obey your father and your mother. The Holy Bible *says* you should honor both your father and your mother. Next time you read the Bible, look that up, and say a few more prayers." He went on about how we should see all these things in the world. We told him that we've already seen stores, and zoos, and airplanes.

"Robert Connor says that he has all of the court behind him," Matthew said.

"Whom do *you* have behind you?" the judge asked.

"We have the entire court behind us," I said.

"Let Matthew answer."

"We have the entire court behind us," Matthew replied.

The judge smiled and went on. "When you grow up, you will see that you have many, many people behind you—you have the court, and many other people, and you have *me*. I am your guardian. Now, I don't want any more leaping out of cars. . . ."

"That was just a mistake," I said. "They are used to having the car locked on the inside. R.C., ah, Robert Connor's car is unsafe."

"All cars can be opened from the inside." Judge Gould looked at me strangely.

"Ours don't open that way. They have safe locks inside so that can't happen. But now the Little Brothers are very careful when in his car," I said.

The judge leaned forward, disregarding what I'd said. "I don't want any more destruction of baseball bats or pictures."

"We didn't break the bats," I said.

Michael spoke up, "Robert Connor told you that."

"I hear things from many places and your mother and your father too," the judge said, sitting back.

"Do the secretaries tell on us?" we asked.

"I have eyes and ears that reach way out. Many things I see myself. It is very important that you obey *both* your father and your mother."

"Our mother gets us what we want. She isn't like our father, who forces us to eat what we don't want," I said.

"Then perhaps you are spoiled? Your father doesn't want to spoil you. Sometimes my children don't want to do things I want them to do, but they obey. Your father does things he feels will be good for you. Your mother is too soft on you if she gives you everything you want."

"No, she isn't," I said. "Everything is so much better at home."

Then he got a very serious look on his face. "Did anyone at the Center tell you to say that?"

"No, but we thought that if we told you, you would tell him to take us there." I paused. "Robert Connor told us that you told him he should take along some of his friends with us."

The judge looked stern. "Is that what the Center told you to call your father?"

"The reason the Little Brothers call him that," I said, "is because the men he brings with him call him that. They also call him 'Bob.' They speak about him like that." My excuse wasn't completely true, but it didn't bother me at all. I knew the judge was trying to prove that the Center told us what to do.

After each visit we would spend several hours with Sister Catherine, Sister Mary Agnes, and sometimes a Big Brother like Brother Boniface, who took care of the legal problems. They questioned us thoroughly as to everything that had happened.

We enjoyed telling them how we would terrify or make fun of R.C. When we played ball we would hurl the ball at him and once it hit him. The day he bought us water guns, we fired them into his face as we were leaving. We threatened to capsize the boat when he took us rowing, and he barely caught his expensive camera, which we tried to drop over the edge of a cliff in a park.

At the army meetings, Sister Catherine would mention how courageous we were. The Little Sisters, I hoped, would realize how clever I had to be to outwit R.C. and the world. I loved it.

"We have a big surprise for you," Sister Catherine said one evening after we had made our report. "We are going to show you some movies which we got for all the Little Brothers and Sisters." We became so excited. She said that they were good movies about fish and lakes and even one about Our Lady of Lourdes. I knew all the sinful parts would be cut out, just like they were in our schoolbooks, so it would be safe. I thought we were being rewarded for refusing to go with R.C. to the wicked movies out in the world. Also, we could now say that we had seen movies.

As we watched movies for the first time in our lives, the children kept exclaiming how real it looked. It didn't surprise me that Sister Mary John turned off the projector's light when it came to a scene at the beach.

The fact of the upcoming court case produced other improvements in the lives of the Center children. They bought us three new ponies, and we had more cookouts. On special feast days we would go out on the lawn with the whole community after Tea and Rosary and eat our own roasted corn with our homemade butter. We had all the hamburgers and hot dogs we wanted. Sometimes we would perform by singing or playing our band instruments when dessert was over. Other times the adults would entertain. I always enjoyed the Big Brothers' and Big Sisters' acts. The Big Sisters would sing songs from their skits. The Big Brothers would do a barbershop-quartet routine. Brother Gregory would sing "Under the Old Apple Tree" and Brother Christopher would play the accordion, harmonica, and bass drum, all of them simultaneously. We would laugh at Brother Isidore, who made faces as he sang "When Major Willard Draws His Gun." Brother Rafael would pretend to frighten us as he did "Anne Boleyn." We giggled as he repeated "with her head tooked underneath her arm she walked the bloody towa." Even the Angels laughed.

Although my stomach ached the whole time, the visitations with R.C. made me less worried about getting in trouble with the Angels. Sister Catherine and the Angels would still punish the others who were stubborn and refused to obey. But when the younger ones were bad on the visits, I would not tell on them if they were already in serious trouble at home.

One evening after supper, Matthew was called to the center of the room. For ten minutes he was scolded, as Sister Catherine and the Angels tried to get him to admit that he had stolen a spool of thread from the sewing machine. He said he just found it in his pocket. The longer she shouted, the more scared he looked.

"Now what have you done?" Sister Catherine said, pointing to the floor. We all looked down. A puddle of water was spreading out from his shoes. The Angels snickered as they moved to clean it up. Sister Catherine dismissed him, saying he had "one last chance" to be good.

At our next report, Matthew told Sister Catherine and Sister Mary Agnes how obedient he had been, and I agreed.

"Pete asked us thousands of questions and I didn't answer any of them," Matthew said proudly. Pete was R.C.'s companion that day.

"What kind of questions?" Sister Catherine asked.

"The usual ones," I said. " 'Have you seen TV?'; 'Ever ridden a bicycle?' Pete even asked if we go to Mass, but I changed the subject. I don't know what Michael told R.C. in the other boat."

"I can tell you what happened," Michael said. "R.C. gave himself away many times. He admitted that he hates you and Father." Michael turned to Sister Mary Agnes. "He pretended he liked you, so we threatened to tip the boat over."

Sister Catherine looked up from her pad. As usual, she was jotting down everything we said. She used a shorthand that we couldn't read. "Did he bring the life jackets in the boat?" she asked.

"Oh, yes," Benedict said, "but we were going to throw them away so he would drown if the boat went over. He was so scared." We all laughed.

"You know he cannot swim at all," Sister Mary Agnes said.

"Yes, you told us before," Michael said. "We thought we would scare him to death. He's so scared of us."

"That's why he brings those boys with him. They are his bodyguards," Sister Catherine said. "Let's get back to what he said and what you said. Start from the beginning."

Michael described the conversations he had in the boat.

"Then R.C. said, 'Do you know my wife?' He called you 'my wife,'" Michael said to Sister Mary Agnes. "Or he calls you 'Loretta.' He said, 'I wish Loretta would be a better woman,' and I said, 'No man would ever say that about a woman.' I told him, I said, 'She is Sister Mary Agnes, and she is our mother and she lives in a beautiful religious order.'"

Benedict spoke up. "He called the Brothers and Sisters 'men and women,' and Michael said, 'You don't love—'"

"Oh, and I remember he said, 'I like my wife,'" Michael interrupted, "and I said, 'You love Sister Mary Agnes? Then why are you taking her children away?' He couldn't answer that. We trapped him so many times."

"I remember you called over to our boat," I said. "You asked, 'Do you like him?'"

"Oh, yes, that's right," Michael said. "R.C. asked us if we liked him, and we answered, 'No.' He said, 'Would you like it if I disappeared and didn't show up again?' Benedict said, 'Yes, that would be wonderful.' Then he asked us to ask the other children, so we called over to your boat."

Paul waved his hand at Sister Catherine, "I said, 'Of course not.' We all told him that we didn't like him. Though Luke said—"

"I was angry that they were talking so much," I said to Sister Catherine, "so when they asked if I liked him, I said, 'We'll talk about that onshore.' I didn't want them to talk until I was with them, because R.C. would make them say the wrong thing."

"Can you remember anything else?" Sister Catherine asked.

"I just remembered," Benedict said, raising his hand. Sister Catherine nodded at him. "R.C. asked, 'Is what I am doing going to lead me to hell?'"

"We changed the subject," Michael said. "He was trying to trap us."

"In the car," I said, "he talked a lot. He asked me if I ever prayed for him, and I said, 'I used to before you tried to take us away.' He said, 'Imagine teaching children to hate their father and mother.' And I told him that in the Gospel Our Lord Himself said, 'Unless you hate your father, mother, wife and children for my sake, you cannot be my disciple,' and he didn't know what to say."

Sister Catherine smiled at that, and I felt proud.

Matthew started waving his hand. "He turned on the radio with the crazy music. First there was shouting and screaming, so he changed it and—"

"Oh, that's right," I interrupted. "He asked us if we liked the Beatles, and I said we didn't want to hear the radio. He said he hated the Beatles. Then later on he said, 'Listen, that's the song that Loretta and I used to dance to before we were married,' and he started humming it."

"Do men dance?" Paul asked.

"Yes, in the world they do," Sister Catherine said. "Robert Connor is deliberately trying to expose you to the wickedness out there."

"Men dance? How sissyish," Matthew said.

"The dances they do are so sinful," Sister Mary Agnes said. She looked like she could slap R.C.'s face. "And God is going to punish him." She paused, and her voice got softer. "We danced only once, at the Totem Pole, and I didn't like it. I left and waited until it was over." She looked as though she were sorry for having done something wrong.

"Connor is trying every way he can to make you like the world," Sister Catherine said. "This is the most vicious way, using our dear Sister Mary Agnes. The dances they do in the world are the most wicked, sinful acts before the eyes of God. The world is ready for another flood. I can't understand how Our Lady can hold back the wrath of God much longer."

"Yes," I said, "I knew R.C. was doing that. I just remembered that he asked, 'If Sister Mary Agnes leaves and comes with me, what will you do?' We said that she would never do that."

After we had told everything, Sister Catherine scolded us for talking so much. She said that we would lose our battle just by talking. From now on we were forbidden to answer any of his questions. If anyone asked why, we should say that we were too miserable to talk.

We obeyed at the next opportunity. R.C. hated it, but there was nothing he could do. I was surprised by the power of our silence.

"If they talk or smile, will they be punished when they get back to the Center?" asked the blond secretary at Judge Gould's office one afternoon. Brother Giles denied it.

At the art museum, where they had all the wicked statues, a guard asked R.C. if the five of us were mutes. We had been trailing behind him all afternoon staring at the floor.

"No, they can talk, they just won't," R.C. said in disgust.

The man at the fair tried to get us to shoot the moving targets, but we wouldn't.

"*I'll* pay *you* if you can get them to even try," R.C. said.

We looked at the ground, dejected, and the man gave up. R.C. laughed.

"How about bowling in a nice cool place," R.C. said.

"We don't mind the heat," we replied.

"No! You're superhumans. I'm human. I mind the heat." R.C. wiped his forehead. I hoped he was getting fed up with us.

Sister Catherine always gave us new ideas to make the visitations unbearable for R.C. She said that he loved a clean car, and if we threw up all over the seats, he might stop taking us out.

"You can do it by putting your finger in the back of your throat," Sister Catherine said, just before one of our visits. I hated to throw up, so I asked if any of the other Little Brothers could do it. Matthew and Benedict agreed to try.

"If that doesn't work, we can give you mustard water, but it would be safer to do it by gagging," we were told. By the day of the next visit, we were ready.

"What's that noise?" R.C. said, glancing into the back of the car. I was afraid that he had caught Matthew with his hand in his mouth. But he drove on. He was angry because we wouldn't talk. I waited.

"Oh, gosh! What was that?" R.C. said as he heard vomiting behind him.

"Benedict is sick," I said. "He threw up."

"Is it much?" R.C. asked.

"It's on his jacket and trousers and the car," I said. I hated the smell, but at the same time I was delighted. I didn't look at the mess.

R.C. pulled into a gas station and cleaned it up. I hoped we wouldn't have to do this often. Just the smell made me feel sick.

"I can clean it better when we get to my apartment," R.C. said. "Do you feel better now?"

Benedict didn't answer. We continued on in silence.

R.C. left four of us with his friend Pete, in the hall, and took Benedict into his room. He closed the door.

"I will give your jacket and trousers to the landlady to wash," I heard R.C. say. "Let me have your trousers." It scared me that he was going to make Benedict take off his trousers.

I knew the Center was trying to protect us from sinful things in the world. I didn't know exactly what they were, but maybe R.C. was about to do something wicked.

I had to stop it. I whispered to Michael to distract Pete by running down the hallway. Then I grabbed Paul and Matthew, and we raced out of the house, down the street, turned right, and finding a dead end, jumped into the bushes. We lay down. No one came by. An hour passed. "Stay here and say your rosary. If I say 'Come,' don't come; but if I say 'Come, ooop come,' then come."

I went back up the street. The house was quiet.

"Ooooh! You scared me," the landlady said as I stole up the back stairs. "Have you seen the kids that ran away?" she asked.

"What kids?" I continued up to the room.

Benedict had a bathrobe on. Everyone was sitting watching slides. R.C. became very angry. We argued back and forth. When he threatened to call the police, I agreed to help look for the others. Pete and I went out. I called, "Come," but they never came. R.C. then went out, but soon gave up.

"I'll call the police. They'll find 'em," he said, exasperated. I didn't want to cause too much trouble, so I called out once more and they came. I was certain we had done the right thing on that visit.

We also had to run away on the visit when he took us to a boys' camp. R.C. said he would take us to the Center to get our swimming trunks before we went to the camp, but we refused to get them. (Sister Catherine had told us never to go swimming at public beaches because of the immodest dress of people there. Also, I was afraid that R.C. might see the marks on the Little Brothers who had received the strap most recently. I thought maybe he would claim that the Angels had punished them for being bad on the visits, even though they had really been punished for something wrong they had done at home.)

R.C. got very angry and said, "Well, if you won't bring your trunks, then you can go swimming without any clothes on, like the boys do at the YMCA."

I was shocked. It was hard to believe that the world was that wicked. I didn't dare imagine what it would look like. It would be a mortal sin to think about it. We drove on in stunned silence.

At the boys' camp, we ran into the woods. When R.C. and his friend caught us, we were taken to the beach. I took a quick glance. None of the boys was naked, but their suits were much worse than any of the new bathing suits the Angels had tried on us that summer. The Angels had splashed water on us in the tub to make sure that no disgusting bulges showed. Then they had checked the length of our new suits by having us turn around and touch our toes. Sister Catherine would be angry if we watched the boys, so I refused to look. It would be sinful.

"You make me very angry," Judge Gould said when we got back to the office. "What has been going on?"

"Nothing, just going out on our visitations," I said.

"What did you do today?" he asked.

"We ran away."

"And on the last two trips?" The judge reached across his desk for a cigar.

"We had to run away on one of them, too."

"You seem to be very stubborn. I don't like to be harsh with you, but it seems to be the only way you will learn. Why do you keep running away?"

"Because we hate it. Can I tell you something?"

"Are you told to run away?"

"We do it on our own."

"I know, but who gave you the idea?"

"We had to do it to get away."

"Who put the idea in your head? Answer me."

"That seemed the only way to get away from it."

"At home, when you told them you had run away, did they approve? I know you are trained to be well behaved, but are you encouraged to do this to your father or not?"

"We decided it on our own," I said. "No one makes us run away, or tells us what day to do it. We do it when we have to."

"Then it is not the adults' fault but yours. And you are responsible. You think you can decide what should be done—but you can't. Listen to your father and obey him."

"Can I tell you something?" I persisted. "The reason we ran away last time was that he took Benedict into his room, and tried to make him take off his trousers without a bathrobe. We were afraid he would do it to all of us. He did it himself, and he made us watch him." Judge Gould started to say something, but I interrupted. "Can I finish my story?"

"Yes, go on," he said. He stared at me.

"We remembered the other time he undressed and made us watch him. When we went out in the hall so he could do it alone, he brought us back. He grabbed and pinched Benedict, and forced him back, and twice he made us watch him. And so last week when he asked Benedict to do it, we thought he was going to make all of us do it. So we had to run away."

"Why do you object to changing your clothes in the same room?"

"Because it is completely against our conscience," I said firmly.

Judge Gould called Robert Connor in. I knew he had heard the conversation because he was very red-faced and embarrassed.

"The children say you disrobed before them," the judge said.

"Oh, no. I never did," R.C. replied.

"Yes, you did," we all said.

"Oh, wait, I remember. Benedict became sick in the car, so when we got to the house I had to send his trousers down to be washed."

Judge Gould turned to me. "You never told me Benedict got sick."

I faced R.C. "His trousers did not have to be washed. You cleaned them very well at the gas station."

"They were really smelling," R.C. said, waving his hand in the air.

"Why didn't you give him a bathrobe?" I went on.

"I certainly did."

"Not until Benedict told you. Also *you* had done it before. You got undressed yourself."

"That is not true," he said, looking at me with a very severe expression on his face.

"Yes, you did. Yes, you did. You did," we all exclaimed.

"You mean, I took off my shirt?" he asked. He seemed to be mad and tired at the same time.

"Yes! And you took off your trousers, too, and made us stay in the room."

"Oh, that is right. I had to change clothes to play baseball." This time R.C. looked very embarrassed, as if he had been caught.

I spoke to Judge Gould, who had been sitting back smoking his cigar. "He made us watch him. We tried to go out in the hall, but he wouldn't let us go."

"You were trying to run away?" the judge said.

"No, we were not trying to run away that day. We just went out in the hall, and he pulled the Brothers back in. He made them watch."

"You made them watch?" the judge asked.

"I just kept them in the room so they wouldn't sneak off."

"We had never run away before. He pulled some of the Brothers in and shut the door. He even pinched Benedict and made him come back, and said, 'Sit here and watch.'"

R.C. looked down and shook his head. His face was so red. The judge dismissed him. I didn't feel sorry for him. This would teach him never to force us into what we didn't like.

"Do you want me to wait?" R.C. asked Judge Gould.

"No, you can go. I will take care of it."

R.C. left.

"I told you very nicely that you should be like soldiers. Obey." The judge turned to me. "You lead the others."

"That is what the Brothers want. They need me—they want me to tell them what to do and when," I said.

"You are supposed to obey your father, whether it is against your conscience or not. Obey your father even if he disrobes. If he wants you to remain in the room, obey him. It's an order of the court. You are supposed to obey. If I hear of you running away again, there will be trouble! You will be punished. It is dangerous to run away like that. I could punish you now, but first I want to give you a warning. I am going to see your mother and have a very serious talk about this running away. I don't want it to happen again."

Several visits later, R.C. called Brother Giles and the five of us into Judge Gould's office. He said he wanted to clear up some accusations we had made. We argued back and forth. When Brother Giles called R.C. a liar, Judge Gould objected. "No one is going to call anyone a liar in my office."

"Benedict, didn't Robert Connor say 'Watch me' when he undressed?" Brother Giles asked.

"Yes," Benedict said.

"Benedict," R.C. said, "look me in the eye. Did I say to you 'Watch me'?"

Benedict hesitated, then said, "No, but you forced us into the room."

R.C. pointed to Brother Giles. "This man here drilled it into you. The reason why I wanted you to stay in my room was because you had already been destroying valuable property. I had to keep you in my sight. You never told me you thought I was being immodest." R.C. looked furious.

Brother Giles burst out in anger, accusing R.C. of destroying the innocence of the children. Judge Gould demanded that he keep quiet, and again he told us to obey our father.

"Even if it's against their conscience?" Brother Giles asked, his voice getting louder.

Judge Gould kept telling us calmly to obey our father, and each time Brother Giles would ask, again and again, "Even if it's against their conscience?"

"Even if it is," the judge said finally.

Brother Giles leaped up and slammed his fist on the desk. "You want to corrupt the minds of innocent children!"

Judge Gould leaned forward. He was smiling, but it was a kind of scary smile. "Do you want to strike me?" he asked. "I am recording this whole conversation, Brother Giles, and this scene has revealed a startling side of your character and the children's environment that I do not like at all."

At this, Brother Giles quieted down. Once more the judge commanded us to obey our father. I nodded. I was too frightened to talk. We left.

In September, visitations were changed to once a week, on Saturday afternoons, because of school. During the week R.C. was at Boston College Law School, and we were in class until three o'clock. He continued to take us to parks and stores. We never talked. On Paul's birthday we refused to blow out the candles. R.C. always seemed angry, yet he no longer tried to force us when we objected. I was worried about what he was planning.

At home, we prepared for the upcoming court case. Sister Catherine and the others feared that R.C. would try to make us look abnormal and uneducated, for he had requested that the authorities investigate our buildings and school. Sister

Mary Salome was made a teacher, because she had a degree. She was to teach us what children in the world knew. We learned the names of the major newspapers and magazines, but I still couldn't remember which was the *Times,* the *New York Times,* or *Time* magazine. Sister Catherine said that our lawyer would fight to keep the five of us from being forced to testify in court. But she wanted us to be ready just in case.

I assured her that we would be ready for whatever the other side came up with. We had just practiced for a whole summer.

Chapter Four

"May it please the court, this is a petition by Robert H. Connor, presently of Still River, for a decree that he is living apart for justifiable cause."

With those words of Walter J. Griffin, my father's lawyer, the long-awaited Connor case had actually and officially begun. It was October 30, 1963.

The attorney continued his brief initial remarks, which he was making instead of a lengthy, formal opening statement to the court.

"It is just another separate-support petition, so-called, with a more or less involved problem concerning the custody of five minor children. There is also pending before you a writ of habeas corpus which was granted some time ago, and that too asks for an appropriate order concerning the custody, care, and support of the children involved.

"I see no reason why all the matters cannot be disposed of under the petition of decree for living apart. . . . I don't think any opening would serve any purpose. I think it is just another domestic case."

It was ten o'clock in the morning, a Wednesday, and the first few rows of benches in Judge Wahlstrom's courtroom in Worcester were filled with parties to the legal matter at hand. Behind them were reporters who'd been sent to cover this most unusual custody case.

Not all the "interested parties" were in the courtroom, however. A dozen or so of the adult members of the Center were in court, but neither Father Feeney nor Sister Catherine had left the Center. Those members in attendance, however, were under strict orders to call the Center whenever *anything* of possible importance took place.

My brothers and I were also back at St. Benedict's, where school had been suspended ("for the duration") and replaced by an air of expectancy. So much depended on what took place in that courtroom in Worcester, where, in effect, the Center's very way of life was on trial.

Mr. Griffin's repeated assertion that this was "just another domestic case" was not accidental. He wanted everyone to remember that even though the circumstances of this case were highly unusual, the same laws of the Commonwealth of Massachusetts still applied.

Much to the distress of Sister Catherine and Father Feeney, the Center was being forced to play by the rules of the outside world, the hated enemy. But that did not mean the Center sat back passively. For weeks there had been briefing sessions, cram courses in legal tactics and terminology for those who would, or might, be witnesses.

Sister Catherine was wise enough to know that if the judge got the impression that life at the Center was *too* different—as far as the children were concerned—from life in the world outside, it would weigh against us. Therefore, certain members had to be most carefully prepared, and of those the one who had to be best prepared was Sister Mary Agnes, my mother.

Sister Catherine probably did not worry too much over the question of how well my mother would do on the witness stand, for it was well-known that Sister Mary Agnes was one of those most devoted to the Center and to Sister Catherine. Also, Sister Mary Agnes was intelligent, quick-witted, and loved a good argument. She would not collapse if the lawyer's questions came hard and fast.

What *must* have worried Sister Catherine (and Father Feeney, though less so in his case because he simply did not know as much as she did about the day-to-day life at the Center), and perhaps even worried her greatly, was whether or not any of the Connor children would be called as witnesses. She did not worry about our loyalty, for that was definitely with the Center. But if we were under oath and were asked a question about punishment, an honest answer might cause big trouble.

Her fears on this score were probably lessened by her knowledge that very few of the adults at the Center actually knew the extent of the punishment, and that Robert Connor was probably no different. Still, she could not be *certain* about this, and that must have distressed her. Sister Catherine was not used to being in a situation that she did not control.

She knew the case would boil down to more than just the

quality of life for the children at the Center; it would come down to the question of normality. If the judge (there being no jury in this type of case) decided, after hearing all the evidence, that our life was not only different, but also different and *harmful*, then he would surely award us to our father and we would have to leave the Center.

At the time, I knew that I did not want to leave and I presumed that Sister Catherine and Father Feeney had nothing but the best intentions for all of us, no matter what that might entail. Later, I learned that my father believed the Center wanted to keep all the children because it would give the order a fresh supply of booksellers, an activity that provided the financial lifeblood of the organization. And what if he won the case and then other parents decided to leave the Center and take their children too? The Connor case could conceivably pave the way for others to leave. The Center did not want a legal decision, a precedent, that went against them.

It took me a number of years to realize that there was a great deal of truth in my father's appraisal of the situation, and that, clearly, Sister Catherine must have worried about the same thing.

From the very beginning of the trial, and although I was only thirteen years old, I was terribly afraid that the Center would do something foolish. I feared an overreaction on the part of some zealous member that would land all of us in hot water.

I knew how angry and even how violent certain members of the Center could get, particularly Father Feeney, and I was afraid that if the "enemy" provoked someone at the trial, we could all end up in jail.

I was not the only one of the children who felt this way, but as we were forbidden to discuss such things, it was not until years later that I learned many of the other children were as frightened by this prospect as was I.

It was just a few minutes past ten o'clock. My father took the stand, was sworn in, and began to give his testimony. His side of the case would be given first, then Sister Mary Agnes would have her turn. Everyone hoped the case would be over in a day or two, but it did not work out that way.

He gave his age (thirty-six), mentioned the date of his

marriage, gave some information about his parents, and recited the names and birthdays of his five sons (noting that I, Robert, was now called "Luke"). Briefly, in answer to the questions of his lawyer, he traced his schooling, his service history, and told the court of his present status as a first-year law student.

Then, as he began to relate the history of his association with the Center, his answers began to get longer and more detailed. Apparently, they were also getting more interesting because the reporters started taking notes—and one of the Brothers slipped out of his seat and headed for the telephone.

Q: Now, during the period that you were visiting the Center as a student at Harvard, was it at that time that you met Mrs. Connor?
A: Yes. . . .
Q: Was she a student at Radcliffe?
A: No, no. She was a bank teller. . . .
Q: And you met her in what year?
A: Forty-eight.
Q: You were a student at Harvard then?
A: Oh, no. I was at Holy Cross then.
Q: When you met her first?
A: Yes.
Q: Refresh my recollection for a moment. You went to Holy Cross when?
A: January of forty-eight.
Q: So, up until the time you left Harvard and went to Holy Cross you had not met Miss Cleary, Mrs. Connor?
A: That is right.
Q: Your reason for leaving Harvard and going to Holy Cross at that time was what?

Mr. Anderson, the lawyer retained by the Center to represent my mother, had a pretty good idea what was coming, so he objected to the question as being too "far afield." But before Judge Wahlstrom could answer, Mr. Griffin agreed to rephrase the question—and this time it was even more objectionable to Mr. Anderson.

Q: Was it as a result of Father Feeney that you left Harvard and went to Holy Cross?

My father was able to say, "Yes, sir. Certainly," before Mr. Anderson made his objection. But the judge overruled it, giving my father a chance to repeat the answer. This time he made it even more emphatic: "Definitely, sir, that was the reason."

He then went on to tell the court about meeting my mother, and he characterized the period of their earliest acquaintanceship by saying, "Our activities were centered at the Center. I would meet her there and we would go to the lectures there. Our whole lives evolved around the Center."

When I first read the trial transcript, years after it had taken place, I wondered if the court reporter had made a mistake, and that he had really said "revolved." Oddly enough, in a sense either word is correct.

The Center members in the audience were not pleased with the testimony about Father Feeney's influencing my father to switch from Harvard to Holy Cross. They did not want the judge to get the impression that Father Feeney or Sister Catherine controlled their lives. They felt all of their major decisions had been the result of their strong faith and their free will. Thus they got visibly upset at the testimony that followed just a few seconds later.

Q: Previous to your marriage to her in July, forty-nine, did you have some conversation with her relative to leaving Holy Cross?
A: Oh, yes. . . . I can best describe it by describing the conditions.

We went to the Center. And on this particular time— usually I went on Saturday—this particular time it was a Sunday. The door of the Center was locked and the lights were on. That was unusual. It was always open at that time. It was the first time it happened.

So as we walked away, Loretta said to me that she knew why it had happened, why the Center was locked. She had been told.

At this, the Center's lawyer objected. He said all of this was "much too remote." But Judge Wahlstrom disagreed, and my father was allowed to continue.

A: She had been told that the Center was getting ready to form, or was forming, a secret order; and they had this religious doctrinal controversy on it, that they were going to start proceeding on it, and they wanted to be sure of certain members of the order. They wanted to have a definite established order.

They told her that she could come with them but she couldn't associate with me also. In other words, I would have— She would either have to break off with me completely and go with the Center, or I would have to come with her. But we couldn't continue the old relationship of her becoming a member of the Center and having me at Holy Cross at that time.

So she put it right up to me, "Right now you have to decide. Are you going to marry me? Are we going to live in the Center and you would leave Holy Cross, or are we going to break up and you go back to Holy Cross?" In other words, I had to decide at that point, that Sunday night. And I decided to be with the Center. That is why I left Holy Cross. . . .

Q: During those first few years in Cambridge, Mr. Connor, will you describe to the court your family life and the circumstances under which you lived?

A: You mean while I lived within this community?

Q: Yes. In Cambridge, to begin with, and how it developed.

A: Well, initially when we first bought the house the second floor was the vacant floor, we moved in, Loretta and myself; and at that time we had just one child when we first moved in. We occupied the back two rooms. By that time several other couples had followed in our stead behind us, had become married, the same situation, so they occupied the two other rooms.

So in other words, in that one floor which would normally be an apartment you would have three families. Then as the top floor moved out, more families came in there. Somebody would buy the next house and so on and so on.

But once we moved down there we didn't eat there, we ate at Dr. Maluf's house. Then when several other houses has been purchased, they moved the dining house down where they heard Mass and everything. So it was a community life.

Q: So at some time did you take vows when you went in there?

A: Yes.

Q: When was that?

A: Well, I believe right in the beginning, January of forty-nine, we had vows. The only element that I can remember about it, in fact the only essential element really, was our promise of obedience to Father Feeney or to whom he might delegate.

Q: And did you live under that rule there in Cambridge?

A: Yes.

Q: Will you tell his Honor, then, how your family life developed in the application of that rule?

A: Well, we were living as husband and wife within this community relationship; and as they bought more houses, they would start switching the families around according to the size of the family—which was the best apartment for them, and so on. But—well, let's see. We had a child in fifty, another one in fifty-one, another in fifty-two. About fifty-two or fifty-three, in that area, they started taking the children away for periods of time for play and things like that; and then that gradually built up until they actually took the three oldest children permanently away—that is, on a complete basis. They would live in a little group of boys. In other words, they would live completely apart from the parents. The parents had nothing to do with those children whatsoever.

Then as the fourth child was born and the fifth child was born, that would also happen to them when they became two or three years old. In other words, between fifty and fifty-five all five of my children were never together; they never knew each other as brother and sister, or brothers. We had no girls.

So all five were not together at the same time. As a matter of fact, even the first two or three years when they were beginning that process, that is, taking them for play and just playing together, instructions, things like that, even at that time other women would come in and help with some duties, you know, the household.

In other words, the point of the thing was to try to make men and women not husband and wife, but religious. And everyone was performing a duty, whether it had to do with his child or her child or what it was. It was more that outlook on it.

Finally, Mr. Anderson objected. It is likely that he did so because his client, Sister Mary Agnes, was so agitated by the witness's repeated use of the word "removed" or the term "taken away from." As she would make clear in her own testimony, there was no element of force involved, which is what she thought my father was trying to imply. But Mr. Anderson failed to make that point, saying only that Griffin was leading the witness. This time the judge agreed with him and told Mr. Griffin to let the witness "do the talking."

Even before the case began, I had thought about the need to lie. It worried me from a moral standpoint, but also from a very practical one too. What if someone from the Center lied, on the witness stand under oath—in order to make our life look "more normal"—and got caught!

I was also worried about Sister Mary Agnes' health. How much strain could she take? We had been told stories of how the lawyers for the outside world would put pressure on a witness by asking many, many questions. I was scared she might crack.

As things turned out, that was the least of my worries.

My father then went on to describe the length of time that each one of us had actually lived with him and our mother, and concluded that subject by saying, "It [the age at which we left] would vary according to how they felt. I never knew exactly what the age was. When they didn't have to change diapers and things like that, you know, the trouble a small child would have, could walk and make talk a little bit, something like that, then they would take them. So that would happen to Paul—or rather, the last two you mentioned, Matthew and Benedict."

Q: And once those children went to live with the others in the community, did they ever again live under your immediate supervision or that of your wife?
A: No, not at all.

Judge Wahlstrom, who never hesitated to ask a question himself if the lawyers hadn't brought out the information he wanted, cut in. "Do I understand they were taken to a place in the Center, or someplace there, where they all live together under the care of somebody?"

A: That is true. But not Loretta, she had nothing to do with that, nor did I.
Q: And you had the boys in one building, a community accommodation, and the girls in another?
A: That is right.
Q: Was that true also of the other children?
A: Oh, yes. That is true of all the children.
Q: You say you lived with your—
The Court: Did you see the children at all after that?
A: We would see them passing in the yard.
The Court: You didn't go to where they stayed?
A: Well, initially they allowed us to talk to them on Sunday for about an hour or two. In the beginning we did have visitation.
The Court: Well, where did you see them?
A: Beside their building in the yard there, say an hour or two hours. But that was done away with after a year or so. So that you saw them only three or four times a year for about forty-five minutes.
The Court: When you saw them pass in the yard to and fro, did you have the right to speak to them?
A: In the beginning, as I say, we did. But these rules became tighter and tighter as time went by. But that was many years ago. Now it is definitely out.

It was almost time to break for lunch, but no one left the courtroom, for now my father had begun to describe the manner in which the married couples "chose" not to live any longer as husbands and wives.

Q: And the order [to separate] that was issued was applied to you and Mrs. Connor as well as the others?
A: Absolutely.
Q: Any conferences between you and Mrs. Connor or either of you and the authorities at the Center, if we describe them as such, that preceded this edict? Any discussion with you about it?
A: Yes, as a matter of fact. . . . About three or four months before this actually happened I was in the office

with Mrs. Clarke and Father Feeney. See, I did a lot of purchasing and buying then and I had to be in the office for many reasons. Father Feeney mentioned that he had this in mind, and he was a little concerned about whether there would be any objections or how they would take it.

But he did not ask me how I would take it. He would never ask you. He would stand there and rub his hands like this and say, "Anybody that doesn't go along or anybody that shows weakness in the methods here is going right out of here." And that is the whole point. If we went out, sir, the children and wife would stay behind. . . .

Q: To begin with, Mr. Connor, did you have at that time some talk with your wife, the subject matter of which was leaving there? Yes or No.

A: Yes.

Q: Did you have that similar talk on other occasions subsequently thereto?

A: Yes.

Q: About how many times?

A: Four or five, six times. I don't know exactly.

Q: Then may I ask you the question did she ever actually leave with you?

A: Never.

Q: During those conversations did she make some threats? Yes or no.

A: Yes.

Q: What were the threats that she made?

A: That she would remain there.

Mr. Anderson: I object.

The Court: That is admissible.

Mr. Anderson: The court will note my exception, please.

The Court: Yes.

Q: What did she threaten?

A: She threatened that she would remain at the Center, that I would be a traitor if I left.

During a good deal of the latest testimony, the judge had been getting more and more interested, and at this point he took over the questioning.

The Court: What is the threat?

A: The threat is that the children would remain with her, and the threat would be that I would lose the children if I left. Because if I left the children and the children remained, that would be the end. I mean, she wouldn't take care of them but would be in the locale.

Q: Following that, this was in 1955, did Mrs. Connor ever live with you again as husband and wife?

A: She did not.

Q: And did you have some conversation with her?

The Court: Now you are dating this from the time that you were ordered to separate?

A: That is right.

Q: And did you ever talk with her about the subject matter, which was resuming your marital life with Mrs. Connor?

A: Yes.

The Court: Well, did you part altogether? Could you see each other?

A: Not any more than we saw the children. In fact, that would be the only time we would see each other; when you went to that play area she would come too.

You must understand this. The very first, say, year or six months they were a little more liberal. I mean, you couldn't clamp these rules down; they were bad enough as it was.

That brought Mr. Anderson out of his chair with an immediate objection—"He is giving a speech here"—and this time the judge agreed with him.

Mr. Griffin then asked my father to tell how the rule of separation was established and enforced.

A: Gradually, rules were put in and first not enforced, but pertaining to silence, pertaining to speaking with other people, pertaining to speaking with your relations, either your husband and wife or your children. Those rules were slowly enforced.

Q: Now, will you tell us what the rules were, as best you can remember?

A: The rules were that you were to speak to only those with whom you had business, and you were inferring that you had no business with your children, no business with your wife, there was no reason for it. And you would only speak, say, if you were working on a job and you had to ask for a tool, you would speak for that; or at certain times like after supper, then you could speak for an hour, or maybe talk in the library. There were certain specific times and certain specific places you would have to go to, what they called a speaking place. They would assign a place like a hallway. If you wanted to talk you would go out there.

Now, that was only between the men. That would be between the men, and the women between women, children between children. . . . When they first brought the children up, the little girls living all together and the boys living together, the little boys were taken care of by the men as the girls were by the women. So, occasionally some of these people that took care of them would be their father, but not as father, as supervisor, it would be as supervisor.

This line of testimony had the Center members visibly upset, but things would soon get worse, at least from their viewpoint.

Q: Now, would you describe what took place at those meetings between you and Mrs. Connor and the children, what observations you made of the children?
A: My observation was they had no allegiance to their brothers at all, no sentiment.
The Court: Would they recognize you?
A: Oh, yes, they would recognize us, yes. And they knew their last name. But I don't think they considered themselves brothers.
Mr. Anderson: I object. Please, that is voluntary.

This, of course, was just the kind of testimony that the Center members hoped would not come out, for—if true—it made the organization appear almost unnatural and perhaps even cruel. But Mr. Anderson's objection went unheeded. He would have to wait and ask about this, if he dared to, during his cross-examination.

My father had just testified that his five children ". . . didn't have any special allegiance to us, so they would be just as apt to talk to somebody else." And that, plus his statement that we didn't consider ourselves brothers (which was certainly true, at least as viewed from his perspective), had produced a discernible buzz in the courtroom. It would continue.

Q: Tell us what you observed concerning the children?
A: I observed that they had as much love and sympathy, or affection, or comradeship, with any of the other boys as they did with their own brothers. There was absolutely no distinction whatsoever.
Q: And any distinction that you could observe between their attitude toward you—talking about your own children now—their attitude toward you or Mrs. Connor as distinguished from other members of the order?
A: I would say they had more affection—in fact, I know they did—for certain members of the order who were assigned to take care of them. Whereas neither one of us had anything to do with them, they would be more apt to go over and talk with them than they would to come over to talk with us.
The Court: Did they recognize each other? For example, your five boys here, did they recognize each other as brothers?

Mr. Anderson must have been steaming inside, for now the question he'd just objected to was being asked by the judge himself!

A: No, I don't think so.
The Court: What relation? I mean blood relationship.
A: Well, they were told that they were, but there was no brother relationship.
Q: As a matter of fact, at some time later you started to tell his Honor about some incident that took place at Still River relative to the fraternity. What was it?
A: Yes. I was doing some electrical work in the building, some communications, and Matthew—he would be the second youngest—came in to go, to use the bathroom, and he, knowing he violated the rules, but nevertheless, came up to me and asked me—
Mr. Anderson: I object. How does he know what the boy thought?
A: I know what the rule was.
The Court: You cannot go into his mind, you see.
Q: Without drawing inference, just tell his Honor what he said?
A: He came up to me and said, "Are you my father?"

My brothers and I were not informed of the developments in court until the evening, but I eventually learned that the lunchtime scene was one of extreme anger among the members of the Center. They were firmly convinced that not only was R.C. exaggerating and lying, but that the judge was already on his side. My mother, Sister Mary Agnes, was particularly upset at what she called the judge's "obvious bias." She told someone that he already had his mind made up against the Center before the case ever started.

They were eager for Sister Mary Agnes to take the stand and tell "the true story." Sister Catherine, no doubt, hoped my father would finish soon and do so without mentioning anything concerning the disciplining of the children. But he had a lot more things to say.

Q: If you will, describe the children's daily activities, insofar as you observed it?

A: Well, they would go through the beginning of the day up to and including breakfast just the same, and after breakfast they would wash dishes, as we did too. Then they would go back to their buildings, where, supposing in the summertime, they would have some activity supervised. They were always supervised every minute of the day. If they were going out in the field or work in the field, they had gardens and various duties they would perform in connection with that. Then they would have their own lunch and their own work in the afternoon again, and they would show up for the services at five o'clock. Then after supper they would go back to their dorms to go to bed.

Q: And did the rules of silence apply to the children as well?

A: They did as far as the building I was in, Saint Therese's House. But over in their own building, in their dormitories, they weren't as strict in silence with little boys, I think, as I know of.

Q: What about recreational activities of yours, the men and women in the organization?

A: Recreation?

Q: Yes.

A: Well, just that half an hour I mentioned after supper and the half-hour at lunch, or fifteen minutes at lunch where you could talk.

Q: Were there any televisions in the institution?

A: No television or radios, anything like that.

Q: No radios?
A: No.
Q: Children see television?
A: No, never.
Q: Taken out to the movies?
A: No, never.
Q: What were they provided with by way of uniform, if any?
A: Well, they dressed in a little blue suit with a white blouse, but they have a military uniform which they put on and they parade up and down the street once a month. They have a parade with a flag and band and bugle and so on; they call it Our Lady's Army. Oh, and their whole life is regulated by this army and by the way they have army meetings.

At this, Mr. Anderson objected, saying, "There is no question before him" because no one had asked my father about the lives of the children being "regulated." It was just such descriptions of our life that the Center wanted to avoid. But again, before the judge could rule on the objection, Mr. Griffin neatly defused the point by rephrasing his question.

Q: Will you describe further what you observed as far as the activities in which the children participated?
A: Well, during the year they had tutoring there. I don't—
Q: Well, the question was particularly directed to this armylike activity you started to mention.
A: Well, when a child is bad . . . [There must have been a sudden tenseness on the part of Sister Mary Judith when she heard those words. I am sure she stared very intently at my father as he finished his answer.] . . . they are told this isn't being a good soldier and they are taken out of certain classifications and put back in a lower classification, something of that nature.

Sister Mary Judith's relief was undoubtedly great, and it probably got even greater when she realized that Mr. Griffin was not going to follow up on what if anything else happens "when a child is bad." There was of course no guarantee he would not return to the subject of punishment, but he had passed up what appeared to be a perfect opening.

Instead, he asked if the children had access to newspapers or "funny pictures," and my father said no to both questions.

Then the attorney began to question my father on the subject of Father Feeney.

By 1963, the time of the custody battle, Father Feeney was no longer the dynamic man he had been during the Center's formative years. He was sixty-six by then and age had taken its toll. But there was no lessening in the admiration and esteem in which he was held by the adult members of the Center. Sister Catherine may have been the power behind the throne, but Father Leonard Feeney was the man these men and women had given up so much to follow. Having turned their backs on their own past, including family and friends, they had embraced the vision of Father Feeney. They had been through hard times with him, for the sake of the doctrine that was the hard rock of their faith, and they would not hear ill of him.

So, when my father testified that Father Feeney was not quite all that a religious leader should be, he earned the instant and everlasting enmity of the Center's members. What sympathy might possibly have remained turned to hatred. It was one thing for a man to lose his belief in the doctrine—as odious as that might be, it was at least not without precedent—but for a person to speak unkindly about Father Feeney was unforgivable.

Q: The subject matter of these lectures given by Father Feeney to which you went, was attendance at them compulsory?
A: Yes, it was.
Q: Were they in the nature of instruction?
A: Yes.
Q: Can you describe some of the instruction that you received in the course of those lectures?
A: Well, for a period of time we— Well, it really amounted to a tirade against the Jews. I don't know, but for a number of years—six, maybe—there was a whole period of time when they were on that subject to show how they were cursed by God and all the different things they did through history that was evil and what they are doing in Boston and the United States, in the world in general, and how they are responsible for communism and everything. That was one particular vein. . . .

Q: Are children in this instruction as well? Are children allowed in this instruction as well?

A: Oh, yes. . . .

Q: Well, are these children at the present time under the control of Father Feeney at Saint Benedict Center?

A: Absolutely.

Q: Now, have you made observations of Father Feeney and his activities that would indicate to the court whether or not he is of sound mind?

A: Oh, yes. Many, many things. . . .

In my capacity of buying things, purchasing, I had to go into the office many, many times for money, and Father Feeney would carry on terribly. He would cry, stamp, slam doors. He would just act like a little seven-year-old that needed a spanking. That's all it amounted to. Of course, he did not make decisions. Mrs. Clarke made decisions. But he would carry on.

If he were in the Common, for instance, and somebody would come up, especially a Jew, and criticize what he said, he would give like the Catholic priest does in blessing, only he would do it, "I curse you in the name of the Father, Son, and Holy Ghost." He would curse them directly. I heard those things; they definitely happened.

There were countless experiences where I had to buy something necessary, something that there was no question but what I had to purchase. I would go in and ask for the money and he wouldn't speak to me for a week.

Q: Were you involved in riots with him?

A: Yes. We had two days of riots in Boston, where we carried around placards criticizing the hierarchy for allowing a chapel to be put up at Brandeis, those three chapels at Brandeis. They were in little groups, about three or four in a group, with these placards, and they were attacked, especially by the Jewish organizations, physically attacked. I myself got hit over the head with a paperweight. And it went on for days, street fighting. . . .

Q: Have you observed any changes in the demeanor of Father Feeney, or his acting in the subject matters from the period since you left the Center?

A: I would say his attitude has definitely deteriorated. I could tell that because I made a tape-back [a tape recording] of some of his talks that were made earlier, say, in fifty-three, and I compared that with him currently. . . . This incident I am talking about, hearing this tape, was about— Well, I left in sixty-two, so it was shortly before that that I heard the tapes. But in his older days he would be advocating no salvation outside the Church. Now, the last four or five years it was just a wild yelling, screaming, and cursing. I heard him call the Pope a dirty wop, things like that.

Q: And was this descriptive of the lectures that you received nightly?

A: Yes. Except the last phrase I mentioned, he would not get that violent in a night lecture, but he would be pretty violent. Anybody who has been to Boston Common can testify to that.

Q: Do you object to this court to your children being under his supervision, care, and control?

A: As much as I could possibly object, I do, absolutely.

When my father began to testify, later that afternoon, about private conversations he'd had with Sister Mary Agnes, Mr. Anderson immediately objected. My parents may have been members of St. Benedict Center and the Slaves of the Immaculate Heart of Mary, and they may have taken vows of obedience and celibacy, but in the eyes of the Commonwealth of Massachusetts they were still husband and wife. And any conversation they had was a privileged matter, except if a third party had been present. Then the privilege no longer applied and the witness could testify about the conversation. However, the judge did not require that the third party be identified.

If any member still felt the judge was neutral after that ruling, that feeling probably went right out the window during the following exchange. My father was testifying about a conversation with my mother.

A: Anyways, so I told her, I told Loretta, that it was a crazy setup, that I wanted to leave. She said, "If you do, the children will stay here with me. I am not going to leave; the children will stay with me." And that is the very thing that held me there the whole time. And she said, "At least in Massachusetts the mother always gets the children, and I am going to stay here. So if you leave, you leave us here."

Upon hearing this, Judge Wahlstrom interrupted. "It may be so in the rest of Massachusetts, but it is not always so in Worcester County."

Although the remainder of my father's direct testimony (as opposed to what he said when being cross-examined by Mr. Anderson) covered several other areas, the one that most interested the press was the conduct of the children on the thirty some visits he made to us prior to the beginning of the case.

Mr. Griffin tried to characterize our behavior as having been the result of "brainwashing," and when Mr. Anderson objected, Judge Wahlstrom told my father to communicate directly with the court and tell what he observed.

A: All right.

At first they wouldn't answer any questions. If you took them to an amusement park, they didn't want to go on any rides. If they did answer anything, it was to tell me how miserable they were, being away from the Center. When I tried to bring them in with groups of other children, oh, like Dr. Pax [the professor of philosophy from Holy Cross who accompanied my father on several visits], who was here this morning, and his family to play with, children about the same age, they would have nothing to do with the children; they wouldn't receive any food or drink. They would just stay together, a closed group, and look at you; and they persist in that.

They ran away twice.

They destroyed pictures of— Well, my first visit, not knowing what to expect, I brought them to my apartment so I could change my clothes; we were going out to play baseball. The first thing they did was take the pictures of their grandparents and destroyed them. They wrote on my blotter, "You are wicked." They took the baseball and bat and proceeded to lose it. That was one day.

We went out boating a couple of times where they tried to beach the boat, tried to upset the boat.

They always had some kind of question. If they said anything, it was always a question they were going to ask. Oh, like some pointed question. I have an unlisted telephone number; they would question that. "Who is your car registered in? Whose name?" and "What do you consider home?" Questions that are highly inapropos for a child of that age.

Most of the times that we went to football games they would sit there frozen-faced, no emotion, nothing. If you asked them if they enjoyed it, they said no, they hated it.

They hated everything. No matter what I did, it was impossible to please them.

I would ask them, "Is there anything I can do to please you?" They would say, "We want to go back to the Center." That is the only thing that would please them.

And then they told me many, many times, "I hope you die. We are going to make you hate these visits."

At that point my father turned and asked the judge if it was all right if he used notes that he had made, after each visit, to refresh his memory. The judge gave him permission to do so. It was ironic: Whenever we returned to the Center after these hated visits, we were taken into Sister Catherine's office, where we told her everything that was said and done—and *she* took notes, in her special shorthand. As it turned out, this note-taking had been a two-way street.

Referring, from time to time, to his notes, he continued his testimony.

A: Well, after the first visit I had to have somebody with me because five boys, driving a car was too risky, your Honor, because after the second visit they destroyed property and all sorts of things, so I had to have somebody with me; most of the visits I had to have somebody with me....

(He reads from a note card.) "Took pictures of Mother and Dad, slid them down from the mantelpiece. They are gone forever. We went to play baseball. Tried to damage the bat, lose the ball; no interest in game, insolent. Came back to the apartment. Sent Luke and Michael to the corner store for tonic." I thought I would give them an allowance; give them some job, some interest in something. That didn't do any good. They didn't want an allowance.

They called me a fake, said they would make me hate the visits. Later, I noticed they wrote on my desk, "Brother, you are wicked." I have a radio in my car. I played some semiclassical music that I thought would appeal.

Michael opened the car door on the way home, in motion that is, and—

At this point the judge interrupted again. Perhaps he was shocked by—or tired of—this litany of misbehavior.

The Court: Well, was there any difference in the actions of any of them?
A: No.
   Luke is the superior, he is the oldest. The others will not answer any questions at all. If you direct a question at Luke and he knows he can answer that question, he will answer it. . . . Well, for one thing, this affects the youngest—they have to go to the bathroom about every half-hour. For instance, your Honor, the youngest were affected by this nervousness; they are terribly nervous when they get on these trips.
   The little one threw up once in the car. The littlest one threw up in the car on the way from Clinton to Worcester. I stopped at the gas station, I cleaned him up the best I could, but still it smelled up the car. When we got to the apartment in Worcester, I took his jacket from him and his pants, gave him a bathrobe. I wanted to wash them. I had the landlady wash them. They were Dacron, they dry fast, and she gave them back. I showed them color slides; it was daytime and it was raining out. So they accused me, through another party, of immorality—now, what child would think of a thing like that—because I had taken the pants off.
Q: What accusation was this that was made?
A: Judge Gould, in his office they accused me of immorality because I took his pants and jacket off, but neglected to say he had thrown up and was washed.
Q: Some incident took place in Judge Gould's office?
A: Yes. A big scene there.
Q: First, who was present?
A: Judge Gould, Brother Giles, the five children, myself, and Pete Trainor, the boy who went with me from Catholic Charities. . . . Judge Gould told the children—by that, he always means Luke, because Luke is the only one that does any talking—now tell Peter what you told me. So Luke said that Peter Trainor said that Father Feeney was excommunicated. That was an accusation. I hadn't checked

with Peter beforehand, but I knew he would never say anything like that. He denied it absolutely. There is no truth in the matter at all.*

Then they accused me of immorality because I had taken the child's pants and jacket off.

And then there was another accusation which escapes me.

In any event, Judge Gould said they were incidental and did not matter. But at that point Brother Giles, the adult here, went into a big scene. He slammed the desk, pounded the desk, and he said, "The children are not going on any more visits. It is against their conscience. It is hurting their souls to take them out and see these things. They are not going on any more visits." And he kept pounding the desk. Judge Gould leaned over and said, "Go ahead, hit me." Because that's the way it was. He was about this far away from his nose. *(Witness demonstrated by holding his hands a short distance apart.)*

And Judge Gould said, "This has changed my whole attitude of you and the Center."

And I also want to say that this was taped, so Judge Gould has a tape of that. That is one incident.

Continuing his description of what the visits had been like for him, my father read:

A: "First of July. Picked up the children at one o'clock with Lee Packard"—he only came once—"tried to take them to see the movie *Tarzan,* a child's movie, the Clinton, children's movie. Children became violent, split up and ran away. Then I asked them to get in the car and go to Greenhill Park. They became insolent. Paul hit me. We all went to Judge Gould's office and he wasn't there, but his secretary told the children to mind. Then we went to Greenhill Park, saw the deer, buffalo.

"Went to Holy Cross and Father Higgins showed them the chapel. The children were very much more docile after the first hour of fighting. . . ."

Here. "The children remarked that Judge Gould was in cahoots with me and didn't care what they wanted. Father Feeney was the only one they would listen to." . . . "Took

---

*My father was mistaken. Peter Trainor actually did tell me that Father Feeney had been excommunicated.

children in two rowboats with life jackets on Lake Quinsigamond. Pete took Luke, Paul, and Matthew in one boat, I took Michael and Benedict with me. We let them row all the time, and they said of all the things they hated doing, this was the most enjoyable.

"Michael kept wanting to argue with me, insisted that I say Father Feeney and Sister Catherine were saints. I wouldn't. At this point they took off their life jackets and threatened to throw them overboard and said they would drown and be done with these annoying visits.

"They said I was going to hell and, for the first time, claimed I was trying to take them from their mother, who they admitted they seldom spoke with."

There was more of the same, as he went on to describe other visits and other acts of insubordination, disobedience, and dislike. He started to tell of the time he took us to the art museum and we walked around so silently that a guard asked him, as we were leaving, if we were all deaf and dumb. But the rules of the court prevented him from repeating what the guard had said. But my father *did* say, "They act as though their minds were left back in Still River."

Finally, he talked about his intentions for us if the judge awarded him custody: "My plans are to give them a normal family life where they receive normal affection, normal family life. All they have had is military life. . . . If I get custody for which I am petitioning for, I will take them back to Ohio. Initially, at least, have them live with me in my parents' house with my mother, father, and myself, because it is a large house. Then there is an excellent school run by the Holy Cross Brothers in our town; it has the very highest reputation. I would send them to that school, which is not faraway. My sister, with six children, lives close by. It will be something they have never experienced, a real family love and companionship."

When my father finished his testimony, it was late in the afternoon, but it was not late enough to quit for the day. Mr. Anderson would have time to begin his cross-examination.

My father must have been emotionally weary. He'd had to talk about a great number of things that were embarrassing and troubling to him. But he had no choice. If he wanted to get us out of the Center he had to tell things the way they had happened. And, even though I did not think so when I first heard reports of his testimony, I now see that is just what he did. Certainly, as the judge later pointed out, he was biased. But he was fair and, in all important details, accurate.

That night, the first night of trial, the five of us Connor brothers were told only that their father had perjured himself repeatedly during the day. That news pleased us. We wanted him to lose the case so we could stay at the Center.

Our greatest fear had to do with the health of Father Feeney, who had collapsed one morning while saying Mass. He remained ill for the rest of the trial, and thus we had no Mass during this period of crucial importance for the Center. We kept Father's illness a secret, but somehow the news leaked out. Even Pope Paul VI made an inquiry as to Father Feeney's health. I was surprised that Rome had found out so quickly.

Looking back, I am sure the worry about the outcome of the trial, the fear that the Center might have to disband, caused Father Feeney to fall sick.

Something very unusual happened that night just as we were about to go to sleep. Sister Mary Agnes came and visited each one of us in our cubicles just before bedtime. I was embarrassed, because I knew that she was not one of the Angels whose job it was to watch over the children, and that she had to have special permission to do what she had done.

I realized why she had made that unusual visit. Also I knew why she was there the next night and why we were dressed up in our Halloween costumes so that a photographer could take our pictures. When I reminded her of the ingenious costumes I had made in previous years she told me she would tell the court.

Before she left each cubicle that second night, she told all of us to pray especially hard for the "brave Big Brothers and Sisters who have to go to court every morning."

There was no in-court session on Thursday, October 31. Instead, the judge and the lawyers for both sides made an inspection tour of the Center. They saw all the places of importance, even where we slept.

Mr. Anderson continued his cross-examination of my

father the first thing on Friday morning. He did not succeed in getting him to change any of his earlier testimony, to any noticeable degree, but he did bring out that my father had suffered from ulcers for the last several years he was at the Center, and it became necessary for him to be placed on a special diet, which meant he could no longer go bookselling.

Mr. Anderson's intention was to show through his questioning of witnesses that St. Benedict Center was no different from any other religious institution and that there was nothing different, unusual, or "deteriorated" about Father Feeney. It was a hopeless task, but he did his best. At one point, early in Mr. Anderson's cross-examination, Judge Wahlstrom chided him to move faster.

Except for a fairly minor alteration here and there, the cross-examination did little to change my father's original testimony.

It must have been apparent to most of the people in the courtroom, and in particular to the judge, that although there were other witnesses waiting to testify, there was really only one more *important* witness: Sister Mary Agnes, my mother.

It was nearing three in the afternoon when she took the stand. She had been immediately preceded by her father-in-law, Judge Stephen Connor, whose testimony supported that of his son, especially in regard to such instances as the confrontation outside the Center when Father Feeney struck Robert Connor. In addition, Judge Connor testified that he was ready, willing, and able to help in providing a home for his five grandsons.

I cannot report how my mother looked when she took the stand and began to testify, for I was not there. But I am positive that she, too—for quite different purposes—was "ready, willing, and able."

Q: What is your name?
A: Loretta B. [Cleary], known in religion as Sister Mary [Agnes].*
Q: Where do you live, reside?
A: I live at Still River, Massachusetts.
Q: Do you live at the Center?
A: I live at St. Benedict Center.
Q: How long have you lived in the Center in Massachusetts, in Harvard?

* This name is used throughout to protect the feelings of my mother.

A: Since January 31, 1958.
The Court: Let me get one thing straight. Is the Center still known as the Saint Benedict Center?
A: Yes, it is, your Honor.
The Court: You have been using another name, Slaves of—
A: That is the name of the religious order, your Honor.
The Court: That is the name of the religious order?
A: The Slaves of the Immaculate Heart of Mary.
The Court: That is the religious order as distinguished from the Saint Benedict Center?
A: From the Saint Benedict Center, right. All of those who live at the Center—
Mr. Griffin: There is no question before you.
The Court: May I warn you now, you are going to be asked questions, just answer them and stop. Witnesses get into difficulty when they add something.
A: All right, your Honor. I am sorry.

Perhaps my mother was sorry, perhaps she was merely being polite, but anyone reading the transcript cannot help but notice that Sister Mary Agnes soon "forgot" the admonition not to add to her testimony. At almost every opportunity, she would try and set the record straight—from her viewpoint—and correct what her husband had said on the stand. This was a deadly fight to the finish, a holy war, and her antagonism came through. So did her cunning and her sense of humor.

She testified that she had five sons, and when Mr. Anderson asked if they lived with her she said, "Yes." This seemed to confuse Judge Wahlstrom, probably because he'd just heard my father say something quite different.

The Court: They live with you at the Center?
A: Yes, your Honor. They live in the same house with me, Your Honor.
The Court: Live in the same apartment?
A: No. They live under the same roof. They sleep in a different section than I do.
Q: Who cooks for the boys? Do you?
A: Yes, I do.
Q: How many times a day do you cook for them?
A: Oh, generally twice a day and, very often, three times a day.

The Court (interrupting): Now, when you say you cook for the boys, do you mean these five boys?
A: Yes, I do.
The Court: Or the thirty-five boys that might be there?
A: I cook for all the children and I serve my own children.

Apparently, the judge caught on right away to the fact that at least in this instance, my mother would put the best face she could on any question that gave her the opportunity. For, when Mr. Anderson asked her, "Have you been cooking for the boys since you came [to the Center]?" Judge Wahlstrom cut in to say, "Well, that isn't quite right, 'cooking for the boys.' Cooking for the children, the boys and girls?"

"Yes," my mother admitted.

Moments later, in answer to her lawyer's question as to how many times a day she saw her own children, she gave a description that was very cleverly put together.

A: Well, I couldn't count the number of times I see them. I see them all day long. You know, I am not with them constantly, as no mother is when they are in school, but I see them the first thing in the morning; I see them for about two hours in the morning before they go to classes; I see them at their recreation and I sit out in the yard and sew while they are playing out in the yard.

I remember being particularly amazed, in 1974, when I first read the transcript at how guilelessly she was changing the circumstances to make everything sound so "normal."

Mr. Anderson then went into a series of questions about the other (onetime) married couples at the Center who had children the same ages as my mother's, in order to show that we all played together. Within minutes, Judge Wahlstrom became impatient to get to the heart of the matter.

The Court: They [another Center couple] are living at the Center now?
A: Yes, they are.
The Court: Are they living together as a family unit?
A: No, they are not.
The Court: What your husband has said, the men occupy

one place, the women another place, and the children are divided in another place—
A: The children are in the same house with their mothers.
The Court: Yes. You occupy one section, the girls one section, and the boys one section?
A: Your Honor, may I say one thing? I don't mean to be contradictory. It isn't as though I never see my children in that house. I see my children in that house all day long, but I do not sleep in the same section with them. I say good night to them and kiss them and they go to their rooms and I go to mine.

That was why she had made that highly unusual visit to our cubicles on the night of the 30th, the first day of the case!

The Court: You tuck them in bed?
A: Sometimes.
The Court: You say prayers with them?
A: Yes, I do.
The Court: Read to them?
A: Yes, I do.

The judge turned the questioning back to Mr. Anderson, who asked about the activities of the Center children, and Sister Mary Agnes told about the pets and the animals and the gardens. Then he asked if we sang.

A: Oh yes. They sing in the fields, you know, if they are playing down in the fields. They sing when they are riding, they sing cowboy songs if they are riding; and they even sing in the water. They are the most singing children I have ever heard. You can hear their voices all over the property all the time.
Q: Do they sing in more than one language?
A: Yes, they do.
Q: Will you name the languages they sing in?
A: As far as I remember, they sing in English, in Latin, in Spanish, in French.
Q: Is that all you remember? In German, also?
A: Oh, in German, yes.
Q: Do you have visitors at the Center at times?
A: Oh, yes. Oh, yes, always.

Q: At times do the children put on a show, singing?
A: Oh, very often. They put on plays to which the neighbors come and people, relatives come from Boston and Cambridge, and even from out of state.
Q: Did they put on a Halloween party the day before yesterday?
A: Yes, they did. No, it was last night. ...
Q: Were they all dressed up?
A: Each child planned their own costumes, but their parents did not know what costumes they planned because the main object of it was to surprise their parents and have them guess who this child is that was inside this strange getup.
Q: How was your oldest son dressed?
A: He had invented the strangest costume I ever saw in my life. He made himself a Chinese midget and he made tiny arms with tiny hands and gloves on it, and he had a black cap with a long braid down the back. He had built out some sort of an arrangement underneath his clothing from which these tiny feet protruded and then he got down so that he came in on the floor. He was about, oh, maybe three feet high. It looked as though these tiny feet were walking. He invented it entirely himself; no one helped him with it at all.
Q: How was your little fellow dressed, Benedict?
A: Benedict wasn't able to come to the party last night because he had a cold. But he was going to be an organ grinder's monkey and he had his costume all ready. ...

Most of Sister Mary Agnes' testimony was marked by arguments between the lawyers, centering mainly on what she could testify to from her own knowledge and direct observation, as opposed to what someone had told her. It must have been clear to observers that Mr. Anderson was not having as much success as my father's attorney, Mr. Griffin, had had in getting his client's side of the story told.

At times, tempers flared. Once Mr. Anderson said to the judge, exasperatedly, "Will his Honor put the question instead of me?" and the judge snapped back, "No. I am not going to try your case for you."

It didn't take my mother long to catch on to the ground rules. At one point, instead of answering her attorney's question, she said, "You see, Mr. Anderson, I am afraid his Honor doesn't want me to say, because, as I said, I was not present at every class."

Mr. Griffin, who probably caught the sarcasm in her tone, said, "Well, the witness does not need to instruct the attorney. I object to it. Now let's have a question."

The issue at hand was that of our education and what specific subjects we were taught. When the judge clarified the question, Sister Mary Agnes answered.

A: I have been present at some classes. I have been present when they studied music, when they were having catechism lessons, and I have been present at their art lessons. That is all I can think of at the moment.
The Court: Well, now ordinarily children in school study spelling, reading, history, and geography.
A: They do.
The Court: And many other things.
A: They study all of those things, your Honor, but I was not present. Most mothers are not present at those classes.
Q: Do they get their reports from the school once a month?
A: Once a month, yes.
Q: Have you seen those reports?
A: Yes, I have.
Q: Do the other mothers and fathers in the Center get reports monthly too, as far as you know?
A: Yes, they do.
Q: Have you ever complained to anybody that your children weren't properly educated.
A: No, I never have. I am perfectly happy with their education.

Mr. Anderson had not asked if she was "perfectly happy" with our education, but my mother had decided early on that—judicial warning or no judicial warning—if she saw a chance to score a point for "her side," she would do so. (She didn't mention that report cards for the parents were begun *after* it was certain there would be a court case.)

When I read the transcripts for the first time I marveled at her boldness, and I was surprised at how easily she fell into the language of the outside world ("mothers" and "fathers" and "parents"—terms that were not used at the Center, except in their spiritual connotations). There was no doubt in my mind that she viewed the court case as another battlefield, and that she had been very well coached.

The differences between the testimony of Sister Mary Agnes and that of the former Brother Mark were basic and fundamental. Unfortunately for my mother, if she had been less extreme in her statements, she might have been more believable.

She also suffered from having been the one who had to defend the unusual, the out-of-the-ordinary; whereas my father had returned to the system (of which the current case was a manifestation of its highest orderliness), she was still outside the pale, a member of an odd and unusual group of religious renegades.

On the morning of the third day of testimony (Tuesday, November 5), Mr. Anderson continued with the direct testimony of Sister Mary Agnes and then let Mr. Griffin start the cross-examination.

Mr. Griffin had my mother read aloud all the letters my father had written to her, and she was not happy at being forced to do so. Finally, she found an opportunity to say what she wanted to about the letters when she was asked to explain why she hadn't sent my father a picture of the children.

A: I had an excellent reason in that he had left them. He deserted his children, showed no interest in them whatsoever. And these, also, are only for the benefit of the court. Everything in those letters is calculated. You wouldn't understand the circumstances, but I know what is behind every line of those letters.

Realizing that her outburst might do my mother as much harm as good, Mr. Griffin replied, "Well, let it stay in the record, if your Honor please. I do not mind."

A few moments later, when recounting her version of the scene in front of the Center when my father returned with his parents, Sister Mary Agnes began to get worked up again.

Q: When Mr. Anderson asked you about what took place

there, is there something that you have not told the Court?
The Court: Was there more conversation?
A: There was lots of conversation back and forth between him and his mother and father and myself, and I am not too clear on everything that was said. I know he asked me if I would speak to him alone, and I said, "No," I would not. And I accused him of being a traitor and I told him he was going to go to hell and he was going to be as low in hell as Judas is.

I told his mother and father that they had no idea what, you know, he was truly like, and that we felt sorry for them.
Q: We?
A: Yes. All the members of the Center. We were like a family. We all loved him very dearly, and we know his family loves him dearly....

I told him, as well as I can remember, that he was going to go to hell and he would be a traitor and he would be in hell with Judas.
The Court: He would—
A: He would be in hell with Judas.
Q: I do not want to get afield, but how do you know he is there? Where did you get that idea?
A: If he is not in hell, no one is in hell.

After a long series of questions and answers, my mother spelled out exactly what she meant when she called my father a traitor.

A: I believed him a traitor because he was false to his vows—both to me and to the order and to our Blessed Mother—that he would dedicate his life to our doctrinal crusade; and because we had agreed together over a long period of time to bring our children up in the manner in which they are being brought up; and, without ever consulting me or letting me know that he had any feelings contrary to what he always professed, he had suddenly walked out.

After she gave that answer, I doubt if anyone in the courtroom questioned her sincerity.

Shortly before the lunch break, when everyone must have been tired, there was an exchange that under any other circumstances would have seemed humorous.

Q: So you have taken a vow to teach to defend that doctrine and engage in a doctrinal crusade for its promotion. Is that right?
A: That is right.
Q: That doctrine is that there is no salvation outside of the Catholic Church?
A: That is right.
Q: So, unless Mr. Anderson, your counsel, joins you, you firmly believe he will have no salvation?
Mr. Anderson: I object to that. I ask that that be stricken out.
Mr. Griffin: I have a right to test this witness's belief?
The Court: I think that is all right.
Q: You believe that, don't you?
A: I believe that Mr. Anderson might very well become a Catholic before he dies.
Q: And if he doesn't?
A: And if he doesn't, he will not save his soul.
Q: If he doesn't save his soul, his soul will go where?
A: To hell.
Q: So without mincing any words about it, you believe that if Mr. Anderson doesn't become a Catholic he is going to hell?
A: That is right.
Q: And that goes for his son, Lloyd?
A: That is right.
Q: And the stenographer?
The Court: Well, do not look too far.
Q: And all our Jewish friends?
A: That is right.
The Court: I think you have come to the end of that now.
Mr. Griffin: Well, I do not like any mistakes about those things.

Time and again, Mr. Griffin would come back to two main ideas that he wanted my mother to agree to. One was that she considered her vow of obedience to Father Feeney (and, by delegation, to Sister Catherine) more important than her marriage vow, and the other was that life at the Center was not—for the children—"normal." She resisted him repeatedly, but even a fast reading of the transcript indicates he got his points across despite her denials. Certainly, he got Judge

Wahlstrom to think about these crucial issues, if he had not already been considering them on his own.

While questioning her about her "common knowledge" of the expense of educating children, Mr. Griffin touched off a series of questions that related to her view of the world.

Q: Your life in the community is sheltered from newspapers that would carry that information?
A: I don't read newspapers.
Q: You have not read a newspaper in ten years, have you?
A: I have read some articles from newspapers.
Q: Yes. If an article is provided for you to read by your superior, you would read it.
A: That is right.
Q: But not otherwise.
A: That is right.
Q: So that generally you haven't read newspapers for ten years?
A: That is right.
Q: That is true of other members of the community, as far as you know, except probably one or two whose duty it is to read them?
A: That is right.
Q: That is so with the children, too?
A: Yes.
Q: So that none of the children are familiar with the funny papers or Orphan Annie or Mickey Mouse?
A: Yes.
Q: You read that to them?
A: Yes. They have comic books.
Q: But not the comics that run in the newspapers?
A: No.
Q: They don't have that?
A: They usually are associated with the lascivious advertisements, so we don't let them see them.
Q: And you feel very strongly about that?
A: I do.
Q: It is because of the lascivious advertisements in newspapers that you do not let the children have the funny papers?
A: Primarily.
Q: Pardon?
A: Primarily.

Q: Well, you haven't seen a newspaper in ten years. How do you know what is in them?
A: I can't help seeing them when I am out shopping.
Q: You open them up and see the funny pages?
A: No. I see newspapers lying around many times, and I am shocked at what is in a newspaper.
Q: Is it not a fact that you were told in the Center that you and the children will be, should be sheltered from newspapers because of the lascivious articles?
A: No.
Q: Nobody told you that?
A: No. We reached that conclusion ourselves when we decided that in that manner. . . .
Q: So the reason the children are not permitted to read the newspapers is that you want to shelter them from the lascivious printings and everything else?
A: That is right.
Q: You consider the world a wicked place, do you not?
A: No, I do not. Not wholesale, no.
Q: But you think the children's best interests are [in] sheltering them from the world, at least newspapers?
A: They are sheltered from anything that is bad for the children; they have every normal aspect of life, American life.

Mr. Griffin asked if the children listened to—or were allowed to listen to—the radio, and when Sister Mary Agnes said yes, he seemed surprised. My father had told him that children never listened to the radio. I think Mr. Griffin suspected that the children had been allowed to hear an hour or two of radio over the past weeks so that Sister Mary Agnes could testify the way she just had. Actually we had heard the radio about three years earlier at President Kennedy's inauguration, because he was the first Catholic President of the United States. Mr. Griffin tried to get her to admit that listening to the radio was out of the ordinary, but he was unsuccessful. He moved to safer ground.

Q: Do they have television?
A: No.
Q: Are they familiar with any of the programs on television?
A: No.
Q: Do you have television?
A: No.

Q: Do you yourself consider that you should be, by choice, of course, sheltered from the programs that are on television?
A: I have no desire to watch television whatsoever.
Q: You have no desire to have the children watch it?
A: No.
Q: By that you mean you do not want them to watch it?
A: That is right.
Q: Is that because you feel they would be exposed to the evils of some form of the world?
A: Yes, that is right.
Q: And you think they should be sheltered from it?
A: I think that they should not be exposed to anything that would corrupt them.

Next, Mr. Griffin spent a long time trying to show that while my mother was thoroughly convinced the Center would pay for all future schooling (including college) of her five sons, she had nothing more than this general belief—in other words, no written agreement.

What stunned me, in reading the transcript years later, was that she actually believed that any of the Center children would be allowed to go to a college of his or her own choice. Such a possibility was simply unthinkable, as far as I and the other children were concerned.

He spent the rest of the time before lunch showing that even though the children had an occasional movie and even though we went outside the Center from time to time, our existence was largely confined to the Center grounds—and our experience carefully circumscribed by our life there. After lunch he brought out the fact that we had never seen our mother's father, our maternal grandfather, and that when he died the previous year, Sister Mary Agnes (his own daughter) did not go to the funeral Mass or to the wake.

He returned to the issue of the smallness of the cubicles, and one of his questions caused Sister Mary Agnes to say more than perhaps she had meant to.

Q: And you think that that (her description of our rooms and the furnishings] is good surroundings?
A: It is far better than the parochial or boarding schools that

I was in as a child. It is much better than what they provided for the little girls at Mount Saint Joseph's Academy when I was a child and visited there. All they had was a little bed and a very small chest right aside the bed and a curtain at night which they pulled about, it had no walls at all.

Griffin countered by establishing that the children she was referring to had homes to return to when the school term was over.

Q: And these [Center] children have no homes apart from this, other than what you described?
A: It is perfectly beautiful.
Q: Please. These children have no homes apart from this? This is their home.
A: That is right.
Q: This is their home?
A: That is right.
Q: Then you intend to keep them in until you say they are grown up and able to make their own decisions?
A: Until we have a new building, and then they will move.
Q: But for the moment, there is not any such new building, is there?
A: That is right.
Q: They have been there now for five years?
A: (Witness nodded.)
Q: Benedict, he is six years old now, isn't he?
A: No. He will be nine in a few weeks.
Q: Nine years old now. He has known no other life since he was four, has he?
A: That is right.
Q: Your intention is to keep them there with whatever education is provided them there until he is grown up and makes his decisions?
A: Within the Center, yes.
Q: During that time you intend to shelter him from the world?
A: I intend to shelter him from evil that would corrupt him.
Q: He knows everything that is good in the world?
A: Yes.
Q: According to whose standards?

A: According to the normal Christian standards that always prevailed up until very recently. . . .
Q: You are satisfied that they remain in these rooms?
A: I am satisfied that they live as they now live.

Just before she left the stand, my mother was in the middle of a long answer about how the children were taught all about the usual professions in the world, and when she finished, Mr. Griffin (by now well aware of her Irish temper and maybe hoping he could set it off) asked innocently, "What do you teach them about lawyers?"

"Well," she replied quickly, "they have had a great course recently."

He jumped on the word "course" and tried to get her to admit that the Center had coached the children in how to behave disobediently on the visits with "R.C.," and he hounded her so thoroughly that she finally had to turn to Judge Wahlstrom for aid.

"I used the term loosely and, your Honor, I would like to take it back. I spoke facetiously."

He said, "All right."

By the time Mr. Griffin had finished questioning her, there could not have been many observers in the courtroom who thought her story was more convincing than that of her husband. And a few people must have remembered Judge Wahlstrom's comment that whatever might be true in the rest of Massachusetts, in Worcester County it was not always true that the mother gets custody.

During the afternoon session, Mr. Haskell, an octogenarian neighbor of the Center, testified that the children were all well-behaved and very happy. Next, Mr. Wilbur Watt, a local farmer, said much the same thing. He was followed to the stand by Mary Ryan, the grandmother of three of the Center children, who described her annual one- or two-day visit to see her son and "his happy children."

Court adjourned at four o'clock.

The next day, the fourth day of testimony, Judge Wahlstrom heard the testimony of more Center members who described their lives.

Brother Isidore said he had not visited or written to his father in thirteen years. He pointed out that the primary love for a person should be directed to the salvation of the soul.

Sister Mary John, the principal of the Center school, testified as to its quality. On cross-examination, she admitted to Mr. Griffin that she had not seen her father for ten years, and that although he had only lived ten miles away, she had not gone to his deathbed or attended his funeral.

Brother Simon, the prior of the Brothers, said that he and Robert Connor had been friends in the navy and that he was shocked when Robert Connor had suddenly left the Center without confiding in him his dissatisfaction with the way of life there.

Near the end of the day, Mr. Griffin began his cross-examination of Sister Mary Judith. It was now apparent that the Connor children were not going to be called to testify, which indicated that no one had learned about the extent and severity of the physical punishment. Nonetheless, Mr. Griffin brought out some interesting statements from Sister Mary Judith, the Big Sister most directly in charge of the children's welfare.

Q: What was the reason for moving your child out of the apartment and down into a group?
A: Well, everything that we did—
Q: What was the reason?
A: We discussed it among all the parents and we decided that since every mother had her own ideas of disciplining their children we would like to choose a common way we all agreed upon and try it out as an experiment, which we did; and it worked out very well. We were very happy with it and the children were very happy with it.
Q: Every mother and father had a different idea as to how children should be brought up, discipline and so forth?
A: Little ways, yes.
Q: And that, you understand, was true in normal family life everywhere, didn't you?
A: Yes.
Q: You were going to experiment with family life as far as children were concerned, notwithstanding the history of the world, and have them go into a common community. Is that what you are telling us?
A: We—
Mr. Anderson: Please—
The Court: Leave out the history part of it, Mr. Griffin, and, I think, your question is all right.

Q: You were going to experiment with family life? That is what you have told us, isn't it?

A: We were going to make a little trial.

Q: A little trial. You used the word "experiment," didn't you?

A: We will give it a trial.

Q: You used the word "experiment"?

A: I think I did.

Q: And you meant it, did you not?

A: We will give it a trial.

Q: Yes. Giving it an experimentation is a trial. And your experimentation was going to be a community life as distinguished from family life?

A: Well . . . we had them in their sleeping quarters together.

Q: I understand. But the experimentation that your Saint Benedict Center was conducting was the separation of children from family life and putting them in community life?

A: We see them all day.

The Court: No, no. Listen to his question.

Q: That was the experimentation that was being conducted, was it not?

A: We didn't feel that way about it.

Q: Please. You used the word. . . . You were going to give it a try to see how it worked out?

A: If we were not all happy with it and the children were not delighted, we would have, you know, stopped it.

Q: Did you ask your two-year-old child if he was delighted with it?

A: We could see they were very happy.

Q: You could see that the three-year-old child was delighted with the arrangement?

A: Yes.

Q: You assumed that he had state of reason, did you?

A: Well, we could see. . . .

Q: That life of separation of mothers, fathers, boys and girls worked out very well, you think?

A: We were all pleased; the parents were pleased with it. . . .

Q: So that you still continued it?

A: Yes. . . .

Q: And you prefer that to the natural, normal family life that you previously enjoyed?

A: We are pleased with it.
Q: You think the children like it?
A: Yes, we do.
Q: And this three-year-old boy of yours, did he ever have any contrary experience by which he could compare it?
A: He was with us for three years.
Mr. Griffin: Yes. Until he was three. I do not have any further questions.

The trial concluded that same day, November 6, 1963. In addition to the four days of testimony, Judge Wahlstrom also had the report of Judge Gould, the special guardian, to help in coming to his decision.

Judge Gould's report said, in part,

> If custody is given to the mother, this will never take place in fact, for while she remains at the institution, the true custody and control of these children remains in the hands of the head of this institution where they are now residing, and I am convinced, that they will never allow the father satisfactory, unimpeded visits with his children.

On November 8, two days later, Judge Wahlstrom awarded custody of the five of us to Robert Connor, our father, with "reasonable visitation rights" allowed to Sister Mary Agnes, our mother.

The Center immediately appealed the case to the supreme court of the state of Massachusetts and, as part of that appeal, requested that Judge Wahlstrom file a "Report of Material Facts" that led him to his decision. His ten page report includes the following findings:

> I find the children to be clean, well-mannered, well-nourished and happy but completely brain-washed and thoroughly educated in those things in which Father Feeney desired to have them know. . . .
>
> I find that the educational system of the Center does not fulfill the standards required by the laws of Massachusetts. . . .
>
> I find that there was no normal family life at the Center and no means were provided for such. I find that

there was no display of affection between husbands and wives or between the parents and the children. . . .

I find that while some children realized they had brothers and sisters, yet this meant little or nothing to them and the family as such was not recognized. . . .

I find that during these visits he has had difficulty in getting the children to speak or to be friendly. It is very evident that they have been coached, brain-washed and that they are most uncooperative. I find that the eldest son, Robert, is the leader and that the other brothers dare not say anything without his approval. When Connor has asked the children about their mother, they have just replied saying "nothing" but that they did admit that they saw her occasionally. I find that the strain under which these boys are living has made them very nervous. . . .

I find that Mrs. Connor, the respondent here, is a charming, intelligent, well-poised, well-spoken lady and of a beautiful personality, but that she, too, has been brain-washed and puts her vow of allegiance to Father Feeney prior to her marriage vows and to her duty to her children and her husband. . . .

I find that while the children are healthy, well-nourished, while they are sufficiently clothed and while they are kept clean and while they appear well-mannered and while they have splendid opportunities for recreations and are intelligent and attend school regularly, yet their education is one-sided. They have no family life. They have no parental care and love. They are not in the custody of the mother but actually in the custody of Mrs. Clarke and Father Feeney, from whom they receive no parental care and love and that the life of the children at the Center is so unAmerican that the welfare of the children requires that the father have custody and that he is living apart for just cause from his wife. Her refusal to accede to her husband's wishes that the family establish a home and live normal lives I find to be desertion of her husband and her family on her part.

CARL E. WAHLSTROM
Judge of Probate Court

From the standpoint of the Center, the judge's report was very bad, but I wonder what it would have contained if he had heard about the daylong silences, the imposed fasts, and most of all the brutal punishments.

I did not see it then, but today I realize full well why Sister Catherine was so worried that the Connor children might have to testify.

Chapter Five

Robert Connor won the case in November, but the Center's appeal would mean many months of waiting. We remained at the Center, and we had weekly visitations with our father. Fall became winter, and then winter gave way to spring. Life went on. It was almost as before.

She kissed the bleeding feet and glanced sorrowfully at the head crowned with thorns. As she turned toward the Little Brothers and Little Sisters seated on the floor, she smiled, and we could see the pain lingering in her eyes. Standing at attention, she raised her arm in salute to the statue. We arose and did likewise: thirty-five arms went into the air correctly, each hand at eye level with three fingers pointed to heaven in honor of the Blessed Trinity. It was army meeting night.

Sister Catherine's voice prompted us to begin the pledge.

> As a soldier in the Army of Our Lady I promise to defend her cause, which is the cause of Jesus, with my life. I promise to be ready to die for her at any moment. I promise to live for her a life so holy that I may win in the battles against her enemies many, many souls for her to give to the Sacred Heart of Jesus.

We paused for breath, and thirty-five hands moved toward thirty-five heads ready to snap outward: "I salute her as my Queen and Commander-in-Chief."

Like everyone else's, Susan's hand completed the salute on the word "chief." She was the oldest of the children, already a high-school junior, and the general of our army. I wanted to catch her eye, but her face seemed focused with royal confidence on the meaning of the pledge.

> I give her the complete allegiance of my heart, and I promise her the complete obedience of my will. I promise to love Jesus and Mary above all things and to have no other love before them.

As we sat down to begin the army meeting, she saw my smile and nodded knowingly. Our surprise was scheduled for that evening after everyone had gone to bed. Her cubicle was directly above mine, and I had discovered a way for us to communicate through a hole in the ceiling near the radiator pipe.

I was anxious, thinking about the details of that night's mischief. The meeting seemed to go on forever, but when it ended, it seemed too soon. The army business was routine. Kathleen Anne, the adjutant, read the minutes from the last meeting. The "soldiers" stationed that week on the corners of the stone walks around the house made their reports, turning in the names of those who had not saluted them properly or who had kicked a stone out of place. After a discussion on plans for the summer, the meeting ended with our good-night hymn:

> Good night, sweet Mary, guide us in your army;
> Thou art our Mother, we are your slaves.
> When we are marching, be thou our leader.
> Dear gentle Mother, good night, good night
> Good night, Sweet Mother, good night, good night.

I suddenly remembered the evening we had sung it by the evergreen trees, named after the saints, called the Fourteen Holy Helpers. In the middle of the song one of the Little Sisters suddenly screamed and pointed in the darkness to something that we all saw immediately. A pale face hung quietly among the branches. The eyes were closed and the lips swollen. We ran into the house, and later found out that it was only Betty Sullivan, who had been kicked out of the Center for disobedience to her superiors. Almost weekly, for the last six years, she would stand for hours at a time, as if frozen on the porch, her eyes shut in stubborn prayer as her hand—the only part of her that moved—tapped rhythmically on the locked door. Her life had become an endlessly futile pleading for readmission. It was an odd thing to remember, but I enjoyed the idea that it had been a real scare. I thought my plans for Sister Catherine that evening were just as eerie.

The lights were out; everyone was in bed. It was quiet. I heard Sister Catherine's whisper at the opposite end of the corridor. She was about to walk down and inspect each cubicle. Mine was in order. My spread was neatly folded, my slippers together on the floor, and my clothes in place except for my bathrobe. It lay on top of the blankets covering my sleeping form. I waited quietly, hoping Susan was ready.

In a little while, Sister Catherine would know that I had been speaking with one of the Little Sisters and had broken a strict rule. She had announced to all of us one day, several years earlier, that if we wanted to be like the adults we should observe complete silence between the Brothers and Sisters. Our agreement was unanimous. No one raised a hand to object, so it became a rule. When, shortly afterward, I wrote a note to one of the Little Sisters, I was told that it was not just talking that was forbidden but communication of any kind.

I knew my planning with Susan was not allowed. Yet, I did not think Sister Catherine would be upset if we made a stunt out of our newly discovered secret. Also, I realized that she was pleased with my performance on the Connor trips into the world. It had been seven months since the Center's appeal to the state supreme court, and my continued cooperation was needed to win the case.

Sister Catherine's footsteps were only a cubicle away when I gave Susan the prearranged signal. Then Sister's shadow crossed my face, and she paused. I thought she was watching me. Maybe she realized that I was really awake. My closed eyelids began to twitch. Just then I felt the bathrobe sliding across my body, down over my legs toward my feet. I tried to imagine what Sister Catherine was seeing: Luke, lying sound asleep, and his bathrobe mysteriously crawling down the bed. I felt it stop and then lift off from my feet. I imagined it climbing like a spider into the air, up, up, toward the ceiling. Sister was standing there motionless. I wanted to look at her face. Was she frightened, shocked? Did she see the thin rope in the dim light pulling the bathrobe toward the tiny hole in the ceiling? I looked and laughed nervously.

She turned to me with a puzzled look. "What is going on? How are you doing it?"

I jumped out of bed and showed her our secret, the hole in

the ceiling by the pipe and the rope Susan was controlling from upstairs. I explained how I tugged the rope twice to let her know when to start pulling so it would make the bathrobe float into the air at the right time. Sister Catherine was fascinated, and she even called the Angel and had us put on another demonstration.

The next day, Saturday, just as I began my lunch, I was summoned to the Office. I was alone, and wondered why. It was a visitation day and the five of us, the Connor children, usually went together after lunch to Sister Catherine's Office. (The court had ordered our visits with R.C. to continue during the appeal period.) There we would receive last-minute advice and be given a few nickles and dimes for emergency phone calls. Nearly a year had passed since R.C. had taken us out on our first visit, and little if any coaching was needed now. Our strategy of silence and misery was routine.

As I walked through the adjoining rooms I wondered if I was in trouble over the previous night's stunt with Susan. Certainly, I thought, Sister Catherine would not mention it just before our visitation with R.C.

I passed the Little Kitchen, where Sister Lilian Marie was preparing Sister Catherine's lunch. She said I should go right in. The door was open and Sister Catherine was chatting with Sister Mary Agnes and Brother Boniface. They looked up and smiled.

"Here you are, darling," Sister Catherine said. "I was telling Sister Mary Agnes about the amusing trick you played on us last night."

There was laughter—an excited wheezing from Brother Boniface as his face brightened with childlike merriment momentarily dispelling his legal worries.

Sister Mary Agnes leaned forward. "I would have loved to have seen it. How do you come up with such ideas?"

I gave a casual shrug, trying to hide the satisfaction I felt at being thought of as clever. I turned to Sister Catherine. "Sometimes my ideas are not that great. D'you remember the time I built a steep ramp out of snowballs so the toboggan would shoot up into the air?"

"Yes, I remember. That was dangerous. We nearly lost several of our Little Sisters. They could have broken their backs or—"

"They lost their wind when it crashed." I looked at Sister Mary Agnes. "I expected it to go sailing through the air and land softly on the snow, but it turned in midair and fell backward to the ground."

"Excuse me." Sister Catherine struggled to clear her throat. "Darling—" she swallowed and looked earnestly at me— "we're going to have to cover up the hole in the ceiling. We have that rule, you know, between the Little Brothers and Little Sisters. You wouldn't want to be the only Little Brother who is an exception."

"Oh, no," I said. "I just thought it would be a good trick to play."

"That's wonderful, dear," Sister Catherine said. Sister Mary Agnes smiled, then grew serious as Sister Catherine continued. "Now we have some discouraging news. That demon, Robert Connor, has petitioned the court to take the five of you to Ohio this summer."

"For how long?" I asked. I immediately thought of summer plans: my vegetable garden, twice as big as the previous year's; my new irrigation syphoning system with my water-storage barrel; and now my lens experiments, whereby I planned to make a real photograph. I hoped it wouldn't spoil my summer.

"Our lawyers are working on it. We are trying to keep any summer visit here in Massachusetts, and for a short time." Sister Catherine paused and looked keenly at me. "We are confident that you will find ways to make the visit unbearable."

"D'you mean like what we've been doing?" I asked.

"We cannot tell you what to do, but with all your ideas, I'm sure you will come up with something."

"I don't know," I said doubtfully.

Sister Catherine inclined her head and smiled. "Little boys can think of lots of things to do if they are forced to stay somewhere against their will." Her eyes searched me for a moment as she nibbled at the end of her pen.

I knew that Sister Catherine was thinking of something drastic. In the past, she had told us not to talk, not to smile, to refuse food and drink and rides in the park, to run away, even to vomit in R.C.'s car. Now she hesitated to suggest something that I had to think of on my own. Her words went through my mind again and again. "Little boys can think of lots of things to do if they are forced to stay somewhere against their will."

I worried about it during the afternoon visit with R.C.

Somehow I felt we would end up in Ohio. R.C. had been threatening it for several months, and it was not impossible.

Already, two Little Brothers and two Little Sisters, the Peterson children, had been forced into the world to live with their mother, Sister Mary Defrosa, who had run away one night a few months after Robert Connor had won custody from the lower court. The Center, we were told, could not afford to take on another case, so the children and their father, Brother William Mary, had to leave. He was now working in the world to support his family. I felt sorry for him and his children. I knew we could easily end up like them. It was all R.C.'s fault.

I had to come up with a good idea. This was my chance to prove myself. I imagined R.C. driving us off to Ohio. We could become sick and force him to pull over. Then we could let the air out of the tires or put water in the gas tank while he was cleaning up the mess. At his house we could accidentally clog the toilet, stain the rugs, and break the ornamental glassware. But they would probably beat us up. Or worse, they would tell the court that the Center taught us to do it, and we would be taken away forever.

The problems looked formidable. How could I control the Little Brothers for *weeks,* when they disobeyed me on the short afternoon visits? Matthew was the worst. He had helped R.C. look for shirts by running down the aisles of the store, he had played with the jukebox, and he had drunk lemonade when the rest of us had refused. He would pretend he did not know any better. Once, when I quietly corrected him with an under-the-table nudge, he said out loud, "Ouch! Who poked me?" Another time he whispered, in R.C.'s presence, "Sister Catherine said we could do it."

Even as I worried about it, Matthew was up to something. It was Saturday, June 6, 1964, visit number 59. R.C. had become resigned to our listless behavior, but on this day he was in a lively mood. He had finished his first-year law-school exams at Boston College.

"Well, here are my happy boys," he joked as we met him outside Judge Gould's office. "I missed you these last two weeks while I was away, and I'm sure you missed me."

We protested vigorously that we hadn't missed him at all.

R.C. turned to Matthew. "I know that secretly in your heart you really enjoy these visits. Weren't you the one that wanted to go to Ohio for the summer?"

Matthew looked at me with horror. "I never said that."

R.C. laughed.

Later in the afternoon, when R.C. took us to the Paxes' house, Matthew tried to amuse us by his mischievous behavior. We were seated on a bench in the backyard. R.C. was inside chatting with Dr. Pax. Mrs. Pax was watering the flowers, and Matthew kept pinching and releasing the water hose at the precise moment it would cause the greatest annoyment. When he got tired of that, he tried to coax the baby over by dragging a string on the ground and calling out with short chirping noises as though he were playing with a cat. As we were returning to Judge Gould's office, Matthew became distracted by an old bearded man who was making little grunting noises and beckoning us to come over.

"Ignore him," I said, "he could get angry with you."

Matthew reached into his pocket, his eyes narrowed with determination, and he muttered with clenched teeth, "If he grabs me, I'll stab him with my jackknife."

I explained my worries to Sister Mary Agnes that evening after we had made our report and the other Little Brothers had gone. She agreed that if the others were like Matthew the task would be impossible. I asked her what Sister Catherine was implying when she said that we could think of things to do if we were forced to go to Ohio.

She hesitated. "I don't know," she finally said.

"Suppose we ran away and I phoned you, could the Center come and pick us up?" I asked.

"No, I'm afraid we couldn't, dear. They would charge us with kidnapping and that would be the end." She changed the subject and asked me about my latest camera experiments. I was relieved to see her so interested and happy. I was afraid she would get seriously ill from worrying about losing us.

Two weeks earlier, she had burst out crying and shouting at us. On that occasion Sister Catherine had called her into our dining room to be present while she scolded Michael, Paul, and Matthew for the badges they had lost.

"And you are the Little Brothers whom we are working so hard to save from the world!" Sister Catherine directed her words at each of them standing at attention, quivering with guilt. Michael had lost his Devotion badge when one of the Angels had caught him making the Little Sisters laugh in the chapel. In grand solemnity before the statue of St. Anthony he had made a double genuflection, which was normally used for the Blessed Sacrament when exposed on the altar. Matthew and Paul had been caught playing with the Malteen. They had tried to pour it from the ceiling and catch the brown goo in a spoon near the floor. Just as the Angel came in, they missed their target.

Sister Mary Agnes stood and listened to Sister Catherine's voice rise in anger. "Children in the world are not protected from evil the way you are. If you continue breaking the rules, disobeying our poor hardworking Angels, and betraying Our Lady at home, then . . . oh, boy!"

Sister Mary Agnes suddenly became transformed. Her hands trembling, her eyes pouring out tears, and with her lips quivering, she shouted, "If you think for one moment that I or any of our Sisters are going to save you from that demon— If you want to go to hell and be tormented with all those who are disloyal to God and Our Blessed Mother, then go AHEAD!" Her face became redder. "I DON'T WANT TO SEE YOU AGAIN!" She turned and left. I was horrified. I had never seen her so upset. I wanted to blame Sister Catherine for calling her in before all the Little Brothers.

Sister Mary Agnes seemed to have forgotten about it on the next visitation, but I felt that, underneath her smiling face and her pleasant talk, she was suffering intensely. But now she seemed relaxed. We talked about the possibility of an Ohio visit, and she warned me not to go out on field trips with worldly children who might do wicked things. I imagined big powerful boys who would take us into the woods and beat us up if we didn't do what they wanted. But she said that girls were the worst. They could be even more impure than boys. I told her not to worry about it. As we parted she said assuringly, "We have the Court of Heaven on our side."

During the following week I learned that it had been decided: We would be going to Ohio for a three-week visitation. A sickening feeling set in. It seemed as though we were losing the battle.

In midmorning on Saturday, June 20, the solemn tones of Cupertino, the bell, resounded across the fields. I saw everyone stop what they were doing and, with questioning shock in their faces, walk toward St. Therese's House. We all knew what the slow gongs meant—Brother Christopher had just died. The whole community filed by his deathbed. He lay white and emaciated; his shriveled mouth hung open with the silent agony of death.

Sister Catherine told us at noon that in his last days, as the cancer grew worse, he had offered his life for the Connor children so that Our Lady would save us from the world. But I felt little hope. The horror of his face in death reminded me only of the futility of this life. I resolved to put up with whatever suffering was necessary for Our Lady's cause. No one could stop me. I was going to oppose R.C. and the world no matter what it cost. They could beat me and torture me; I would never give in. If I died, I would be happy forever in heaven.

In compliance with the court's decree we were delivered to R.C. in Clinton at nine o'clock, Monday, July 6. Sister Catherine had finally let us know what she wanted us to do in Ohio. I thought it was going to be risky for the Center and certainly very difficult for the Little Brothers to go all the way. But I remembered Sister Catherine's assurance; "They cannot blame the Center, Luke. It is entirely up to you. You can bring us victory. The supreme court will not give five boys to a man who cannot even keep his children healthy for three weeks."

R.C. seemed nervous and in a great hurry. He said we would be at our grandparents' house in Akron, Ohio, by eleven o'clock that night. As we neared the Massachusetts Turnpike in Auburn, Michael suddenly vomited in the car. R.C. cleaned it up and we continued on in silence.

"What is that rattling noise?" R.C. asked. There was no answer.

When he stopped for lunch, he rearranged our suitcases in the trunk. I stood there tense. I wondered what he would do when he discovered our plan. We sat down at the counter in the restaurant.

"I have to leave the room," Benedict said, using the Center's idiom.

R.C. took him to the washroom.

"Now, here is our first test," I whispered when R.C. had gone. "But it is okay for you, Michael, because you were sick." The waitress approached. She could be a spy for R.C., I thought.

"How are you boys today?" She gave us the menus and commented on our "cute" blue-and-white uniforms. She treated us like little children, though I was fourteen, and Benedict, the youngest, was nine.

"So what are you going to have for lunch?" R.C. asked when he returned. He leaned over Matthew's shoulder. "If you cannot talk, at least point to what you want. The Center won't mind; there's nothing evil about pointing."

"I'm not hungry," I said.

R.C. looked at me surprised. "Oh, come on now. How about a grilled cheese sandwich and some hot tomato soup? Doesn't that sound good?"

The waitress paused for our order.

"Michael, what would you like?" R.C. asked.

"May I please have some tomato soup and a grilled cheese sandwich?" Michael said moodily.

"How about you, Paul?" R.C. glanced at me to see what I was doing.

"I'm not hungry," Paul said.

"Oh, you can eat something, Paul." R.C. turned to the waitress. "I'll have a hamburger and coffee. And Matthew, what will you have?"

"Nothing," Matthew said quietly.

"I'm not hungry either," Benedict said.

R.C. looked at me as though he had just realized our plan, but didn't quite believe it. "Listen, Luke— Oh, never mind. Make it three grilled cheeses and two tomato soups," he said with finality to the waitress.

"Anything to drink?" she asked.

"No, the water is fine, thank you," I said, and the others repeated it.

R.C. sighed and shook his head. "Luke," he began, "it doesn't matter what you do, you will still be out here for three weeks. So please don't make yourself miserable and spoil it for everyone else." He paused. "You know, if you keep this up and I have to call my attorney, there could be serious trouble."

He placed a half cheese sandwich before each of us. Benedict frowned at Michael, who ate his lunch. But the rest of us refused to touch the food.

"Luke, go out to the car and wait," R.C. said.

At first I wouldn't go, but R.C. got angry and grabbed me by the arm, pointing out the door. Everyone was watching. I left. The sandwiches were still untouched when R.C. brought them out to the car. He put them in the front and back seats.

During the afternoon the Little Brothers poked holes in them and then licked their fingers. Matthew even ate a small piece when he thought I wasn't watching.

I realized how difficult it was going to be to keep them from eating for three weeks. But I had to show the Center how capable I was.

"Here you are," Grandpa said as we opened the car door. His round glasses flashed in the lantern light at the base of the walk. It was nearly eleven o'clock at night. A huge dark house sat at the top of the lawn. A terrible feeling came over me at the thought that we would be living there for weeks. I had fears of unknown sins of impurity that I knew were routine in the world. We might be forced to undress in the same room before wicked eyes, and if we refused, they would say we were "abnormal."

Grandpa lumbered around slowly, pretending to be friendly. "And you're Benedict, the youngest, nine years old." His teeth grinned hideously. I grabbed two of our suitcases and walked up the driveway. The others followed me. As we entered the cellar through the garage door, Grandma appeared.

"You made it all right," she said. Her thin voice quivered and her eyes seemed exhausted with pain.

I looked away, showing my misery.

"Come right through here," she said. "But be sure to wipe your feet on the mat. We have so many kids traipsing mud all over the rugs in this house." Greeting us by name, she watched each of us enter. "You look so tired. It must have been such a long hard trip. I know. Steve and I have made that trip several times, and at the end I'm so sore and exhausted."

"Mom, they haven't eaten all day," R.C. said as he came in with Grandpa. "They wouldn't eat lunch or dinner."

"Well, I can take care of that," Grandpa said. He led us upstairs to the kitchen. We went through a large room with couches, bookcases, and in the corner the dreaded TV. Fear flashed through me as I anticipated the struggle we would go through refusing to look at its wicked pictures.

We sat dejected in the breakfast room.

"How about some milk and cookies?"

"No, thank you."

"Maybe something hot, like a boiled egg?"

"Oh, no, Grandpa, they don't want eggs now," Grandma

said. "They're just so tired that they're not hungry." Her high lilting voice put me at ease. She did not seem as though she would let them beat us or force us into doing things we didn't like.

"We're doing very well," I said as we huddled together in my room. "But we'd better not talk about it here. They might have recording devices hidden in the rooms."

I accompanied Paul and Michael to their room on a floor above us. They had their own bathroom also. I couldn't find any suspicious wires hidden under the beds.

"R.C. said we could be in terrible trouble if we continue," Paul whispered.

"Don't worry," I said as I left for my room below. "There is nothing they can do if we really are too homesick to eat."

There were two beds, one bureau, and a chair in my room. Benedict and Matthew slept in the twin bed and I took the cot. The house became quiet. A sad train horn reminded me of the strangeness of the place. It was the first time we had slept outside of the Center. I could hear sobbing coming from the big bed. It sounded like Benedict. Everything must seem eerie to him, I thought. We were abandoned in quiet darkness hundreds of miles away. A car light swept a moving pattern across the walls and ceiling.

I took out my rosary, praying to Our Lady to bring us back immediately. Fingering the smooth hard beads, I chose the sorrowful mysteries. The first was the Agony in the Garden. I imagined Our Lord sweating blood as He thought of the horrible torments He would receive: the Scourging at the Pillar, the Crowning of Thorns, the Carrying of the Cross, and finally death by being nailed to a cross.

It was boring. I had pictured it daily all my life. My mind wandered. I saw pictures of R.C. in bed plotting how to force us to eat, and Sister Mary Agnes crying before the sanctuary lamp in the chapel at home. What mystery was I on? The beads ceased to move through my fingers.

Noises. It was light. The twin bed in Ohio. Was I hungry? Fear flowed to my stomach. "The coffee is ready." Grandma's voice. I wouldn't eat all day and never again until I was home. We should get ready for daily Mass, I thought. I dressed and went downstairs.

"There's an eight-o'clock Mass at St. Vincent's Church if you want to go," R.C. said. I felt humiliated that he was in charge of us.

I got the others up and we saw our first worldly Mass. The church was nearly empty and there was no sermon. I wondered how people could think they were holy in such a strange place, a huge chapel with microphones. Though we still claimed to be homesick, we received Holy Communion because hosts were small.

At the house, Benedict became sick to his stomach. There wasn't much of a mess because he hadn't eaten for a whole day. But I knew it was caused by our trip; he wasn't one of the children at home who usually vomited at breakfast.

"Remember: no milk, just water. We can get thin fast that way." I led the Little Brothers downstairs. We stubbornly ignored the exhortations of our grandparents. Only Matthew drank a little orange juice.

"Why don't you write a letter home," Grandpa said after clearing the dishes. "It will make you feel better." I thought that Grandpa would read it, so I warned Sister Mary Agnes at the end.

> Dear Sister Mary Agnes,
> We arrived at Akron last night at about 10:45. Benedict and Matthew and I live in one room and Michael and Paul in another. We are very homesick. Michael got sick before we got on the turnpike and Benedict was sick just this morning (July 7). They are begging us to eat but we can't because we are homesick. We all hope that we will come home before three weeks.
> Grandpa and Grandma plus our father are living in the same house.
> Grandpa asked me if I wanted to write a letter to our home and, I said, "Yes." He said that he would mail it.
> Yours in Our Lady,
> /s/ Luke, Michael, Paul, Matthew, Benedict

In the back of the house, a steep wooded hill dropped away into a gorge that was covered with bushes and vines. We found a safe place hidden from the view of the house. After successfully refusing lunch, we huddled together in our hideout and plotted the strategy for the next meal.

"It is getting too obvious," I said. "We should at least pretend we're trying by taking tiny bites, you know, like a pea or two or whatever it is. Okay?" They agreed.

"Grandma is really worried about our health," Michael

said. "I heard her talking to Grandpa in the kitchen. She thought he should promise to let us go home early if we ate."

"I know they're worried. If we keep it up, we're going to win," I said. But I felt my assurances were getting dull as our hunger increased.

That evening, I could see the torture in the pained stares and empty swallows of the Little Brothers. The alluring smells from Grandma's special potato-and-cheese casserole, her steaming beans, cool salad, and fresh bread strained even my determination. And all was set in a display of fine white linen, sparkling china, polished silverware, and purple and yellow flowers.

"But I'm not hungry." The words sounded fake. It was useless. Each Little Brother was served a small portion, the nearer for the smell and possible bite, an irresistible temptation. Our grandparents pretended not to be concerned.

"At night, raccoons steal the food from the garbage cans," Grandma said.

A smile crossed Grandpa's face. "You should see their cute little black faces," he said. "They even come up to our door, and sometimes I feed them cookies from the cookie jar."

R.C., however, wasn't interested in the raccoons. He urged Benedict to try a taste of food, but he wouldn't. Our grandparents seemed oblivious to the silent tension building up, as we watched them eat and drink in guiltless pleasure. Sideward glances—like an invisible fence—held us back. Matthew tormented his beans, poking them into different formations around the spreading juices of his casserole. Paul built a dam of potatoes. When Grandpa saw it, he grew angry.

"Poor Grandma has spent the whole day working to make this big dinner for you boys and you don't even have the decency to try it. What kind of respect do they teach you at the Center? If you had no intention of eating, then I think you ought to have told us earlier, and all this food wouldn't go to waste. I asked you, Luke, if you would eat dinner and you gave me your word."

"Grandpa," I said, "I told you that I thought we might be over our homesickness by then, but now I realize that it is just getting worse. There is no way I can tell what will happen in the future. Maybe we'll be homesick as long as we're away from home. I'm trying to get better, but I still don't feel like eating."

I could see Grandpa's face growing redder. Grandma urged me to try a little bite, and I decided to do it. I put a quarter fork-load of her potato casserole into my mouth and slowly swallowed. It was disastrous: all the others started to eat immediately. They were following my example. Paul went with half a fork, so did Benedict, and then Michael. But Matthew decided a small nibble was a fully loaded fork followed by a couple more, "to make it look convincing," as he told me later.

I sat on the bed in the midst of the Little Brothers in silence. I hoped they could see my fury. Matthew spoke up.

"You told us to eat a little, tonight."

"But you ate much too much," Paul chided.

"I don't think you are strong enough to do it," I said, exasperated. "I bet I'll be the only one who comes home really thin." I turned to Michael. "I saw you drink the melted ice cream."

"Aw, it was practically nothing," Michael said, embarrassed.

"They deliberately left us to clean up the food from the table so we would sneak a few bites when they were gone," I said. "The way you're going now, I'm afraid R.C. will get us for the Christmas vacation too!"

"Oh, no," Matthew said. He was horrified. "You mean we'll have to go through this not eating all over again?"

I was amused. I encouraged Matthew by saying that we would win the court case and never have to fast again if we were stubborn and didn't give in now. I told the Little Brothers not to follow me at the table, but to pretend to try to eat no matter what I did. They were very good the next two days. But by Friday, the fifth day of starvation, they had slipped again.

"Someone is eating sugar and cookies," I said. "Grandma said she could feel the sugar on the floor, and she's angry that we refuse her meals yet eat the cookies in the jar. She knows that someone is really hungry." They all looked at me innocently and denied that they had done it. I knew I'd never find out, so I threatened them.

"Well, remember," I said sternly, "it will be obvious when we get home who lost the most weight. Sister Catherine will know who had the courage to fight and who were the cowards. I've already lost eight pounds."

I reminded the Little Brothers of the Fatima children, who

133

had finally been released from jail when they refused to give in.

"It takes a lot of courage, and I'm going to go all the way even if you give up." They promised that they would be brave and never abandon me.

By the end of the first week we began to feel perpetually tired. We no longer felt like playing outdoors, but preferred to sleep or read in bed during the day. I had phoned the Center on Thursday, July 9, by hiking out to a phone booth I had seen every morning on the way to Mass. The Center had encouraged me to continue our strategy, and to ignore the Connors' threats of trouble. Now I was too weak to make the long walk (over two miles) to the phone, yet I needed advice from the Center. R.C. had offered to take us home one week early if we started eating.

On Saturday, July 11, we received a letter from Sister Mary Agnes. She wrote that she really missed us. It was the first time I had heard her express such affection for us, and I felt embarrassed. I thought she was required to stoop to such words in order to appear like a normal mother just in case her letter was intercepted. She encouraged us to say our prayers and described to us all the exciting things that were happening at the Center.

There was a paragraph for each of us. Benedict learned about a baby kingbird that survived after falling out of its nest. Michael found out that the Center might buy some geese any day. Paul was happy to know that his homemade wheelbarrow was still working, and Matthew was touched by Sister Mary Agnes' concern for his sore ankle. Lastly, I was urged to be courageous and have faith, even though Our Lady asks very hard things of us. She also mentioned that there might be a jeep at home when I returned.

The next day, Sunday, we wrote back. I told Sister Mary Agnes that I prayed for her and that I thought of her every morning at Holy Communion. I concluded: "We are longing to go home and we are told that if we eat more than we are eating we will come home Sat." Paul wrote: "I want to come home and see the sheep, cows, and ducks and I also want to play with my wheelbarrow." Benedict started with: "I miss you very much," and Matthew ended, "We send you and everyone all our love." But Michael was the most poetic: "I wish with all my heart to come back home, and you and everyone else there seem to be close in one way, but very far in another way."

"Here's a letter for Sister Mary Agnes," I said to Grandpa as we lined up around the table for Sunday dinner. I had sealed the envelope carefully so the Center could tell if it had been opened.

"I will mail it first thing tomorrow," Grandpa said. He bowed his head to say grace. As he thanked God for His gifts, I prayed for strength to resist. Then I sank back in my chair staring at the scrumptious meal. I imagined myself jumping off the bank of a medium-rare steak and into its pool of bloody juices. I swam between the golden rings of floating grease, and when I reached the porcelain shore, I dove in again. The currents seemed irresistible. If only I could just taste, but I couldn't.

"Just because a man wears a collar doesn't mean he cannot get out of hand," Grandpa began. "There are scoundrels all over the world hiding behind religious garbs. But Feeney has got to be mentally ill. Anyone who would tell children not to eat—I don't know—he must be mentally deranged." He paused for another bite. During meals, only his hunger would interrupt his angry words.

We continued in staring silence. Michael was smirking at R.C.'s struggles with a stubborn piece of meat and sinew. A fly landed on the edge of the beef pool. After a brief taste the fly landed on my plate. It almost seemed to be rubbing its arms with excited anticipation of its next sample of the forbidden meat. I envied its freedom to eat as it chose.

I thought of the feasts we would receive at the Center. Sister Catherine had assured me that three weeks of fasting would be little trouble for "our cooks" to undo. The spark in her eye told me the unlimited range of culinary delights she could command for our reward: our own fresh corn on the cob with melted butter and salt, new potatoes baked crisp and steaming white inside, and succulent potato steaks of tender beef. At breakfast we would have coffee rolls with raisins in the white topping, chilled applesauce, squeezed orange juice, and omelets with cheese and ham, or maybe fried eggs with bacon. At lunch . . . Grandpa, interrupting my fantasies, was at it again.

"New England is noted for its wild growth. The Puritans went around hanging people, condemning women as witches. That area is a hotbed of fanatical groups. The Shakers lived there and they didn't believe in marriage either. There are an awful many crazy religions messing up peoples' lives. Feeney and that Mrs. Clarke are really messed up and they are responsible for all this. They took advantage of the youth of the students at Harvard."

"What I can't understand . . ." Grandma stopped to clear her throat. "What I don't understand is Mrs. Clarke, what's her name there—Sister Catherine. She tells everyone that they should separate and not live as a married couple, yet she herself goes home to her husband and family several nights a week. Now that's ridiculous." She sat back, apparently overcome by the thought of such injustice.

"It's crazy," Grandpa said disgustedly. "The state should go in and close up the place and get all the children out of that unhealthy environment."

"Come on, Benedict." R.C. leaned over, cutting a small piece of meat. "Eat this little bit." Benedict's mouth remained closed. He looked at me.

"This has got to stop." Grandpa put his fist down on the table, pushed his chair back, and rose. "Now I'm telling you, Luke, that if you think you are helping your cause you're wrong. I've been a judge for many years, and I assure you that any institution that puts minors in such a state that they won't eat is going to have to be shut down. We tried to be nice, to politely ask you to eat a little bit, but you are the most stubborn obstinate children I've ever seen. And it is over."

Grandpa's face was flushed. He walked around the table, pausing behind me. I cut a small piece of meat and held it on my fork, hesitating. Grandpa's arm came over and he moved my hand toward my mouth. I froze. He wasn't going to force me. As the fork got closer, I turned my head away. I could feel the anger mounting behind me as Grandpa drew a slow breath. He broke into a tirade against the Center, Father Feeney, and Sister Catherine, but I hardly heard it. I was battling a sudden surge of helplessness. My strong will seemed to dissolve, and as I felt it collapsing, I rushed headlong with it in despair. The Center would probably be wiped out, I thought, but I did my best. I struggled to fight the tears coming up. I was embarrassed. Everyone was going to see it. I burst out sobbing, and once my weakness was revealed, I didn't try to hold it back. It was too late. The world had collapsed around me. Grandpa left the room. I gradually gained control and calmed down, but the tears kept coming quietly.

"I sympathize with you, Luke," Grandma said. "You are caught between the devil and the deep blue sea. If you eat, they will punish you at the Center, and if you don't, we give you a rough time here. And it is not your fault. You were born into this situation. I really understand. We don't mean to be harsh. We are trying to help you. If you can't eat, then I guess there is nothing we can do. But we don't want you to get sick."

I wanted to eat to please Grandma, but then that was her trick to get us out of the Center, I thought. I had to be strong and fight back.

When we got upstairs, I told the Little Brothers that my crying was mostly an act, and that whenever it was done convincingly it could help us. Matthew said that R.C. had walked into his room when Benedict and he were crying, and they had told him that they were crying from homesickness.

"I am too weak, I'll never make it," I said to Paul and Michael on Monday, the next day. "It is a very long walk to the phone."

"We can easily do it," they said enthusiastically. They were thrilled with this unexpected responsibility.

"Tell Sister Catherine we have been without any food now for one whole week and the Connors are almost out of patience with us," I said. "Tell her that they are fighting with each other over what to do, and that Grandma wants us sent home immediately."

The Center was overjoyed at the news.

The next week it was easier to keep from eating, but extreme fatigue made any exercise a real chore. Grandpa decided to take us on trips in his car. We had already attended a baseball game on Friday night, July 10. It was a depressing experience of lights at night, of crowds and loudspeakers. They said Cleveland beat Baltimore 8 to 0. Grandpa took us to the Cleveland Zoo, and my favorite spots were the benches where I could rest. We went to Danville to see relatives. I dreaded each stop when we had to get out and walk to the house.

Then someone named Uncle Justin died. Matthew woke up feverish and shaking that day, and he couldn't go to the wake. Benedict and he were usually cold and tired. They would lie down on the nearest couch no matter where they were. When Grandma wanted them out of the house, they would curl up on the backseat of the car. Michael was often up at night with bad attacks of asthma. Only Paul was well, though also tired.

On Thursday of the second week R.C. told us that we were going to see a doctor the next day. I felt so exhausted that night that I couldn't walk up the stairs to my bedroom. I waited until everyone had gone, and then I quietly began to crawl on my hands and knees, step by step. I paused and rested on the midway landing. I could hear R.C. coming up from the TV room. He stopped when he saw me.

"Luke, what are you doing there?" He walked up the stairs to where I was sitting. I leaned against the wall with my hands on the carpet.

"Tying my shoes," I said, and I moved a shaking hand toward my feet. It was quiet for a moment and I could hear my heart beating.

"If I take you home a week early, will you feel better and start eating?"

"I'm homesick. I want to go home immediately."

The grandfather clock clicked, and the cuckoo called out eight times.

"Luke, look at me." R.C. paused. "Do you really think I'm doing this to be mean to you?"

"No." I looked down and I felt the tears beginning. I had probably said the wrong thing. I put my face into my hands and cried. I wished R.C. would go, but he waited until I stopped.

"Please, you're only hurting yourself," he said quietly.

"I told you, we don't want to leave the Center, and I'm determined to fight all the way."

R.C. left. I was ashamed of myself for crying, and I felt deeply humiliated by my weakness. I crawled on all fours, like an animal, climbing the remaining stairs to my bedroom.

"Now look at her—just skin and bones," R.C. said, pointing to a stretcher in the hospital corridor. A pale emaciated girl was wheeled by the room where the doctor had examined us. "She had no choice," R.C. said, "she would do anything to be healthy like you."

The doctor came out of his office. "Well, I see no problem.

They are as healthy as horses. They should have no trouble holding out for three weeks."

I was downcast by the doctor's optimism. It was Friday, July 17, our twelfth day of starvation. We had nine long days to go. As we left, I heard the doctor whisper to R.C., "Leave plenty of candy and cookies around the house for the younger ones." I knew then that the doctor was R.C.'s friend.

That afternoon I sent Paul and Michael out to phone the Center. "Ask Sister Catherine if it is worth eating to get a few days off, or if it is better for our case to come home looking terribly thin," I said. They returned with the answer: It was up to us.

"It looks like we will just have to stick it out for the full three weeks," I said to Paul and Michael as they got into bed. "This morning I was hoping that the doctor would tell R.C. to send us back immediately."

Paul looked at me and smiled. "D'you know what I was thinking the other day?" He went across the room and showed me a trap he could set for R.C. when he came to get them up in the morning. There was a heavy metal folding bed standing against the wall at the top of the stairs. Paul explained how it could be rigged with a rope tied in the stairwell. When R.C. walked up, the bed would collapse on him, and he and the bed would go tumbling down to the landing below. If it killed him, that would put an end to our misery. I laughed at the idea, knowing that Paul was trying to show me his determination to fight.

I went to bed early that night and slept well until I was startled by a desperate gasping noise. I rushed out of my room and looked over the banister. At the foot of the stairs was R.C., his eyes bulging, his face sweating and red; he was grasping his throat. I had the horrible feeling that one of the Little Brothers had tried to be good and poisoned him. R.C. slowly climbed the stairs, reaching out to me as though I were responsible. Just then I awoke and tossed in bed, relieved but feeling terribly guilty. I assured myself that it wasn't even remotely possible for one of the Little Brothers to go that far. We all knew that it was a mortal sin to kill no matter how wicked the person was.

"We're going home." It was hard to believe—one week early, Monday, July 20. R.C. had suddenly given in. We packed the car, nibbled at some toast, and that was all.

Grandma seemed relieved to have us go, and Grandpa said nothing. I thought he was planning his revenge.

R.C. drove along the highway in silence. He acted indifferent. I was proud of myself and the Little Brothers. R.C. was defeated. We had won. I thought about the glories of home: Sister Catherine awarding us the highest medals of honor and bravery as we stood together before Our Lady's Army and the whole community. It had taken great willpower, and now everyone would know how courageous I was. I thought about the feasts of food we would be given to make us regain our weight. I was the worst off. I had lost over twenty pounds, after two weeks of only water. Benedict had lost sixteen pounds, and the others slightly less.

"Time for lunch," R.C. said, and he pulled off the highway. I told him that my appetite had come back a little. I ordered a ham sandwich, a glass of milk, and an ice cream for each of us. R.C. watched quietly as we finished it off.

The whole community had gathered at St. Therese's House. It was nearly ten o'clock at night. I strutted in with the others, thin and exhausted, but proud. Everyone's eyes were on me. I imagined what they were whispering to each other. "There's one thing that has to be said about Luke, he's got tremendous willpower which no one can break." I felt their quiet admiration, but I knew I'd never be told how wonderful they thought I was. They feared it would "go to my head."

But the glamour I anticipated never happened. There were no special dinners (though for a while we did receive a midafternoon snack), there were no sermons of praise (though we got the army salute for "bravery under fire"), and there was no jeep as Sister Mary Agnes had mentioned in her letter. I was just another Little Brother who was no exception to the rules.

"Young man," Sister Catherine said sternly one morning, "you have been riding too high these last two weeks. I don't know who you think you are. We are proud of what you did, but don't forget for one minute that it was Our Lady's victory, and it was due to the countless prayers of our Brothers and Sisters who stayed up nights before the Blessed Sacrament storming heaven for your release. You'll never know how much we suffered for you."

I swallowed and nodded. Sister Catherine said that she would be at the pool that afternoon, and she wanted to see me swimming like all the other Little Brothers. I tried to explain that the water was often too cold for me, but she said it was nonsense.

Sister Mary Agnes and several other Big Sisters arrived with Sister Catherine. I sat on the bank shivering from the cold, refusing to go in despite the Angel's urging.

That evening I was summoned to the Office, where Sister Mary Agnes and Sister Catherine scolded me.

"I was disgusted," Sister Mary Agnes said. "All the other Little Brothers were in the pool, but you sat like a coward shaking in the wind."

I became angry. "I am not a coward. The other Little Brothers do not mind the cold as much as I do because they're heavier." I was convinced that I was being treated unfairly and I would not give in. Sister Catherine rose up to her full height. Sweeping her hand in an arch from the shoulder to her side, she ordered me dismissed from the swimming program.

"And I hope you are proud of yourself," she said. "When all the children perform for the Big Brothers and Sisters on Field Day, you can sit by yourself and pout."

I made up my mind to get back at them. Michael and Paul agreed that Sister Catherine was being totally unjust, and they suggested that I disregard her advice on our weekly visitations with R.C.

"Let them find out how helpful their prayers are without us," Michael said with a gleam in his eye. But I felt that God would punish us if we did not oppose R.C. It was sufficient, I thought, for Sister Catherine to worry that I might not cooperate. So I refused to report the visitations, answering in the briefest deadpan monosyllables and claiming that there was nothing to talk about. After two weeks Sister Catherine let me return to the swimming program if I would do my best. In another two weeks I had forgotten about my offended pride, and I began to talk again with my usual enthusiasm. I completed the program and received my junior lifesaving badge.

Miss Foley had been our teacher. She was a middle-aged professional swimming instructor and a longtime friend of the Center. When R.C. had criticized our education programs for lack of qualified teachers, she had been called in to run our swimming classes. In the fall she led the P.T. (physical training) classes for both the Little Brothers and Little Sisters. However, one time she showed up at our class in a short dress, giving us an unprecedented view of legs as she demonstrated the exercises. After that, she disappeared. Sister Catherine explained that Miss Foley would not be able to teach us anymore due to "poor health."

But there were several Little Brothers who missed her weekly presence, and among them was Alexander. He was in my class and therefore of the same age, fourteen. One cold autumn night he climbed out of his window and ran several miles to the nearest phone booth. When he discovered that he couldn't make the call without money, he went to a nearby house and asked to use their phone. The operator, not knowing where Miss Foley lived, could not give Alexander the number. He then told her he needed help because he had run away from home. The police were summoned, and Alexander was returned to the Center, where his absence from bed had already been discovered by Sister Mary Judith on her nightly inspection. His running away was never mentioned nor was he punished for it, but several weeks later he incurred the full extent of the horrifying wrath of Sister Catherine.

I saw nothing unusual about the class that day except that Alexander was missing. Sister Mary Salome ended the prayer with her characteristically bold but devout intercession to the "whole Court of Heaven." Silence resumed. I was called on to recite a poem by Robert Frost, and being unprepared, I managed to divert Sister's attention by asking if it were true that Frost was the late President Kennedy's favorite poet.

Sister Mary Salome explained that Father Feeney had been President Kennedy's favorite poet in the early days of the Center, and that Father had put Al Smith's brown derby on Jack's head, claiming that he would succeed where Al Smith had failed. According to the story, Kennedy had humbly denied that he would ever be the first Catholic President, but he was grateful for the honor of wearing the famous derby given to Father in gratitude for his well-publicized poem, "Al Smith's Brown Derby." I already knew all of this, but expressed keen interest, realizing that Sister Mary Salome enjoyed talking about Father. Then the knock came.

"Everyone out!" Sister Catherine stood by the new magazine rack in Our Lady Seat of Wisdom Room. The brightly colored magazines that we had been forbidden to look at were gone. They had been put there originally to convince the town's school officials that, contrary to R.C.'s claims in court, we were well-educated in current affairs.

"We have removed the magazines because some of you cannot be trusted," Sister Catherine said when all the Little Brothers were assembled. She gave no individual smiles to anyone, but remained coldly serious. I wondered what had happened. She nodded to Sister Mary Judith, and we followed them over to St. Therese's House.

Entering the lower door near the garage, I began to hear howling from the back room in the basement. The door opened and we were led in. Alexander stood bloody in the middle of the cement floor. He was stripped of his shirt, and blood covered his purple-striped back, stomach, and his pummeled face. I saw the terror in his eyes when Sister Catherine ordered the whipping to resume.

Two Big Brothers lashed leather belts across his back and side. Alexander screamed in pain, and his body shook with the force of the blows. The powerful slashes of the belt resounded through the tense room. And when he struggled to get away, he was punched in the face. He coughed and pleaded, spitting blood over the floor and walls, and then I realized how the huge drops of purple blood had become so scattered about the room. My knees weakened and I leaned against the wall. The Little Brothers stared in cold fright as the flogging continued. When the Big Brothers paused for a rest, Sister Catherine spoke, "I want everyone of you to know that at this very moment Alexander has one foot in hell."

One of the Big Brothers, aroused by Sister's anger, bit his lip, and the beating continued. He called Alexander a filthy, wicked, rotten boy. He shook his head in disgust and raised his arm for the next blow. "And you—doing that to our dearest Sisters." Alexander pleaded that he would never do it again, that he didn't mean it, but this only increased the intensity of the blows. It went on and on, and Alexander fell against chairs and tables. After a while he didn't even try to speak. We were told, through intermittent breaks in his punishment, what he had actually done.

Workmen constructing the new addition to St. Anne's had accidentally left a newspaper behind. Alexander had found it, cut out some pictures of girls advertising underwear, and labeled them after the Angels. Sister Mary Judith had discovered the pictures hidden under some clothes in Alexander's drawer.

I knew that most of the souls in hell were there because of impurity. It was such a serious sin that horrible floggings were needed to instill the fear of God's fiery eternal punishments. Years earlier, a similar dramatic punishment had occurred when one of the Little Sisters had been turned in for exposing herself in the woods to satisfy the curiosity of certain Little Brothers. The innocent Little Brothers and Little Sisters were made to stand in the center of Slaves' Field and listen to the terrified screams from the surrounding woods where Sister Catherine and the Angels whipped the wicked bodies of the guilty children. Alexander, ten years of age at that time, was the oldest of those punished. I wondered why he had not learned. Certainly he would never do it again after the Big Brothers were through with him, I thought. For the next two weeks Alexander remained hidden from the community. He was in bed, recovering.

Nonetheless, my fear of earthly punishments was not as great as the fear that I would be taken into the world, where I would lose my soul and be damned to the fires of hell for all eternity. But when Sister Catherine asked me one day if I wanted to become a postulant, the first step toward lifetime membership in the order—the Slaves of the Immaculate Heart of Mary—I hesitated. I wanted to help the Center and to save my soul, but not necessarily as a religious Brother. I was hoping that Sister Catherine would conclude that God wanted me to be a scientist who would invent ingenious devices that could bring in thousands of dollars to help support the Center.

"Now we want you to choose freely," Sister Catherine said finally. "The five oldest Little Brothers, except you, have already asked to become postulants. They will live and eat in a separate section and will not be permitted to talk to any of the other Little Brothers. If you are admitted to the postulancy—and I see no reason to keep you out, since all the Angels tell me that your behavior has been very good—then you will not be excluded from their activities."

Immediately, I imagined the disgrace of being associated with the younger Little Brothers during meals, in class, and in chapel. The Big Brothers and Big Sisters would think that I was not good enough to be a postulant. I decided to join.

"Yes, I do want to be a postulant."

"That is wonderful," Sister Catherine said, smiling gently. "It is going to be so exciting. The new addition to St. Anne's House was especially designed for the new postulants. You will have completely separate cubicles, a separate living room, kitchen, and bathroom, so you can avoid the other Little Brothers entirely. The younger ones will look up to you, and someday, if they are worthy, they will follow in your footsteps."

"But suppose R.C. wins, you know, suppose the supreme court gives us to him as he predicts will happen?" I asked.

"You need not worry. Our Lady will be so pleased that you have dedicated your life to her. She has given us victory in all of our many legal battles. We have never lost even one, thanks be to God."

I was happy to be reassured, yet I felt uneasy about my new life as a religious. I asked Sister Mary Agnes at my next report if I would still be allowed to talk to her anytime I had something important about the Connor case. She said that I had to observe the rules like every other Little Brother and get permission.

On November 24 I became a postulant along with three other Little Brothers and eight Little Sisters. I donned the long black cassock and responded proudly to my new name, Brother Luke. We celebrated with a special breakfast served with grape juice, and that evening we had our first taste of lobster. We began a new life with stricter rules of silence and more prayers. Each morning before Mass we would kneel quietly in chapel for our "meditation." Then we would sing the Monastic Hour of Terse, a traditional sequence of psalms and prayers. Every other week we had a chapter meeting, a ceremony wherein each Brother took his turn and knelt down with bowed head in the midst of his fellow brethren as they accused him of his faults. If any Brother was above reproach, due to his "perceived perfection," then he was obliged to accuse himself. The sin of pride was always there as a last resort for those who had difficulty with self-accusations.

In early December, the Connor case went before the Massachusetts supreme court. Representing the Center was a prestigious law firm from Boston. They contended before the supreme justices that the strength of America lay in the diversity of its beliefs and ways of life. No court, they argued, should condemn a sect as un-American out of bias to its religious tenets. Robert Connor's attorney, Walter Griffin, characterized life at the Center as "fantastic," and certainly unhealthy for the upbringing of children.

On the last day of the year, 1964, the Supreme Judicial Court of Massachusetts upheld the lower-court decision and cleared the way for Robert Connor to take his five children out of the Center. When Brother Boniface, the Center's "brother lawyer," heard the news, he sighed in defeat. "We'll see what happens. The children are our best bet."

Countrywide news coverage of Robert Connor's victory prompted worried relatives of Center members to send him letters of congratulations and inquiry. They asked for any information about their daughter or sister or son. A letter from Mexico said that the "appalling" article in *Time* magazine (January 1) was the first definite information she had had for years concerning the Center where her sister was "trapped." Another letter asked for the address of R.C.'s attorney so "us parents" can "blast Feeney out of business." A shrewd grandmother, whose daughter had recently escaped from the Center, but who could not yet win her children's affection, warned R.C. to take his five sons as far away as possible to avoid continued alienation through Sister Catherine's influence. *The Saturday Evening Post* requested an exclusive interview for an article about life with Father Feeney's movement. But Robert Connor was too busy with the worst part of his struggle, which he knew lay ahead. The caption in a full page feature article in the Boston Sunday *Herald* [January 10] summarized it: "A FATHER'S DILEMMA—CAN HE WIN THE LOVE OF HIS 'BRAINWASHED' CHILDREN?"

Though *legal* victory had been achieved, R.C. worried about the Center's determination and how it would affect us. Already, by our intentional starvation, we had succeeded in weakening his parents' support. After that summer's visit, Grandpa wrote to him: "I think you will find it impossible to handle those children." He advocated compromise with the Center. Again, on January 10, Grandpa wrote to Mr. Griffin:

> ... Mrs. Connor explained to Bob that she no longer possessed the physical strength that would be necessary for the care of five hostile children. Unless someone there now comes forward to help him, it would appear that the Court decision will turn out to be an empty victory indeed.
>
> I do not feel that I am able to assume any financial burden beyond the bill that you rendered me and the expenses Bob will incur in finishing his work in Law School. ...

R.C. was halfway through school, heavily in debt, and now he faced the task of providing for his five alienated boys. If he waited a year and a half until he finished law school and had a better job, he feared it might be too late to recover his children. He consulted with Bishop Flanagan, Father Robert Drinan (then dean of the law school), and Monsignor Dewey, Director of the Catholic Charitable Bureau of Boston. A plan was developed so that he could take us to Akron, Ohio, and with support from the Catholic Charities find temporary foster homes while he finished his schooling.

The Center realized R.C.'s financial difficulties and drew up a bill of $21,753.54 for the cost of our support over the previous two years and nine months since R.C. had left. Using information from an observant friend in Boston, Sister Mary Agnes suddenly appeared at the time and place where R.C. usually met a young woman, a law-school classmate by the name of Conchita Morales. Sister Mary Agnes told him that she knew that he really didn't want her to rejoin him. On Friday, January 22, the attorneys for Sister Mary Agnes informed the court that she would leave the Center if given custody. R.C. could support her and the children in an apartment nearby. Judge Wahlstrom, thoroughly exasperated, dismissed the appeal and ordered us to be given to R.C. on Monday, January 25.

The Center's lawyers countered that Sister Mary Agnes would abide by the decree and return with the children to her husband, provided they were not taken to Akron, Ohio. Mr. Griffin claimed hypocrisy, saying that the Center was using delaying tactics and making a mockery of the court's decisions. The judge reiterated his order postponing the modification of the decree, and offered to issue a writ of habeas corpus if the children were not released from the Center.

The night before our departure the five of us gathered in the cold misty darkness outside a large house. Sister Catherine had agreed to try my plan. The door finally opened and Governor John Volpe stepped out. I begged him to use his power to halt the execution of the supreme court's decree. If he could appoint the supreme justices, I reasoned, then he could bring pressure to keep us from being taken away. I broke down crying. The governor said there was nothing he could do, though he would look into it. The next day we were flown to Ohio.

The jet blasted off and I felt the power of the world

against me. The airport grew smaller and smaller. Down there was Sister Mary Agnes, crying uncontrollably, her heart broken. She would get sick and die, I thought. The last scenes of that traumatic morning flashed through my mind. I had cried before the whole community when I went to receive Holy Communion. Later the Little Brothers, tears in their eyes, were huddled into the car. Sister Catherine looked into our windows, and I volunteered that we would lay down our lives rather than give in. She told me not to go too far; Our Lady would help us. I saw Sister Mary Agnes running to the plane, her black habit flying in the wind as we descended the steps and embraced her. The attendants said we were holding everything up, and, still crying, we separated. I waved at her through the plane's small window, but she never saw me.

I was not going to let the Center down. I would keep my promise and fight to the end.

"No, thank you," I said to the airline hostess. "I'm not hungry."

Chapter Six

It was traumatic being forced into a world that appeared to me to be a waiting room to the never-ending torture chambers of hell. Only the prospect that I might not be away from the Center forever gave me hope. As it turned out, it was for ever for three of the five of us—and for all of us eventually.

On the surface, the story of what I did next seems like a vicious fight against my father and those who were part of the alien world he had thrust us into. Yet, beneath the obvious conflict there was a more seductive struggle going on. The very signs of the world's evils, which I shunned—physical affection, love, family life, romance, and certainly the sins of the flesh—had a subtle attraction that grew in time.

I got out of the world after seven months of intrigue. To the Center it appeared to be a victory for their side. Later, I'm sure, they must have seen it quite differently. I had become tainted by the world in those few months, and that corruption gradually rotted away my lifelong commitment to the Center.

By coincidence, my first two days at St. Vincent's High School in Akron turned out to be retreat days. During a retreat (which means a "retreat from the everyday world") regular schoolwork is set aside and the time used for prayer and examination of one's faith, which should have been easier for me than some of the normal classes would have been. Coming from the Center, my dedication to religion and my knowledge of the Faith would certainly be greater than that of these students who had been raised in, and were a part of, the world. But it didn't turn out to be that way.

Suddenly, there I was rushing around with crowds of strange students while buzzers rang and the voices of priests echoed through the public-address system. Except for a few large sporting events, I had never seen so many people crowded together, nor had I ever heard so much noise of all kinds. And there were times when *what* they said was worse than the way they said it.

At one conference in the school auditorium, the priest began to talk about the fact that boys my age were actually approaching marriage. I put my fingers in my ears. He had said we were at the stage of adolescence—or some word like that—and I knew Sister Catherine would not want me to hear it. I managed to block it all out.

Several weeks later, in what they called religion class, another priest told us a story about a girl and a boy who were "going steady." The girl ended up "pregnant," which I suspected meant that she had a baby inside her. Our assignment was to write a paper explaining exactly when the boy had put himself in an "occasion of sin" (a situation that he is morally bound to get out of).

I was truly scared, for I didn't know what to write. The Center had been urging me to do well in all my courses, because my good grades would help convince the school board back in Harvard, Massachusetts, that the Center's school was worthy of official approval.

Yet, when Sister Catherine heard the story the priest had told, she said it was filthy. And she groaned in despair that it was "all over"—I had already been corrupted.

Sister Mary Agnes urged me to forget everything I had heard, not to do the assignment, and write a short note condemning the priest for corrupting the minds of innocent children. I followed her advice and got a D for my efforts. The other students could see the grade when the paper was passed down the aisle. Afterward, the priest told me that the children in his classes already knew what he called "the facts of life," and therefore his assignment would only protect them. Although I still disagreed, this time I did not tell him about it.

But the most wicked thing happened after gym class. Boys walked around the locker room entirely naked, and they all took showers together in one big room without partitions. (I heard that the girls did it too, but that it was considered wrong for boys and girls to take showers together.) I had never imagined that such wickedness could take place in a Catholic school. I always managed to avoid the showers, and I stayed home sick the day they were to be compulsory. Though I was the fastest runner in my class, I refused to join the track team out of fear of what might happen in the locker room. The boys talked and joked about things I didn't understand, but all of which I suspected were very impure.

I had been in my new school for about two weeks when I found out just how little I really knew about the ways of boys in the outside world. On that occasion one of the juniors took a dessert away from a boy who happened to be sitting next to me at the freshmen table. He sat down at his place and began to eat it. Furious at this blatant dishonesty, I jumped up and ordered him to return it, as he had not paid for it. Startled, he stopped eating the stolen dessert and just stared at me. Quickly, several of the other boys at my table told him that he had better not get mixed up with me because I "knew judo." I was surprised at their intervention. It had never even occurred to me that anyone would fight over such an obvious infraction of a rule.

The junior, awed by my audacity, returned the dish and left. Later, my classmates said I should never challenge an upperclassman, and I was very lucky he hadn't taken me on. (In the months that followed, I never got into any fights, but all of my younger brothers did.)

In class, I felt that I was considered different by the other students. I had told the world-history teacher that the world was not millions of years old, and that I could recite in Latin the entire Biblical genealogy from Adam to Jesus. In religion class I said the book was wrong—there was *no* salvation outside the Church. I denounced the "English Mass" and new hymns as protestantized and designed to corrupt the True Faith. One day there was a cheer in class as I entered, and I later learned that my classmates had been betting on the number of consecutive days I would wear the identical color combination of sweater, shirt, and pants. I saw no reason to change the same uniform I had worn all my life.

However, in English class I became the admiration of all. I had been asked to recite the part of Shylock in *The Merchant of Venice*. Assuming I was supposed to talk like a Jew, I merely imitated Father Feeney's frequent and derisive mimicries of the Jews—performances I remembered very well. With uplifted shoulders and hands, and with eyebrows upraised in question, I spoke in a voice vacillating in pitch from a high intensity to a deep guttural tone that lingered on the ending consonants. My whole manner, face and all, showed a total repulsion for having to stoop to communicate to "that other thing." The nun in charge seemed rather amused, and the children thought it was hilarious. After class I was stopped in the stairwell by classmates who wanted their buddies to see me do that "Jew dialect." I was surprised that everyone liked it.

I managed to get on the honor roll for both quarters at St. Vincent's. The Center had helped by sending a translation of Caesar's *Gallic Wars*, which I used in preparing my Latin II homework. (I saw no dishonesty in this; doing well for the Center's sake was clearly the higher good.) I also received, from the Center, the answers to the weekly tests in current events that appeared in the *Junior Review*. There was no other way I could match the names of the world leaders with the pictures of faces I had never seen before, and the Center certainly didn't want me to start reading the newspapers or watching television.

If the Center was helpful in school matters, it was even more so in regard to our "domestic problems." Sister Mary Agnes, our mother, found the separation far more difficult than one might have imagined it would be for a mother who did not directly raise her own children. She wrote long and unusually emotional letters, at first daily and then several times a week. She described watching the plane that flew us to Ohio pass over the building. She said she ran across the corridor and watched it disappear in the clouds, carrying a more precious cargo than any plane has ever carried before. Most of her time, she wrote, was spent in the chapel at St. Therese's House. She left only late at night because she had to be nearby should we have a chance to phone.

Her mention of the telephone was no exaggeration, for it was the main weapon in our battle, or at least our chief line of communication with headquarters.

Because the first one had been so successful, we began another hunger strike as soon as we were settled in our grandparents' house. But when the Center thought this over, it decided on a different tactic. The court battle and the cost of their son's legal education had put a severe financial burden on the senior Connors. Realizing that our hunger strike was only hurting us and saving them money, we gave it up after two weeks. We then began to eat the Connors out of house and home. We demanded better food, more clothes and shoes, and we ran up huge long-distance phone bills with our frequent calls to the Center.

When they complained of the expenses, we accused them of being stingy and of loving their money more than us. Also, we spread vicious rumors at school about the "cruelty" of Judge Connor, who we knew would be running for reelection the next year.

I went to the Safety Department and told the police that dangerous weapons (guns and bullets) were kept in the house, and I brought along as samples some bullets Michael had stolen from a relative's house.

In religion class, when we were discussing the sin of perjury, I stood and announced that my father had done it, that he had lied in court under oath. The class was shocked that I would say such a thing about my own father (or, as they phrased it, "your old man"). The teacher shut me up with a warning, and a knowing look.

At nearby St. Sebastian's School, Michael burned his "heretical" prayer book, exclaiming that it was "the best chemical reaction" he'd ever seen.

Although we never showed them any affection, in private we had to admit to a degree of grudging respect for the patience and kindness of our grandparents, who had to contend with our behavior without the help of their son, the only person with any semblance of control over us. R.C. was back in Massachusetts for his second year of law school at Boston College. He knew what he was up against. His only chance to get a decent-paying job was if he had the law degree, and he would need a salary large enough to support us and pay for a house and someone to take care of it—and us.

In 1965, both Grandma and Grandpa Connor were in their mid-sixties, and our continuing disruptive behavior was very tough on them. We had been with them for about a month when Grandpa wrote his Harvard Law School classmate, the same old friend who had helped him find a lawyer for his son several years ago. "Our son brought the children to our home January 25. After subjecting us to a hunger strike for nearly two weeks, they have adjusted reasonably well. I believe they would settle down satisfactorily if their fanatical mother would desist in her appeals to them. It's a big problem, perhaps too big for Mary and me at this late period in our lives."

On February 7, my fifteenth birthday, my father wrote to me: "Someday I know that you will look back on all this and see the ones who really loved you and have done their best for you." Perhaps so, but at the time I did not believe it.

The first really good time we had in Ohio was in mid-February, when Sister Mary Agnes came out for *her* first visitation under the rules laid down by the court. We all met at the Shebans'. The Shebans were our only close friends in Ohio. Mr. Sheban, a very successful lawyer and businessman, had been raised in Lebanon with Fahkri Maluf, who later joined the Center and, like everyone else there, ceased to communicate with the outside world. The Sheban family was overjoyed to hear from him when he called on our behalf, and readily promised their help. They opened up their home to Sister Mary Agnes and the five of us for once-a-month weekend visits.

The first two visitations, February and March, were held at the Shebans, and were most enjoyable. They took us to parks, lakes, and waterfalls, and in the evening we could bowl all we wanted for nothing. Mrs. Sheban stuffed us with T-bone steaks, tossed salads, and fruit. She did her best to make sure that we had a wonderful time with our mother.

The Shebans had three children. George was fifteen, my age; Karam was a few years younger; and Jenine had just turned eighteen. For her present on that special day she had received a Cadillac convertible, which she called her "toy."

Jenine was beautiful—long black hair, dark eyes, and a smooth tan complexion that contrasted sensuously with her flashing smile. I was totally fascinated by her fresh and rebellious attitude toward her parents and by her tender and charming manner toward all of us. Because Jenine's family was obviously worldly, Sister Mary Agnes warned me not to be shocked by the ivory statuettes in the bathroom or by the clothes Jenine would sometimes wear.

One warm morning as we were all getting ready for a hike in the park, Jenine came out of her room holding her sweater up above her waistline. "Sister," she whined, "are these too tight?" With a mischievous smile, she turned around so all of us could see the revealing grip of the jeans about her thighs. An embarrassed Sister Mary Agnes quickly dismissed her, saying the pants were "passable."

Unfortunately, the Shebans did not live close enough to the Connors for convenience' sake, so the next few visitations took place at the home of a Mrs. Sipe, in Akron. There was not the affluence in this house that had been all around us at the Shebans', but we had fine times at Mrs. Sipe's. Sister Mary Agnes would cook us fancy omelets, exactly the way we liked them best, and we could see how much she enjoyed doing it. At Eastertime we took our own pictures in a booth downtown; we inserted a quarter and then sat making faces as the lights flashed. Another time we went to a rummage sale, bought bikes for a few dollars, and learned to ride them the same day.

We also enjoyed the relative lack of supervision on these visits. Once, when no one was watching us, we five boys went to a busy intersection and played "cripple." Using a broom and a pair of crutches we'd found in the basement, we devised a game to harass impatient drivers. Just as the light turned green, one of us would start to limp across the street on the crutches.

Then, realizing that he was blocking traffic, the poor crippled boy would attempt to wave the cars on, and begin to limp back to the curb. But invariably the drivers would decide to do their good deed for the day and would wait. The cripple would hobble slowly across the street. When the patience of the backed-up drivers was at the breaking point, one of us would run into the street, hit the cripple with the broom, and then take off, whereupon the boy on crutches would give up his act and sprint off after his attacker.

As the rest of us stood on the sidewalk doubled over in laughter, the drivers would react with anger at having their best intentions made fun of. We learned a whole group of new swear words from the worldly drivers.

These visits, however, were too few and, as far as we were concerned, too far between. For the most part, we spent the first months in Ohio making life difficult for the people around us.

Our grandparents admitted that taking care of all of us was too much for them. Michael, at thirteen the second oldest, had already been sent to live with Uncle Hugh and his family, and by the end of March Matthew (eleven) and I were taken in by the Souers, a large Catholic family in Akron. (The Souers owned a lake cottage in Indiana, where, we feared, we would be sent for the summer.)

We all continued at the same schools, but now only twelve-year-old Paul and ten-year-old Benedict still lived with our grandparents. Some of us behaved better than others, but none of us was exactly what could be called "good."

Michael was particularly hard to manage. He had been sent to still another set of relatives for the summer, and after one week he had caused so much trouble that his aunt wrote to Grandpa that she had "the urge to use a baseball bat on him with pleasure," terribly strong language for that ladylike person. Soon Michael had been through a camp, a foster home recommended by a Catholic welfare organization, and finally ended up back with Grandpa and Grandma.

At the beginning of the summer, when Matthew and I arrived at Clear Lake with the Souers, the five Connor brothers had all been fighting, one way or the other, since late January, to get back to the Center. The judge could order our bodies, but not our hearts and minds. Our father had been fighting, even longer, to get us to change our attitudes. It was a stalemate.

Although I did allow myself to have some fun now and again, especially in the water, I vowed to continue the fight as long as was necessary. The world was wicked, and I did not want to be a part of it.

It was nearly nine o'clock on the night of August 12, 1965. I was alone in a phone booth on the southern shore of Clear Lake in Indiana. That afternoon, my brother Matthew had been taken away. Now all of my younger brothers were in different places, not just separated but *scattered* throughout Ohio, which made it difficult for me to encourage and direct them. R.C., our father, still would not relent and let us go back to the Center. Now, with the taking of Matthew, I was desperate.

"But, Sister Mary Agnes, don't worry. They can't blame you because it's all my idea!" When I hung up the phone I was still furious. In his determination to break us, R.C. ignored me as if there were no chance of my stopping him. He would see. I had a plan that I would implement tomorrow.

I swung my leg over the seat of my old red bike and began the four-mile trek back to the Souers' cottage on the opposite side of the lake. I felt guilty. I knew it was wrong to disregard Sister Mary Agnes' advice, but I was sick and tired of the Center's legal cautions. I was resolved to see victory for all of us—Sister Mary Agnes, the five Connor brothers, and the Center. And I didn't care what it took to ensure it.

The letters that my mother had written in January and February, right after we had been taken away, had burned themselves into my memory. I had never known how strongly she felt about us, and the memory of her anguish and unhappiness was something I would have given anything to erase.

When the first separation occurred and Michael was sent to Uncle Hugh's house, she cried out in rage that such brutality was unbelievable in these United States, and in her anger she threatened revenge, saying that our entire story would be made known all over the country. I admired her spirit, her determination to fight, and I felt that she would be proud of me if I were successful. I would succeed, I thought. I was fifteen years old—old enough to do things on my own.

My heavy bike squeaked along the dim road that wound between the lakeshore cottages. Its rusty noises set dogs barking behind the wood-slat fences. And I could see the eyes of cats as they looked up from the rubbish barrels. I had bought the bike for seventy-five cents, "marked down" from the asking price of five dollars. Children laughed at it, but I didn't care as long as it would get me to the phone booth every day. The phone was the fastest and safest way to report to the Center and to relay instructions back to my brothers. It was the phone that had made our strategies against Connor so effective. (In the winter, we had substituted "Connor" for "R.C.") Connor thought that we would be adjusted to the world and would have overcome our hostility to him by June, when he returned from Boston College Law School. Instead, we were still driving our grandparents mad, causing them to gradually separate us until by midsummer only Matthew and I had remained together.

I paused on the top of a small hill to look at the silent lake below. On the opposite shore a dark silhouette of pines cut the last ribbon of an orange sunset. The water caught the rising moon, full and yellowish. I loved it. Occasionally I would sail out onto the lake at night. Lying down and looking beyond the damp sail and into the stars, feeling the darkness, and hearing the hiss of the bubbles in the wake of the boat gliding over the black water, there was nothing to worry about. All was peaceful and beautiful. It would grip me deep down and hold me fascinated, and truly these were my happiest moments. I could just *be*, and it was all there for me to enjoy. I wondered if the Little Brothers at the Center could ever imagine what they were missing.

Connor, I thought, was hoping I would be corrupted by the sun and fun of summer at the beach—swimming, water-skiing, and sailing. And to a degree I *had* given in. I learned how to sail the sunfish and to water-ski (though I pretended I didn't enjoy it). I saw more of the pleasures of summer fun than I would ever admit to Sister Mary Agnes.

She was worried about the purity of my soul, which was tempted by the wickedness of the underdressed teenage girls at the cottage—bodies on the couches, bodies on the dock, and bodies in the boats. She warned me not to associate with such girls and never to forget my early-morning three Hail Marys to Mary Immaculate for my holy purity.

The summer cottage was not rented, but belonged to Doctor Souers, who was an eye specialist. The Souers had seven children, four girls and three boys: Pat, twenty-two years old; Tim, twenty-one; Terry, nineteen; Cathy, sixteen; Mike, thirteen; Joe, ten; and Mary Bridget, eight.

Most of the Souers had left that day, except for Cathy and Mrs. Souers' parents, Grandma and Grandpa Cochrin. Because it was unusual for me to be out that late, I wondered if they would be suspicious.

I parked my bike near the gasoline tank used to fuel the motorboats. The tank always reminded me of Connor's visit that summer. He had arrived while I was away from the house one morning, and he took pictures of Matthew having a good time swimming and water-skiing. When I arrived, sunburned and wearing short pants, he seemed delighted. He commented on our "marvelous adjustment."

"Even the way you sit on the chair, Matthew, with one leg sprawled over the armrest—why you would never do that at the Center," he said.

I was furious. He was trying to say that we were giving in; and so, when he drove off later, I imagined myself pouring gas over his car and igniting his departure. He was so sure of himself, but there was always *that* incendiary lesson I could give. I hadn't entertained the idea seriously, but I liked telling it to Sister Mary Agnes to prove my loyalty to the Center.

I hesitated at the door of the cottage. Inside, Cathy was laughing. I liked her, so sweet with her blue eyes and blond hair. She always talked with such tender concern, even though, as I well knew, she regarded me with suspicion. What would she think after what I had done that day? I had stowed away in a hidden compartment in the Souers' Buick station wagon, the car that eventually took Matthew away. But I was caught, and Dr. and Mrs. Souers stared in wonderment as I laughed off my "prank"—just a joke, of course.

I entered with what I hoped was a casual air. There was nothing unusual, I told myself; only I knew what would happen the next day. The cottage was spacious inside. Along the south wall on my left was the kitchen, then three bedrooms, the last one separated by the stairs leading up to a huge room that Matthew and I had shared with the two youngest Souers boys. One spacious room occupied the center of the cottage and faced the stone fireplace on the north wall. At the far end of the house was the rumpus room, with the water-skis, Ping-Pong table, and the assorted couches set against the screen windows that looked onto the lake where the boats were moored—two sailboats, two motorboats, and a pontoon raft.

"Hi, Luke," Cathy said. She was seated with two of her girlfriends, and the glow from the fire reddened her face. "How are you?"

"Oh, fine. I've been watching the moon over the lake. It's a full moon tonight; you should see it."

Cathy offered me some pizza and made me feel comfortable, though I wondered about the smirks on the other girls' faces. Perhaps she had told them about my attempted escape. I slouched back on a chair and watched the red coals for a while. Then, tired and worried, I bowed out, saying I had to be up early for Mass at St. Paul's Chapel. That was foolish, I thought later. Cathy certainly knew that there was no Mass on weekdays.

At eleven o'clock I was still tossing in my bed, worrying about what could go wrong the next day. The laughing voices of the girls downstairs reminded me of the night I heard children splashing in the water outside: skinny-dipping, which I'd heard meant they had no clothes on—completely naked in the water! And their laughter and screams fused into the cries they would yell from the fires of hell when the time of their punishment came. The girls flaunting their sinfulness in taut bikinis as they walked around the house were so wicked, and they didn't even know it. They were laughing their youth away, getting closer and closer to the brink of never-ending torments in hell which would be doubly painful because of the scandal to the innocent. I had warned Matthew that Sister Mary Agnes forbade us to look at the girls in bikinis.

"But why? They are more modest than the boys, who don't wear any shirt," Matthew said. "At least the girls wear something on top."

I was amused, and explained what I had just recently learned myself: that the world considered wearing nothing on top to be okay for men but not for women because women were made differently. But, I cautioned him, we should continue wearing our shirts when swimming as we had always done at the Center.

I wondered if Matthew had caught on that nakedness was sometimes allowed in the world, even by supposedly good Catholics. I learned that nakedness of boys among boys and girls among girls was okay, but not between them. However, I suspected that in marriage the rules were different, because Michael had told me that Uncle Hugh and Aunt Lydia would get undressed in the same room. I found that horrifying.

I thought about my plans again. During the summer I had saved up nearly two hundred dollars, working as a dishwasher seven days a week for six or seven hours a day at the Lakeside Hotel. Mrs. Moreland had liked me and gave me the job at thirty-five dollars per week. I wasn't quite old enough to be employed (you had to be sixteen), but she was kind, though the other boys made fun of her and did wicked things when she was gone. There were three boys from Kentucky and they were the worst, ripping out street signs after dark, swinging dummies from trees over the road to make cars swerve, and getting "stoned" with their own brew. Once I saw Roy, the oldest of the Kentucky boys, reach under the dress of one of his girlfriends and squeeze her bottom, and she laughed, saying he hurt her sunburn. I never went with them at night, except the time they told me that the girl with the knit bikini would be at a dance nearby. I finally quit the job, after nearly six weeks, when I had more than enough money to accomplish my plan, which included, if necessary, a round-trip flight to Boston.

The Center had said my idea was much too risky. But I was determined. Anyhow, I had plenty of money for the next day; if any trouble developed, it would be *my* fault, not the Center's.

I could still hear Cathy downstairs. I had seen her older sisters at the wild rock-'n'-roll dance, where the girl with the knit bikini was supposed to be. Sister Mary Agnes often told me that the dances in the world were extremely wicked. The night of the dance I was trembling with guilt as I entered the shack. I expected to see satanic visions, naked bodies writhing with the pounding that I had heard from the outside. But everyone was wearing something, and the place was very warm, with strange odors. At the far end, men with unusually long hair were screaming into microphones and beating out their anger on the drums as sweat poured down their faces and bare chests.

Then I saw the Souers girls. Terry was swinging her arms around and laughing, not in the least bit afraid of all the yelling. Pat was bent forward, her head almost touching a tall guy with long black hair like the Beatles. She waved her arms over her head, and her body shook in hideous convulsions. Even though she wiggled her hips in a disgusting way, she seemed completely unembarrassed. Suddenly, she started mouthing the words, first smiling, then almost crying, her eyes seeming to remember past fits of such pleasant horror.

Shocked, I left immediately, without even seeing the girl from the hotel who wore the bikini made out of a see-through knit of black yarn.

When the girls left and sleep finally came, I dreamed that I was hitchhiking away from the lake and that the boys from the hotel came by, picked me up, stole my money, and left me stranded on the road. Then the Souers found me, my plan failed.

Early the next morning while the house was still asleep, I got out on the road. Dressed neatly in a white shirt and long blue pants, I walked along the side, afraid to flag down the cars that passed by. Sister Mary Agnes had warned me how dangerous it was to hitchhike. I had lied to her over the phone, saying that the bus came right by the cottage; I knew it was about twenty miles to the station in Angola.

Worries raced through my mind. Maybe Grandma and Grandpa Cochrin heard me leaving and would come looking. What would they do when I didn't show up all day or even when it grew dark? Would they think I had drowned, like the eleven-year-old boy who broke his neck in a diving accident the previous week? If they were called, the police might search all the highways in the area. I had to get a ride, but no one stopped for me and I continued walking, mile after mile along the lakeshore road.

I had gone four miles when I reached the South Shore Grocery, the place from where I phoned every day. The lady at the store asked me where my bicycle was. I had confided in her during the summer, telling her about the separation of my brothers because of the cruelty of my father.

"I need a ride to Angola," I said. "No one will stop for me."

She saw a tall man come out from his house across the street and called to him, asking him to drop me off in Angola on his way to Fort Wayne. The gentleman was friendly and seemed satisfied with my story that I would be meeting friends at the Angola bus station. We drove along in silence.

The trip, as I had planned it the previous day, was to take me by bus from Angola southwest to Fort Wayne, then east to Canton, and from there north to Akron. I expected to arrive at about 9:30 in the evening and take a cab to Grandpa's house, where I would confront Connor and belligerently inform him that I had enough money to get around on my own. Also, I hoped to see Sister Mary Agnes who had arrived in Akron two days earlier.

On the bus ride to Fort Wayne I watched the trees fly by, and I quietly prayed the rosary, promising ten more in thanksgiving to Our Lady if I arrived safely in Akron without being stopped by the police. But at the Fort Wayne terminal, while I waited for the next bus, other trouble developed.

I noticed that a muscular young man with short brown hair and what looked to me like evil eyes was following me around the station. He would look me over and then stare down at the bulge of money in my trousers pocket. I was nervous and crossed to the other side of the room. He came over, pretending he was interested in other things, but I would catch his eyes glancing down. I thought he wanted to steal my wallet with all my money, so I went to the phone away from the crowds and dialed a random number.

"Hi, there. Yes, Bill has arrived and the rest of the men should be here very soon." I hoped the man would think that I had friends around and leave, but he continued watching me as he leaned against a nearby wall. I couldn't call the police because they would find out I was running away.

I made a collect call to the Sheban residence in Ohio, where I thought Sister Mary Agnes would be.

(I wondered if we could all get together, now that Sister Mary Agnes was also in Ohio. Michael was already in Akron. He had just been released from the hospital, where a doctor had taken a piece of bone from his hip and put it in his wrist, which had never healed properly from an old injury. Matthew, who'd been taken from me yesterday, was on his way to the YMCA camp outside Akron. Paul and Benedict

162

were in Danville, Ohio, living with relatives; Paul was with Uncle Wilford, and Benedict with Uncle Charles, both of whom were farmers.)

Suddenly, out of the corner of my eye I saw the tough-looking young man approaching me. I got up and walked away as casually as I could. I turned, went out the door, and walked down the street. At the end of the block I looked back. He was coming!

I did an about-face and headed back to the terminal, going past him and stopping only when I got to the ticket window. He entered the station, looked around, and sat down opposite some boys playing the pinball machines. I was sure now that he was after my wallet.

I decided on a bold plan; I would scare him off by confronting him and hinting that I knew he was a thief. I sat down beside him, holding my elbow against my left pocket so he couldn't slip his hand in without my feeling it.

"Hello," I said, looking sternly at him. "Do you know how to play those pinball games?"

He turned and smiled at me. "Do you want to play a game?"

"Me? No, there are too many pickpockets around here who could easily rob someone playing those games."

He laughed, unafraid, and remained seated. I asked him what he did for a living.

"Clerk at a hotel."

"Doesn't look like it," I said. "How come your arms are so tan? I bet you're outdoors most of the time." I had seen through his lie, I thought. Now he would see that he couldn't outsmart me.

He asked me if I liked to drink, and offered to give me some "booze," which he kept at his apartment. He was trying to trick me into going to his room, where he would get me drunk, then steal my money and maybe even kill me.

He started talking about the games boys like to play in the bathroom. I didn't understand. There was one game where he got something eight inches long. It sounded impure and horrible, and for the first time I became really frightened. When I told him that my bus was almost ready, he said it had already left, but there was "plenty of time till the next one." I went over to the booth to check, thanked Our Lady that I was not mistaken, and boarded the bus a few minutes later.

The ride to Canton was long, with frequent stops. I arrived

in Akron at about 9:30 at night. Everything was the same—the dingy station, the tall gray buildings across the street, St. Bernard's Church, probably empty now. I took a taxi to my grandparents' house.

I left the cab on the quiet street where my grandparents lived and where I knew Connor was staying that summer while he worked as a bailiff for Grandpa. Old houses of different sizes and styles, each beautifully landscaped, were all around in the dark. I walked toward Grandpa's large two-and-a-half-story house. Built of brick and dark wood like the English houses I'd seen in the travel movies at the Center, it stood at the top of a small hill. I was very familiar with the inside of the house, its ten rooms, five baths, and the deep mahogany woodwork on the doors and panels everywhere. I passed silently through the attached garage on the basement level and paused at the entrance to the recreation room. I could hear the TV.

The grandparents and Connor were probably sitting in there, I thought. Connor might become furious and slap me around the room. Of course, if he did, I could always use it against him in court, as I had threatened at Eastertime when he hit Paul. He had come out for a week from law school to visit us. We ignored his urgings to us to be more grateful to Grandpa and Grandma for all their pain and trouble; instead we enjoyed insulting them. Then, one afternoon, Connor lost his temper and hit Paul for some fresh remark directed at Grandpa. I knew then that Connor was getting fed up with us.

Shortly after that, the Connors sought to weaken our strategies of disruptive behavior by separating us more. By midsummer nearly all of us were living apart with various relatives and foster parents. I knew that even if we ceased our hostilities, Connor could not afford to raise us together in a home until he graduated from law school and got a good job. Now that he had taken Matthew away from me, I intended to show him how useless his efforts were. I wondered how long it would take him to give up.

I peeked into the room. The grandparents were sitting on the left, and Grandpa was dozing. Connor was lying on the couch against the wall. Then I saw Michael in the corner absorbed in the wicked entertainment of the TV. I was shocked. For all those months I had scrupulously obeyed the Center and totally ignored TV, radio, movies, magazines, and the newspapers. When the Souers had a TV dinner, Matthew and I would turn our chairs around and eat quietly. When Mrs. Souers placed the morning newspaper near my plate at breakfast, I put it aside. Now here was Michael, casually committing mortal sins as he sat there comfortably in his chair.

"Hi, there." I stood smiling in the doorway.

Michael turned around, and his face flushed with guilt. (He told me later that he wasn't watching TV, but had just paused in the chair for a few seconds to ask Connor a question.)

"Luke! What are you doing here?" Connor said, "I thought you were at the lake. Did the Souers take you back with Matthew?"

"Oh, no, I came on my own."

"What? All the way from the lake?" Connor got up from his chair.

"Yeah, I've been riding the buses all day. It's fun being independent with plenty of money to travel."

"You . . . you ran away? Do the Souers know?"

"No, we better tell them. I think they must be worried by now."

Grandpa had also gotten up, and Connor gave him a look, shaking his head. Michael was delighted, and he congratulated me. As Connor got on the phone, Grandpa groaned in exasperation. We learned that the Souers were terribly worried and had kept hoping I would suddenly show up. They were about to call us.

Connor said I would be returned to the lake the next day. My response was that I had enough money to make the trip back "ten times."

I worked myself into a fury, saying that all of this would come out in the new court trial in September. Connor was seeking a divorce, and the Center was planning to contest it and force Connor to return us to our mother. I would testify how cruel a parent he was for separating us; any decent judge wouldn't stand for such inhumane treatment. The papers, I said, would be full of the stories of our deplorably neglected condition. I paused to see what Connor would say. I had not forgotten that Grandpa, the judge, did not want any publicity that might hurt his chances for reelection.

Surprisingly, Connor didn't flare up, but he studied me. He mentioned that he was sick of my rebellious attitude, and he started to say something more, but then he cut it short and left the room. Later that evening he told me that I might be sent to a boarding school in the fall.

That worried me. My four months at St. Vincent's had been bad enough. I was always afraid that I would be forced into some wicked corruption or learn something terribly sinful. Boarding school, I feared, would certainly be worse.

The very worst prospect of being trapped in a boarding school was the possibility that I wouldn't be able to use a phone. Without my direction, the other former Little Brothers would succumb to the world and Connor would win. I would be desperate in such a place and would have to use any means, even violent ones, to get myself out. As school was less than a month away, I would have to force Connor to give up immediately.

To my total surprise, Connor changed his mind the next day. I would not be going back to the lake immediately, but instead could visit Sister Mary Agnes over the weekend. I did not know then that I would never return to the lake or ever again live with the Souers family. I had no idea of all the pressures, family pressures, on Connor to simply send us back to the Center.

Our lawyer in the pending Ohio court case was Mr. Christoff and it was from him that I learned that there were strong disagreements among the Connors over what to do with us. Grandma and all the relatives who had taken their turn with us felt that they had done their best, that our situation was hopeless, and that we should be returned to the Center. Grandpa and Connor were determined to stick it out. They argued that it was their duty to ensure our future welfare and happiness.

Uncle Hugh, Grandpa's brother (and the lawyer for Connor in the new case), was simply fed up with us. His wife, Aunt Lydia, exhausted by four months of trying to manage Michael, had convinced Grandpa to send him to another set of relatives, Uncle Wilford and Aunt Gertrude, for the summer. (It was Aunt Gertrude who had written to Grandpa, not even a week later, that she found her job to be almost unbearable and that although she could handle Paul she wanted to use a baseball bat on Michael, whom she described as "deceitful and hateful.")

Grandma Connor had found our mischief and intrigue nerve-racking. She had come to the belief that the emotional strain on us was not worth the benefits of keeping us out of the Center. It seemed to her that we would never adjust, and when I heard that, I took it as a grand compliment. Jane Peterson, a woman who had left the Center after the Connor case and taken her four children with her, wrote to Grandma that all we needed was love and some time, that our happiness lay in never again seeing "those hateful people" at the Center. But Grandma no longer agreed.

My strategy was that as long as we were hostile and behaved badly we would be separated, and that the longer the separation lasted, the worse it looked for Connor, who had won our custody so he could give us a "normal life." I hated all of us being separated the way we were, but I felt it just might work to our advantage eventually.

Earlier in the summer I had written to Judge Wahlstrom to let him know about the terrible situation we found ourselves in.

> Dear Judge Wahlstrom:
>
> I am writing to you because I want you to know how terribly we are treated.
>
> I and Matthew live in Indiana and my other three brothers live somewhere in Ohio. I think two of them are in the lower part of Ohio, and Benedict is either in Akron or on a farm somewhere. We are really miserable and no one is changing our situation because our father and grandfather do not love us and, therefore, they don't care what makes us miserable.
>
> Our lawyers say that you never meant such a thing to happen to us. We have no home and we are separated from each other. Our relatives out here don't want us. They have told us so. We are homesick and miserable.
>
> Our father said to Michael, "I can't pay for keeping you around." Michael and Paul are working on a cattle farm for $30 a week each. Our lawyer here was told by Grandpa that he intends to have us in this way—separated—until such a time that they can get established. He gave us no definite time. Our father said that he will only keep about two of us when he gets a house.
>
> Certainly you would do something to have us live together. You know how much we want to be with our mother and with our brothers. I heard that you knew what was going on, but I doubt it, because no one would

stand by and watch us suffer like this. Please write to me as soon as possible.

Judge Wahlstrom replied that he was terribly disturbed by my letter. He said he would look into the matter immediately and do whatever he could to correct what seemed to be an unfortunate situation. But, after hearing Grandpa's explanation through Walter Griffin, Judge Wahlstrom told me to stop subverting my father's efforts. The court had decided that I shouldn't be returned to the Center, and the judge begged me to try to cooperate.

In Grandpa's letter to Griffin explaining why he had separated us, he wrote that together we were "impossible to control." Michael was "terribly hostile" and I acted like "the Center's field marshal in relaying instructions from the Center to the younger children." He ended by saying that the younger three were "adjusting to a normal life," but that he doubted the two oldest boys would ever make the adjustment if the "active influence of the Center" continued.

My running away from the Souers was about the last straw. For three weeks I lived with Sister Mary Agnes at the Sipes' house in Akron while the "negotiations" were going on. Occasionally Matthew and Michael would be allowed to visit. Once we went down to Danville to see Paul. In the last few days all six of us were together. I could tell that Sister Mary Agnes was enjoying our company immensely, though it was also apparent that she was deeply troubled by the consequences of her decisions in the dealings.

The bargaining began in earnest when the Connors announced that they would let Michael and me go back to the Center. In return they wanted an uncontested divorce, no alimony, and almost no visitations and communications with the remaining three. They insisted that Paul, Matthew, and Benedict should be allowed to adjust, free of the Center's influence. Michael and I were considered too far gone, but they thought they had a chance with the others.

We knew that the Connors feared the court case coming up in September and the inevitable publicity. The whole case, custody and all, was to be tried over again but this time in Akron. Also, by Ohio law, children fourteen years and older (that would include Michael and me) were free to choose the parent to be their legal guardian.

The Center was thrilled by the Connors' offer. The bell,

Cupertino, resounded four times in the middle of the day. Brothers and Sisters left the fields and barns to hear that victory was at hand. Meetings, phone calls, and lengthy discussions with lawyers in Massachusetts and Ohio occurred late into the night. The decision was: take the deal and run. But first they wanted to make sure they were getting the best deal possible.

Both sides began to call each other's bluff, so utmost secrecy was needed. I always had to leave when Sister Mary Agnes got on the phone with the Center. Though they said they trusted me, they couldn't take the chance that I might accidentally let something slip out. Sister Catherine would go out to different pay phones to take the more important calls because she believed that our enemies had tapped our phones. I was used to such cautiousness: I had swapped the birthday watch Grandma gave me for another one, fearing that it had a listening device inside it.

The Center had Sister Mary Agnes ask for custody of Paul as well. Then we tried for better visitations—possibly even paid—but Connor wanted no visitations. So the original plan stalled, and the Connors countered with an offer of an apartment in Akron plus sixty dollars per week. All five of us could live with Sister Mary Agnes but she could not take us back to the Center, she would not have custody. We accepted the deal, provided the monetary aspects were more realistic and provided Sister Mary Agnes had complete custody. At one time Connor confronted Sister Mary Agnes and asked if she were being honest in accepting the apartment deal. The confrontation ended in a shouting match, and nothing was accomplished. The new deal fell through and the original offer was made again.

After nearly three weeks of haggling, it was finally accepted. Sister Mary Agnes got reasonable visitation rights—Christmas, Easter, and the third weekend in October. The question of summer visits was left open for further negotiations. However, communications between those of us at the Center and the three in Ohio were strictly limited—one letter per month between each individual and no phone calls except on birthdays. They had learned the importance of the telephone.

All during the negotiations, Sister Mary Agnes spoke to me as though she felt she was abandoning her youngest children by agreeing to the divorce in exchange for Michael and me.

Could Paul, Matthew, and Benedict carry on and eventually get back to the Center on their own? That was the question. To my surprise, I got the impression that Sister Mary Agnes was at odds with the Center on several occasions. Twice during those three weeks she was asked to return home, and only Christoff, our lawyer, prevented it by saying he needed her nearby.

Sister Mary Agnes knew that all of us had been equally faithful to her throughout the court case. Now only Michael and I would be rewarded because we happened to be fourteen and over. Each of us had expressed our loyalty in our own way.

I reported daily by phone, got on the honor roll at St. Vincent's High School, and wrote long factual letters giving possible ammunition to be used against Connor. I ended one of my letters with "Our Lady can't wait until she is ready to drop her foot on our torturers."

Michael's loyalty was expressed with much more affection. It was during those weeks of negotiations that I first began to think that Sister Mary Agnes loved Michael more than me. Michael would pour out his feelings and I wouldn't. His letters to Sister Mary Agnes, though written to impress Aunt Lydia, who censored them, were full of phrases expressing his love. Aunt Lydia claimed that Sister Mary Agnes was a nun, and therefore not a normal mother. Michael tried to show her otherwise. He would begin with "Dear, dear loving Mother." Words like the following were common in his many letters: "You know how much I love you." "This telephone [Aunt Lydia's] is not worthy to carry your welcome voice to me, your almost destitute son." Concerning some fudge Sister Mary Agnes had sent, he wrote, "It seemed a little bit of you."

He wrote about us in the same passionate way. "I got permission to visit my lonely brothers whom I'd die for." About me he wrote, "Luke is so brave. Though I never say it directly to him I admire him tremendously. His shrewd maneuvers behind this Iron Curtain are or seemed to be inspired. . . ."

In the heat of his anger Michael would lash out, "Who ever heard, in this U.S.A. of ours, supposed to be free and just, of five sons being mercilessly separated from their mother who brought them up. The thought of this horrid outrage turns my red American blood cold and white with rage and unlimited fury. I'm sorry for this outburst of true heartfelt feelings but what boy of my age could help not restraining himself under these conditions. . . ." Another time he wrote: "My grief in this separation is unexpressible. . . . Maybe on Easter day my father will be ———! You know what I mean. Don't worry about anything. We will fight on!" (Many of the letters like the one just quoted were never seen by Aunt Lydia. He mailed them out secretly.)

Though Paul, Matthew, and Benedict did not write as much, they continually reiterated their love for Sister Mary Agnes and their resolution not to give up. Paul wrote: "A soldier and a missionary must go through hard suffering for God. I send you and all of you my deepest love. But again I say don't be discouraged and pray hard. . . ."

On Friday, September 3, 1965, we met at the lawyers office and watched Sister Mary Agnes sign the agreement that would allow her to take Michael and me back to the Center. Everything she felt about Paul, Matthew, and Benedict must have been vivid in her mind. Her hand was shaking slightly, and tears ran down her face as she applied her signature to the document. She was now divorced from Connor, who would keep the three youngest of her children in Akron, Ohio.

I went to the Souers' house to pick up the rest of my clothes. Mrs. Souers was very cold to me. As I stepped out onto the porch to leave, she stopped me and looked directly into my eyes.

"How can you do this to us, who have worked so hard trying to help you?"

For the first time, I felt really guilty. Up until then, the cause of the Center seemed so important that everything I did to achieve victory was justified in my mind. But now I felt I had hurt an innocent family. I admired the Souers. I knew how good their intentions were when they took on Matthew and me. Grateful to God for their own seven children, the Souers had applied to the Catholic Charity and offered to help out a poor child in need of a home. They had never expected to encounter such difficulties. I could see that Mrs. Souers was greatly distraught. She had a heart attack one week later, but she recovered. It was shortly before that that she had decided that they could not help the Connors any longer. Matthew would have to go elsewhere.

There was something strangely sad about those last few days with my brothers. I knew I would go home to the Center victorious, yet I suspected that I would rarely see my brothers again. (And I was right. Over the next two years, Sister Catherine allowed us only one visit. The world was a distraction to my religious life, I was told.)

I decided to have fun in giving away my possessions. I had to dispose of my wristwatch, my bicycle, and some loose change. Matthew said he would do anything for my belongings, so I decided to take him at his word. The rest of us laughed as I had him polish my shoes or comb my hair. He ended up with everything worldly I owned. The money I had saved from work that summer ($168 was left) I eventually gave to Sister Catherine. It was the least I could do after all the expenses the Center had incurred to get me back home.

Michael and I talked a bit about why the Center forbade us to speak to the Little Sisters. We had both realized that in the world boys and girls formed friendships before they got married. We thought Sister Catherine wanted to prevent that from happening.

We said good-bye to Paul, Matthew, and Benedict at the bus station. I encouraged them to continue fighting as we had done over the last seven months. Victory would come eventually; it only took perseverance, I said. I promised to come out often and help them think up new strategies to frustrate the Connors. No tears were shed on our parting because we hoped it would only be a short separation.

The three brothers who remained behind were soon to be separated once again. Paul remained at Grandpa's, Benedict went to a foster home, the McCarthys, and Matthew was sent to Parmadale orphanage in a suburb of Cleveland about an hour's drive away. The Catholic Social Workers recommended that Matthew be put in an institution somewhat similar to the Center. Both the CSW and Connor said that the discipline of the institutional life there would help Matthew make the adjustment.

Connor returned to law school in Boston for his last year. He had been unsuccessful in transferring his credits to a law school in Ohio without delaying the day when he could start earning sufficient income to support the remainder of his family. In Boston, he was seriously dating his classmate Conchita Morales. After his civil divorce, the archdiocese of

Worcester sent him a letter declaring his marriage to Sister Mary Agnes "null and void on the grounds of defect of substantial form." That meant that he could once again marry within the Church.

At Christmas that year, Connor asked to visit with us for an afternoon. After two hours of trying to break our glum silence he gave up and returned us to the Center. "You win, boys," he said. "I hope you are happy."

Back in Akron, my three youngest brothers continued their hostile behavior. But no one suffered as much as Matthew, aged eleven. He found the institutional life unbearable because the nuns could so easily punish him for his defiance. Their chief threat was the cutting off of his only emotional supports—his letters and the twice-a-month visits with his two brothers still in Ohio. He was extremely lonely amid strange boys and bullies who would set him up in fights for their amusement. His letters to Paul and Benedict (sometimes written in code to us at the Center) were tragically lonely. Paul decoded them after they had survived the nun's censorship and he secretely mailed them to the Center.

While the boys watched TV, Matthew wrote letters and reread his old ones. While they slept in, he attended the early-morning Mass, and while the boys dressed up for parties, such as at Halloween, he excluded himself from the fun. If the nuns used force, he would fight back physically, becoming totally belligerent. Once he even smashed a catsup bottle on the wall of the cafeteria. When some of his precious letters hidden under his shirt fell out, and one of the nuns maliciously tore them up, he went straight to the principal and wasn't satisfied until she was rebuked. When all courses of retaliation against the invincible institution seemed closed, he would refuse to eat, refuse to attend school, or just run away and call the Center. He spent one entire winter night sleeping on the stairs of the administration building with his sweater rolled up under his head.

We encouraged him, in the belief that he would be the next to go back to the Center. Thus he continued his bad behavior: He flunked all his courses and openly defied the authority of his teachers; by March his weekly meetings with the social worker had been discontinued; and he was removed from the ordinary life of the boys of Parmadale. Mr. Kingsley, a psychiatric social worker, wrote both my father and Sister Mary Agnes, saying that Matthew's behavior had deteriorated to the point of full-blown rebellion, that he was grossly unhappy, and that they had to place him in the intensive-treatment unit at Parmadale.

Brother Boniface, the Center's legal strategist, was worried about Matthew's long-term welfare. He wrote to an old law-school classmate asking him to help. In his letter he said that he did not want Matthew to develop any bitterness from a sense of frustration and abandonment that would leave permanent emotional scars. He hoped that his friend would get a lifeline to him.

Though Sister Mary Agnes had visited Paul, Matthew, and Benedict for three days both at Thanksgiving and Christmas, it was only a small respite in the midst of a growing crisis. Matthew's condition was now almost out of control. As Sister Mary Agnes planned her Easter visit, arrangements were made to visit Mr. Kingsley. It was hoped that he would use his professional influence and have Matthew returned to the Center, where he would be happy again. Sister Mary Agnes asked her lawyer, Mr. Christoff, to prepare some legal action. She wrote that Matthew had gone through a grim cruel experience and had lost one year of his life. She said that she was extremely upset to have her children's childhood ruined by that kind of treatment.

At first, things went smoothly for Sister Mary Agnes' Easter visit. Mr. Kingsley agreed to recommend that Matthew be returned to the Center if that would make him happy, and a final meeting was set up for April 13, at 8:00 P.M. Attending was Matthew, his grandparents, Mr. Kingsley, and the principal of Parmadale. But the outcome was totally unexpected and its details wrapped in secrecy.

All we learned was that Matthew had suddenly changed his mind. He would be good from now on. He would return to school at Parmadale and be released in June, when he would join his brothers and his father to live together in Akron. And that is what happened.

Sister Mary Agnes was confused, but she suspected that Paul had turned traitor. She had scolded Paul for getting good marks in school when the Center no longer needed that proof to get their school accepted; it was more important now to *flunk* courses, as Matthew was doing. Paul never replied to this scolding and Sister Mary Agnes felt he had secretly turned against the Center.

She was right. She warned Matthew and Benedict over the

phone that Paul had possibly turned traitor and, pretending they agreed with Sister, they let Paul listen to the conversation. The three of them secretly pledged their loyalty to their father. Matthew wrote "everything is going good now" and Benedict assured "Dad" that he wouldn't give in: "I promise, I won't break. They [Center members] are turning my brothers [Michael and me] against me. . . . I'm going to tell Michael that one of the reasons I don't want to go home to the Center is because of the cruelty of the Angels. Michael will think [about it] because he gets a lot from them. . . ."

Paul wrote: "I still think Michael wants to get out of that money-making Clarke place, but Luke hangs on his every move. . . . Luke is his same old clever, sarcastic self, yet he would be quite persuading to Benedict only I was listening instead. . . . They [Center people] want Matthew to call Sunday [today], but we'll see about that! Just the way they cut off communication with us so I will cut off their only communication with all of us. . . . Grandpa is well informed of all they say. . . . Affectionately, /s/ Paul."

Grandpa was delighted and he wrote to Griffin: "The three children here, Paul, Matthew, and Benedict, have come completely over to our side. They have developed strong anti-Center feelings. I believe they will be cooperative hereafter. We anticipate that the Center group will resort to diverse steps this summer to recapture them."

When Sister Mary Agnes started out for her visitation in June, she did not know that she had lost the loyalty of her three youngest children. It was a traumatic visit for her and the last one for a long time. Paul described the visit a few weeks later in a report he filed for my father's records.

A condensation of Paul's report of June visit, 1966:

> On the first day, Monday, we were picked up by Sister Mary [Agnes] . . . who came in a cab. She hugged Matthew and Benedict, but only smiled a greeting to me. We arrived at the Sheraton with our baggage and Sister signed for rooms 737–739. Things went smoothly in the morning. In the afternoon we decided to go bowling at the nearest bowling alley, which is the Akron Recreation Center. As we neared the bowling alley, Sister started to interrogate Matthew, pumping him for information. . . . I was quite far ahead of them, leading the

way. . . . Benedict came up and told me what Sister was doing. Sister, of course, knew what he was doing. We came to a crossing and I put this question to her.

"What is going to happen when St. Benedict Center falls apart?"

She became enraged and attempted to strike me. I stopped her hand and the unexpected impact knocked her glasses half off her face. I made to re-adjust them, but she did it herself. All the while she shouted at me saying, "How dare you, you vile little traitor—you wicked little traitor. . . . Everybody is going to whisper behind your back, 'He betrayed his mother' and you're going to hear in your sleep, 'I betrayed my mother.' "

I held down her frequent and futile attempts to hit me, repeating when she paused for breath, "You're not going to hit me, Sister."

And she would say, "Oh, yes, I am."

She carried on like this for about 15 minutes. . . .

We had turned back to the Sheraton hotel and she started asking Matthew how he felt about returning to the Center. He told her eventually that he did not; then she asked Benedict and he said that he did not want to go back to the Center either. After this Sister seemed to forget about it and was engaged in making and receiving phone calls, buying gum for Matthew, and playing cards in the hotel room.

The next day [Tuesday] all went smoothly until early afternoon. Sister received a phone call and gave directions as to where her rooms were. A few minutes later, someone knocked and Sister invited in my two older brothers, Luke and Michael. They had just arrived on the bus from the Center after she had sent for them the day before. Sister and Michael left shortly to get something. Luke then began by asking us where we were living (as if he didn't know everything about it). I replied by telling him that we all lived at Woodside Drive. To which he said, "All three of you, I thought that you were supposed to be giving Grandma a hard time."

"Not anymore; she isn't having that trouble from us anymore," I said.

"But that way you'll never get home [Center]," he said.

"We don't want to go back," I said.

"Well, if that is so," he now addressed Matthew and Benedict, "you must have some very good reasons."

Matthew and Benedict knew their own feelings, why they shunned going back, but they were afraid to express them in full through fear of immediate punishment from Sister, Luke, and Michael. Sister and Michael had just come in. . . .

Sister then stood up [and] . . . started indoctrination in full. She accused Dad of perjury and wickedness and hatred of sacred principles; she spoke of the unholy and vile persecution of St. Ben. Center's righteousness in defending "no salvation outside the Catholic Church." She and Luke and sometimes Mike kept up a never-ceasing tirade against Dad and sometimes me. She and Mike heated up beyond control, though Luke kept his self-control. She accused me of speaking extremely disrespectfully of "Our dear Father" (that's her superior Father Feeney) and of striking her in the face and knocking her glasses off in retribution of her slapping me. Mike stripped off his jacket and threatened me with his fist in my face, daring me to get up and fight him. I got up to ask Mat. and Ben., (the only other witnesses of the events of the previous day, Monday) what had really happened, saying that I never struck my mother. Mike kept on standing in front of me, daring me to fight. My mother had in the meantime got up and she came over in front of me. She, Mike, and Luke were all raising their voices at the same time. Then Luke and Mike stopped and remained more or less behind her. Her rage had not abated at all and she hit me on my right cheek all the while working herself up into a greater rage each time. I would not let her slap me more, so she said, "If you don't put your hands down so I can slap you, I'll have your two brothers hold them." I put my hands down and she slapped me as hard as she could six times on the right side of my face after which I stopped her hand. She then hit me once on my left cheek after which I did not let her hit me again. She returned to her chair still calling me a vile little traitor. For a half-hour at least she and Luke and Michael kept it up. Gradually they stopped and we started a card game.

Luke and Michael slept in another room which she

had rented for that night. Things went fairly smoothly after that except for short periods of indoctrinating remarks. That night we had some more card games and Mike and Mat. and Ben. were tired and became quite giddy. All other times before and after this Michael's attitude was contemptuous and insolent. When I awoke in the morning Sister was telling Mat. and Ben. (who were still in bed) stories of old-time martyrs and comparing their persecution and their bravery to the persecution of the Center and its bravery. She then spoke of some young traitors who betrayed one of the Catholic priests under Henry VIII and her meaning was very evident.

All this is not pretty at all and serves to make the visitations unhappy and an ordeal for us. I, personally, never wish to see her on visitations again—nor anyone else she might bring. . . .

Sister Mary Agnes, Michael, and I returned to the Center. She waived her visitation rights for August, Thanksgiving, and Christmas. Paul sent a Christmas card saying that he, Matthew, and Benedict were happy and hoped that we were. Her next visit was not until Christmas of the following year, 1967, and then only at the request of her children.

In the meantime, my father married Conchita Morales. The wedding took place in August, 1966, in San Juan, Puerto Rico. Paul, Matthew, and Benedict went to live with them in Akron.

I imagine that my father now had great hopes that he could live a relatively normal life with at least part of his family. That was not to be. As usual, it was Matthew who acted up, until finally his behavior got to be too much for our father. From then until he joined the navy at the age of seventeen, Matthew was in and out of a variety of foster homes.

He had prided himself on his skill at survival. He bragged that he could "borrow" a car for two hours and return it to the exact same spot without its owner ever knowing, and that he had borrowed our father's car ten to fifteen times (usually between the hours of one and three in the morning). Though Connor never found out, he did become furious when he learned that Matthew had borrowed, without permission, of course, Grandma's car and been involved in an accident.

Oddly, Matthew's moods could change very quickly. If he got angry with someone, he could more than make up for it moments later by a generous show of kindness. He never seemed to stay angry for very long. (Years later, when Robert Connor successfully campaigned for judgeship in Akron, Matthew was our father's most tireless worker.)

Finally, Grandpa Connor was happy. He had been reelected, which helped his peace of mind, but most important, he saw his son remarried and three of his grandsons happily free of the Center. It should have been the time for his retirement, for he was past sixty-five, but because of the many years of helping us and his son, he had heavy financial responsibilities. He would have to work a little longer.

Then, in March 1967, he was struck by a massive heart attack and died. The front page of the Akron paper read: "JUDGE STEPHEN CONNOR DIES AT 68." And that same week the Ohio state senate issued a resolution in tribute to his memory.

Back at the Center, Michael and I heard the news personally from Sister Mary Agnes.

"Darlings," she said, "I have news for you. I received a letter today from Paul." She paused, and I noticed that her arms were folded tightly about her body, but her fingers were nervously working away at the ends of her coat sleeves. She took a deep breath.

"Judge Connor is dead. Thank God, the biggest gun in our enemy's camp has been silenced. I'd hate to speculate as to the state of his soul right now."

Suddenly I felt very sorry for my father. I wondered how he and Grandma were taking it. I remembered Grandpa's determination to get us out of the Center. During the recent weeks and months, and especially when I had realized I was often bored during the long hours of prayer, study, and work, I had begun to see things somewhat differently.

Grandpa had really loved us, I now thought, and—unlike my mother—I had a sudden fierce hope that he had saved his soul.

Chapter Seven

It took more than a year for me to readjust to life at the Center, which surprised me. I had not thought my seven-month sojourn into the evil world had affected me very much, but apparently it had. As the months wore on and I plunged harder and harder into a regimen of work-study-prayer, I finally came to realize that I was often fighting, not the temptation to sin, but simple boredom. I pushed such thoughts out of my mind and again busied myself, but soon the feeling of boredom would recur.

I had been back for more than a year when I fell ill with a high fever and had to remain in bed for several days. As I lay sick in my cubicle at the farthest end of the corridor, I had too much time to think. Almost all of that time was given over to reflection on my life at the Center.

I came to see that I frankly resented Sister Catherine's determined efforts to make me into what *she* wanted. It didn't seem to matter that I might not want to be a religious. God had given me a vocation, I was told. It was obvious to me that the Center was taking great pains to protect it.

I had tried to show my unhappiness by constant complaining, which of course always got back (as I knew it would) to Sister Catherine. I wanted to study more science, and when I could get someone to listen, I would argue that science was not opposed to the Faith, but was also a part of God's creation. I had told some of the Little Brothers that we did not have to believe all those fanciful tales of the saints; they were obviously, I said, fictional. Sister Mary Judith was very upset when I stated that we should use our God-given reason and not accept everything on blind faith. In that way, I argued, we would be better prepared to defend the Faith against its intellectual enemies.

My skepticism had begun years earlier when I first realized that our superiors sometimes lied to us. I was about ten years old the first time that we received Christmas presents. Sister Catherine told us to write notes to Baby Jesus, asking for what we most wanted from Him. (I, like most of the other Center children, had never heard the story of Santa Claus.)

There were two things I wanted: a wild deer to ride through the snowy woods, and, even more important, an assurance that He had forgiven all my mortal sins and that I would not be sent to hell.

Instead, I got a top, some candy, a teddy bear, an Indian chief's headdress, and some holy cards. The gifts that I had made for Baby Jesus had disappeared during the night.

Baby Jesus never relieved my worry about mortal sins, but Sister Catherine tried to. She announced that once we tell our sins in Confession they are completely forgiven. I had played doctor with one of the Little Brothers when I was about five years old. I was still too afraid to confess it, and I had hoped that Baby Jesus would come to my rescue. I became suspicious that Sister Catherine had read my note. I then wondered if there really were a Baby Jesus.

My doubting was strengthened by other deceptions. I knew our superiors were lying when they told some of us who asked how we were born that we were found under the tree, or under the sink, or other places. I confirmed more suspected lies by asking my special friend, Brother Fabian. I even wondered if the Catholic Faith was a Center fiction, but I dismissed that idea when I saw how many books on Christ were in the Center's library.

A year or so later, I began to wonder if my experience of colors was the same as someone else's. Maybe my sensation of green is your sensation of red, I queried. I went further. Maybe my whole twelve-year-old's perception of the world— the trees, the stars, the Brothers and Sisters—was all a concoction of my mind. How could I be sure it wasn't, I asked a Big Brother one day. He answered, "You punch the skeptic in the nose and don't let him blame you for something he believes is his own imagination." Father hated skeptics, and for years after that I felt everyone considered me to be one.

When I heard Sister Catherine coming down the corridor that afternoon as I lay sick in bed, I knew I was in trouble. There was little chance I would be beaten, because at sixteen I was too old. In anticipation of the confrontation, I had perfected some "irrefutable" arguments. But now I suddenly became afraid. Perhaps I was just weak and tired from the fever, which had been the worst I had had in many years and had even brought back one of the horrible repetitious nightmares of my childhood.

I thought of it as the dream of the head. I would see a head, a big head with no hair on it, no features, no eyes, nose, or mouth. There was nothing there but a big head. Yet, when it would first appear, I would be surrounded by the most overwhelming terror. As the head came closer, growing bigger all the time, my fright grew worse. The head would loom before me, and then I could feel it occupy my brain. I couldn't get away from it. I could feel something mounting and increasing inside my head. It would go faster and faster until I woke up. When I was little, I would try to yell at the top of my voice, but nothing would come out. My whole body would seem paralyzed. Often the dream would repeat again and again during the night. I had not had that dream for many years, and when it returned, I was surprised.

Sister Catherine's footsteps stopped halfway down the corridor. I heard her whispering to Sister Mary Judith. Then the two of them went back to the Angels' closet where secret Angels' discussions took place. I feared they were talking about me.

I was a novice, the second step toward becoming a full member in the Order of the Slaves of the Immaculate Heart of Mary. I found that life of strict rules to be tedious, especially after experiencing so much freedom in the world. In the early morning there was meditation. I would doze off and my book would fall, waking me up. Then we had to chant the Office, followed by Mass, which could go on for an hour or more. Throughout the day there were rules of silence surrounding our work assignments and classes. The only free time might be for an hour at lunch and a half a day on Sundays.

Chapter meetings seemed to me like another form of control. We would sit in folding chairs arranged in a circle. One Brother would have to kneel down in the center of the floor, kiss it, and bless himself. Then Sister Catherine would nod, and each one of us in turn would accuse the kneeling Brother of his faults. "Dear Brother in the Immaculate Heart of Mary, sometimes you break silence." Or "You are proud." Some brothers would just say "Nothing" when their turn came. Sometimes there was a subtle tit-for-tat battle of accusations.

When the rounds were through, Sister Catherine would make a few reprimanding or encouraging comments, always ending with "Do you promise to overcome these faults?"

"Yes." (No one ever dared argue back).

She would say, "You may rise."

We would kiss the floor, get up, and return to our seats. Sister Catherine would say "Next," and the process would start all over again.

But there was something I resented far more than the controls of religious life. Ever since I had returned from Ohio, Sister Catherine had taken away from me any kind of responsibility as far as helping my blood brothers get back to the Center. I couldn't go out to visit my brothers, and communications with them were held to a minimum. I felt the Center thought that my vocation was too frail to be exposed to worldly news. Even the letters from my brothers had already been thoroughly read by several other people by the time I saw them. It was the custom for a religious superior to read all incoming and outgoing mail. Father Feeney, for example, would go to the post office every morning, pick up the mail, read it, then show it to the various people to whom it belonged. Usually they would just read the letter and return it to Father. Some mail, I later found out, was never passed on to the addressee.

The only time Sister Catherine allowed me to see my brothers was when Paul, Matthew, and Benedict had turned against Sister Mary Agnes and the Center. Sister Catherine called us in and, as a last effort, let us go. I got the impression she was getting fed up with religious members trying to continue family relations out in the world. She made some comment to me about helping Sister Mary Agnes decide what she really wanted to do. But Sister Mary Agnes never gave any indication that there was a conflict between her and Sister Catherine over my three brothers in Ohio.

I had been in some disputes with my superiors already. There were some kits from the telephone company in the school, and I spent all my free time working on those projects. My physics teacher, Brother Saturninus, accused me of having too much interest in science and not enough in my religious life. I said that there were great saints who had studied science, and no matter what he said, I intended to continue. My arguments with Brother Saturninus were reported to Sister Catherine. I argued with her, and she eventually allowed me to pursue my interest in science.

My projects were the only thing that compensated for my boredom in the religious life. When the walkie-talkies (Christmas presents) broke down, I adapted them so I could turn on the lights in the house by voice from outside. Starting from scratch, I built a toy electric car with remote controls and a tiny electric motorboat. I told Sister Catherine that I hoped someday to make a major invention. I wanted to patent it and bring in thousands of dollars to help support the Center. She seemed pleased with my idea.

I liked the idea of helping to support the Center. When I had returned from Ohio, I had $168 left from my summer's earnings, and I proudly turned it over to the Center. The checks were written in my name, so I had to cash them myself. Father took me to the bank and tried to take the money directly from the teller; the Big Brother who was driving got Father to restrain himself until I got outside the bank door, where I handed over the money.

I always felt that Father and Sister Catherine were not just keenly but overly interested in money. The first adult member admitted to the Center after fifteen years of no new recruits was a wealthy woman. She turned in her engagement ring, and within a day or so Father had taken it down to be appraised. He found that it was worth about six thousand dollars. I made a comment about Father's and Sister Catherine's interest in the monetary value, and I was soon called into the office. Sister Catherine told me that each day she and Father took the expensive ring out of the safe and doted over it. I nodded politely in agreement, though I was puzzled why she was telling me, whereupon she became very angry that I had so readily accepted her sarcasm. She said that my grandparents, the Connors, were vicious in saying that she and Father were just greedy people amassing their own wealth. I was surprised that she still remembered this comment from years ago; I realized that it was a sensitive point for her.

The Angels' closet door creaked as it opened, and I could hear a squeaky swish. Only Sister Catherine made that noise when she walked. She pushed open the door that separated our part of the corridor from the rest of the Little Brothers who were not postulants or novices. The four oldest (including myself) had become novices that July, and five younger brothers, my brother Michael being one of them, had become postulants in September. Now there were eight of us, all living together. But, because everyone was busy in the fields, no one was in the corridor at the time Sister Catherine strode up to my cubicle.

Though no one could be more gentle and loving at times than Sister Catherine, she could also communicate terror in the very manner in which she stood—shoulders back, stomach in. Every movement was deliberate, nothing haphazard; even her walk seemed more like military paces.

At no time did her power seem more terrifying than on Friday nights—the nights of badges. I would twist my napkin into all sorts of shapes (a habit since early childhood) as she stood erect against the doorway separating the Little Brothers' and the Little Sisters' dining rooms. On that night she would decree the punishments. When she got angry, she would rise on the balls of her feet and her hand would swing out, royally, in an extended position. Her finger would be pointed up as though she were balancing the world.

So, when I saw her position herself only two feet from my bed and when I saw her face, drawn tight with severity, looking down at me, I instantly resolved to give in to whatever she wanted.

"Young man," she said, "I understand you have been complaining and griping about our rules here. Is that true?"

I began to explain that it really wasn't the rules. It was just a little argument I had concerning some of the ancient stories of the saints.

"Well," she said, "if you don't appreciate what we are doing for you, you can just march yourself right out of here now." She said it with such a determined motion that her arm dropped behind her back. At once I felt the full impact of her power.

I didn't want to be thrown out of the Center. I didn't want to be thought of as wicked by all the adults, by Sister Mary Agnes, and by all the Little Brothers. Alexander had been dismissed in disgrace after his horrible beating almost two years ago. We had never talked to him again. Sister Catherine would tell stories about his strict life in the military school to which he had been sent. We heard how sergeants beat him up, how Alexander would spend hours marching in the burning sunlight, and how other kids would threaten to push him through glass windows if he didn't do what they wanted. The only Little Sister who had been dismissed, Barbara, was also a disgrace.

I immediately backed down and begged Sister Catherine's forgiveness. I told her that it would never happen again. After a while she seemed appeased, and left.

I felt guilty that I had thought so ill of Sister Catherine after all she had been trying to do for us. I realized that I had forgotten what I used to think of her, that she had always been an understanding person who knew how to make us happy. It was Sister Catherine who had thought up each of our pleasant surprises. We would do our best, keeping our rooms clean, washing the dishes, scrubbing the floors, or doing all the many odd jobs such as digging dandelions out of the lawn or picking up the rotten pears from under the tree. She would reward us with little prizes: holy cards, pins, or even jackknives.

She organized Our Lady's Army. When we drilled, following the various military commands—"About face," "Forward march," or even the change of arms, using sticks as guns—she would always compliment the good soldiers. Some of us received medals, and the names of those who passed the army inspection and had the cleanest cubicles were proudly announced. As we got better, we were given fancy blue uniforms with gold braiding. We wore white gloves and an army hat with a blue pom-pom on top. The Little Brothers wore white puttees. Dressed up in all our glory, we would march before the whole community every first Saturday of the month. Since musical instruments cost a fortune, as Sister Catherine would say, we were lucky that Mr. Haskell, our neighbor, bought most of them for us.

Those of us who were good in school, or kept the rules, would be taken for rides with Father Feeney. We would see firemen or soldiers at Fort Devens. Later, we got to see baseball and football games played by a nearby high school. (We eventually got our own bats and balls.) Sister Catherine let us go out on afternoon rides as long as we were careful to protect Father from his enemies. Our strict orders were to jump in front of Father if someone attempted to shoot him.

During the growing season, we were always busy with the farm chores: cutting potato eyes, weeding, picking strawberries, beans, tomatoes, corn, peas, and digging carrots and potatoes. Then there was the canning, putting up the vegetables and the pears and apples for the long winter. Sister Catherine encouraged us and promised special surprises. For months we would look forward to going to Day's Ice Cream, to eat fried clams, or to spending a day at the ocean (but at a safe distance from the sinful public beaches).

It was Sister Catherine who arranged for us to have the swimming hole dug out of a ravine where a brook was flowing. She got us the ponies and horses to ride. Sometimes she would "spring a surprise," as she would say, and we would all go down to visit the cows in the barn. She announced the cookouts and called the community meetings, which were so much fun. She even allowed us to go to some of the skits put on by the Big Brothers and Sisters for Father's and her feast days. Though she was very busy, she would organize army projects, like collecting field stones to build the chicken coops or clearing a new pasture for the pigs.

After the Connor case, when more of the outside world was allowed in, Sister Catherine was the one who introduced each new, exciting change. We started watching rented movies, going on trips to the ocean or mountains (sometimes more than once in one summer). People in the world would tell our superiors that they had never seen such happy and healthy children. We would yell and scream for joy just walking down the road to Bearhill Pond. Those were the happiest times, and Sister Catherine, who knew how much we loved it, was trying to make us happy as a reward for our hard work on the farm.

When guests started coming to the Center, we performed for them. Father showed us off by having us recite long litanies of saints, and he called us the most brilliant theologians in the world. But the guests seemed to prefer our choir. We would be reminded to smile before we went in to perform, and invariably they would say how beautifully happy we were. Sister Catherine told us that Charles Malik, a former president of the U.N. General Assembly, wanted to send his son, Michael, to our school after watching one of our performances.

Though we were never allowed to speak to "outside people" without an adult present, Sister Catherine made an exception when the Valencia Choir came to the United States to perform at Lincoln Center in New York. Because the director was the brother of one of the Big Brothers, half the choir (college students) spent a few days with us. They rode the ponies, walked our fields, and sang their hearts out. We became so attached to them after their two- or three-day stay that most of the children were in tears when they left. They had brought us such happiness. Even though I never got up the nerve to speak to her, I had become fascinated by one of the Spanish girls. I held my tears back when I saw her crying and kissing the Little Sisters good-bye. Some of the children were allowed to write to them, and did so for years afterward.

Sister Catherine was always busy with very important things, yet she found time to listen to my special projects. She let me have my own vegetable garden, and I would bring her the best fruits of a whole summer's work. The Sister who cooked for Sister Catherine would prepare it especially for her, and Sister Catherine always made a point of thanking me, which made me proud.

Telling me that she remembered my one ambition was to get a microscope, she showed her concern for my interest in science by buying one for the school with the money I had brought back from Ohio. I was very touched, and didn't spoil her generous feeling by telling her that it was a *telescope* I had always wanted. She let me use the microscope for a few days, but then it became off bounds and was put in the science lab for the school inspectors to see.

Another reason why I hoped that Sister Catherine would eventually realize that I didn't have a religious vocation was that I had become particularly interested in one of the Little Sisters, Sister Mary Kristine, whom I suddenly found very attractive. If I went through the final vows and became professed as a Slave of the Immaculate Heart of Mary, I knew I would never be able to marry, and that idea began to bother me. I would daydream that Sister Catherine would tell me she had decided I shouldn't be a religious, but should marry one of the Little Sisters who also didn't have a vocation. Sister would tell us the facts of life. We could love each other, yet do it in a holy way so we wouldn't go to hell. If only that would happen, I would be so happy, I thought. I would cry in bed at night just thinking how much I wanted Sister Mary Kristine to be part of my life. I couldn't speak to her, but I tried to catch her eye continually. Occasionally, she would give me a look that kept me happy for days. But most of the time it was despairingly painful.

A month before I was professed as a Slave of the Immaculate Heart of Mary, I graduated from high school. I was seventeen years old. Sister Catherine gave a speech before the community commending each of us. There were four in my graduating class, John, myself, and two Little Sisters, Mary Joan and Mary Demontfort. I graduated with high honors. Sister Catherine mentioned in her little speech that I had shown great ability in the scientific areas, and that it was hard to tell in what ways God would use my talents. I was flattered to hear that, and I hoped up to the day of my profession that she would change her mind about my religious vocation. Maybe some special arrangement could be made where some of the Center children could get married and live on the property. I could go about my scientific inventions and help support the Center while the others went ahead with their bookselling.

The night before I was to be professed, I gathered up all my courage and went in the office to tell Sister Catherine that I had other interests in the world and that I thought God hadn't called me to be a religious. She just listened. I told her that I didn't want to be considered wicked like Alexander and Barbara, who had been dismissed in such disgrace from the Center. Sister Catherine said that I was a very good Little Brother.

"But if I leave, would I be considered wicked like them?" I asked.

"But you would never leave, Brother Luke. You are not like them." She said that Saint Theresa on the night before her profession had also been tempted by the devil, who was trying to prevent her from giving herself to God for the rest of her life. She told me that I would probably be drafted into the army if I went into the world, and that I would be very unhappy. I agreed with Sister Catherine that it was probably the devil tempting me. (I was afraid to tell her of my romantic interest in one of the Little Sisters after all the troubles she had gone through trying to prevent such a thing from happening.) The next day I went ahead with her plan.

Surprisingly, life as a professed brother was actually better than before. We were moved over to St. Therese's House under the Big Brothers' charge and were given more responsibility. During that summer Sister Catherine bought me a wonderful sailfish kit for about $350, and we took it out to a nearby lake. I spent my free lunch hours sailing, and I would skim close by the public beach. Out of the corner of my eye I would guiltily glance at the bikini-clad bodies of girls jumping off the diving board.

When school started in the fall, I was made a teacher. I was the first Little Brother allowed to teach high school, which made me almost like an Angel. I taught algebra, general science, and Latin. At the same time, I started with the college courses being taught at St. Therese's.

From the first day the philosophy courses fascinated me. I learned that I had once thought like a solipsist, believing in no existence other than my mind. Minor logic gave me the rational tools I had wanted, and I went to work, freely asking questions about the Faith and science. Cosmology left me dazzled by the probings of the meaning of motion, time, and space. I felt more at ease now that our teachers, the Big Brothers, allowed us to ask any questions, no matter how skeptical they sounded.

Sister Catherine continued teaching advanced catechism for a while. The oldest Little Brothers and Sisters would sit in the library and listen to her explain in greater depth the catechism we had learned as children. We had taken her class for several years. Once we planned a show for the community where she would pretend to ask us random questions. Actually, Sister Catherine had told us ahead of time who was going to be asked what question, but we never got to it that fall because Sister Catherine became ill.

In January 1968, as my eighteenth birthday approached, I went to Brother Simon and asked him to tell Sister Catherine that I was convinced that I did not have a religious vocation. I told him that I would want to get married someday. He said the devil was tempting me with what he called "temptations of the flesh," and I should try to overcome it. Sister Catherine, he said, was too ill to be troubled with my problem.

In the spring of that same year, Sister Catherine became very sick. Then one Tuesday in early May, Father interrupted us during our noon visit in the chapel. He stood up before the altar and said that Sister Catherine was dying. I was horrified. He started to cry, but managed to control himself. In a quivering voice, he said, "What will we ever do without Sister Catherine?"

Sister Catherine asked to see all the children. In small groups, we filed over to St. Pius X's House, where she had been staying during her illness. The doctor said that Sister Catherine might pull through, because she was putting up such a fight to live. We heard that she didn't believe she would die yet, because God would not abruptly cut off the work He had given her to do.

Sister Catherine was in a small room and all the windows were wide open. Brother Simon and Brother Isidore were at her bedside. I was shocked by what I saw. Her hair seemed brown instead of golden red, and her face was chalk white, emaciated, and dried out. Her eyes were shut, but her mouth open as she gasped feebly for air and moaned faintly. Occasionally she would groan some indistinguishable words, and Brother Isidore would take a glass rod with drops of water on it and moisten her tongue and lips. Brother Simon announced us as we came by. I said, "Hi, Sister Catherine," and forced a smile, though my lips were quivering. She immediately opened her eyes and looked at me. She mumbled my name, and then slipped back into her groaning sleep.

At noon the following day Cupertino rang very slowly. It resounded throughout the property, and we all knew that Sister Catherine had died.

The whole community gathered at St. Pius X's House. I felt my knees begin to shake, and I thought I could no longer remain standing. I saw Brother Simon in the kitchen; he was crying. One of the Big Sisters rushed up and hugged Sister Sylvia, saying, "Now you are our superior." Amid the muffled sobs were some less-controlled outbursts of grief. There were some strangers around, and I guessed that they were the part of her family, which she had never mentioned to us.

We filed through the death room. Sister Catherine was lying there, her eyes shut, her mouth open, her face worn with agony, but cold and white. In her hands someone had placed a rosary. It was rumored that she had died of throat cancer. She lay in the room for several hours until the whole community had seen her.

Stories about her last days and hours went all around: Sister Catherine had remained heroic to the end. Even her table manners, which she had taught us, were scrupulously observed in the quiet loneliness of her room. When she could barely lift the spoon, she still carefully wiped it on the edge of the bowl, which she kept tipped away from herself in the proper manner.

I heard that I had been the last Little Brother she spoke to, and Sister Mary Kristine the last Little Sister. She had said to Brother Simon, when the children had left, "They do not know how much I loved them." A few hours later, at 11:00 P.M., she had slipped forever into unconsciousness, and death came at noon the following day, May 8.

That night as I lay motionless in bed past the hour of ten, eleven, twelve, and through the hours of the morning, I kept crying quietly to myself as I realized how much I had misunderstood Sister Catherine. She had been so self-sacrificing in her efforts to work for God. She had given her life to the Center's cause for the Catholic Faith.

I had never told her of my interest in Sister Mary Kristine while she was alive, but now in heaven I knew she knew all about it. I asked her to help me resolve my problem, to let me go free from the religious life if I could still save my soul. She wanted all of us to be saints, and that was all that mattered. My grudges about the severity and fear with which she raised us children seemed trivial now.

I remembered the last army meeting, a couple of months before she died. She had mentioned that it would be fun to learn how to square dance. I was surprised to hear this, and wondered if she had changed her mind. Would I actually be able to dance with Sister Mary Kristine? Perhaps she had finally decided that some of us really shouldn't be religious, I had thought. Now it seemed like perhaps it had been just the indecisive gropings of her mind in its last months.

About one o'clock in the morning darkness, I could hear a mockingbird singing. I had never noticed it before. Its voice in the quiet of the night sounded like Sister Catherine, crying out that she was still with our community. Everything that we had, every regulation, every detail of our lives, had been developed under her careful supervision.

I wondered what would happen to the Center and especially what would happen to Father. Sister Catherine, and not Father, had run the day-to-day affairs of the Center. Father's office was really Sister Catherine's office. The one desk there was Sister Catherine's. Father Feeney would sit in the big red cushioned chair and listen to what Sister Catherine had to say. Though Sister Catherine always seemed to humbly defer to what Father said, he never failed to follow her advice.

Sister Catherine lay in wake in the front room of St.

Therese's House. Guests from Boston and neighbors and friends from the town of Harvard came by to offer their condolences. They all talked about how charming and endearing Sister Catherine had been to them. Sister Catherine's family also came by. Her husband (an old man broken with grief), her daughter, and her son and his wife were there. We heard that both her son and daughter were adopted children. It was rumored that a few years after her marriage and years before the married couples at the Center had done it, Sister Catherine had taken a vow of celibacy.

Sister Catherine was buried on the edge of the lawn near St. Therese's House. Beside her were the bodies of four other members of the order. Our Lady's Army gave her the final tribute by parading to the burial site in grand solemnity. On her tombstone was written: "Sister Catherine, Foundress of the Slaves of the Immaculate Heart of Mary, Commander-in-Chief of Our Lady's Army."

Father had been very shaken during Sister Catherine's last illness, yet almost within the hour she died he became transformed with new energy. For months afterward he repeated to us, "Before Sister Catherine died I was almost in despair, yet somehow after she died I felt a new strength. I'm sure she is up in heaven now, looking down on us. I can feel that she is still with us." He would sometimes add, "If Sister Catherine isn't in heaven, who is? I'm not canonizing her, but if there ever was a saint, she was." For years Father carried around a golden relic case with a clear view of a large lock of Sister Catherine's hair. When he wasn't taking it to and from the altar for daily Mass, it was kept on the mantelpiece in the front room of St. Therese's House.

There were some problems, however, now that Sister Catherine was gone. Father no longer had someone to keep him in check. His manners could be embarrassing, now that Sister Catherine wasn't around to keep him from sticking his fingers in our cake, or warn him lest he wipe the frosting off his chin onto his cassock. When we had to recite for guests (growing more bored by the minute), Sister Catherine wasn't there to intervene. Everyone quietly groaned when we had to sing the lengthy "Te Deum," which might well be followed by our recital of the Hail Mary in seven different languages. Or we could recite the last gospel in Greek, or some factual lists that could include the 100 Franciscan saints (there are over 5,000 Benedictine saints, but we didn't have to learn their names), the 27 Jesuit saints, the 30 Doctors of the Church, the first 33 Popes, the 14 Holy Helpers, all the saints who had died at the age of sixty-seven, the 15 men with Mary in their names, the 42 Old Testament saints, the genealogy from Adam to Jesus, and the sign of the cross in Gaelic.

If Father thought he saw someone yawn, he would break into one of his defensive arguments: "Imagine saying you love the Mother of God and not knowing the Magnificat, the prayer she said every day after receiving Holy Communion. Say the Magnificat." We obeyed.

(When I was about ten years old, I took the saints' feast days very seriously and memorized the names of three to five saints for each of the 365 days in the year. For some of them I knew the years they died. Thus: January 1—St. Fulgentius, 520; St. Odilo, 1049; and St. Vincent Mary Strambi, 1824; and so forth throughout the year.)

Despite the problems with Father, within days of Sister Catherine's death, life at the Center resumed its normal pace. I began to really enjoy the college courses we were taking. My favorite was philosophy, taught by Brother Albert, whom I considered to be brilliant. He would become so enthusiastic in his teaching that it was contagious; at last, because of his instruction, I had the rational tools to destroy the heresies of our day. Sister Mary Salome taught church history. In great detail, she pointed out all the "little demons" throughout history who had attacked the Church. We also had courses in theology, English, mathematics, Greek, and chemistry.

In theology class I began to get a greater realization of the world-shaking importance of the Center's teaching of no salvation outside the Catholic Church. It was fundamental to the traditional life of the Church. Persecutions, martyrdoms, missionary work, the sacrifices of the monastic life, prayers for conversion, prayers in the Mass, the Athanasian creed, and so many other things were meaningless if one religion were as good as another. Father Feeney had predicted that such liberal beliefs would lead to loss of vocations, and that seminaries, convents, and monasteries would be forced to close; the traditional liturgy of the Church would become embarrassing, and changes would have to be made. Everything seemed to be coming true. We were the last ones with the Truth. Someday we hoped the Church would recognize us, and we would be reestablished. While everyone else's vocations would be disappearing, ours would be growing.

My personal religious life, however, was still a struggle. But I was helped from day to day by the growing feeling of superiority: on the one hand I could put down the worldly short-term pleasures as inevitably leading to never-ending torments in hell; on the other, I could look forward to my own eternal rewards of inestimable bliss. My suffering might be despairingly bitter now, but someday God would reward me with a love and happiness that could not even compare with the joys of the most imaginably beautiful girl on this earth. After all, I reasoned, God made both my *desires* for a beautiful girl and the beautiful girl herself. If peace and happiness were the proper matching of *desire* and *object,* and if God made me for the prime purpose of knowing and loving Him, how much happier I would be when *that* perfect match took place. What is more, it would last forever. On this earth, every pleasure passes away in time.

I learned to motivate myself intellectually, although I found it impossible to feel toward God the kind of love and sweetness that swamped me when I thought Sister Mary Kristine had given me a loving look. I would try to remember and concentrate on Sister Catherine's description of Our Lady as an eighteen-year-old girl.

In my strife, I would turn to the beauty of nature and convince myself that it was a reflection of the eternal beauty of God. I would find such peace in just looking at the snow falling quietly in the woods. For hours I would lie on the lawn, convinced that my soul was "burning with the earthly despair" because I didn't have a girl to love, yet I would find peace in the stars. One such night I wrote a poem:

The Stars

The permanence and peace of every silent star
Arrests us in the restlessness of earthly strife,
Today—no more, the star the same for years thus far
Aloof it mocks the vain pursuits of mortal life.
Yet honors man, ethereal infinity,
Who seeks from starry density
To grasp from this reflection of Divinity.
Eternal Peace, Immutable Immensity.

The long hours spent in chapel were becoming increasingly, crushingly boring. I found it impossible to keep my mind on the repetitious Latin chants, although there were times when I felt powerfully moved by the music, such as the passionately sorrowful chants of Holy Week. Then the whole community moved through incense and purple cloth, holding candles or palms and lamenting the death of Christ. Sorrow was the most frequent emotion I would experience, and I loved it. (My favorite Gregorian chant has always been the "Dies irae, dies illa," which is sung only at a Mass for the dead.)

The rest of the year I bowed and genuflected with the community, but my mind was on Sister Mary Kristine or the design of my latest invention. Most of my major inventions occurred in chapel. I would continue to rise and to sit down and to bow as everyone else did, but my mind would be inventing a machine to sort tomatoes by color, or a bean-snipping machine, or the precise geometry of a system of reflectors to produce a death ray of solar energy, or figuring out the binary system and how a computer could work using the numbers of just 0 and 1. I had asked Sister Catherine many years earlier how a computer worked, but she wasn't able to give me much information. But I knew that it worked on the binary system, and so I eventually went about designing a machine made of wooden moving parts and rolling marbles that could add, subtract, multiply, divide—and play games. I enjoyed showing it off to the rest of the community. Everyone was impressed by my ingenuity.

Each Christmas we would make Christmas projects for the larger religious community. Traditionally the children had made projects for the adults, and when we became religious, we continued to do it. Over the years I had built a toy electric car, toy electric motorboat, and several other similar gadgets, all from scratch. But no one knew that all the designs had been done in chapel.

When I was much younger, I had always tried not to have distractions in chapel. One day after Holy Communion as I was kneeling in my pew, I began to feel tired, but I was so determined not to have any distractions that I decided to punish myself and remain kneeling. I would say my prayers again and again, and if a distraction slipped in, I would start all over. Suddenly I found myself being carried out of the chapel. I had fainted.

During the year, I was kept very busy working on the farm, taking college courses, and doing my daily work assignments around the house. My unhappiness was temporarily suppressed by the intellectual stimulation of scholastic philosophy, a newfound pride in the life and history of the Center, the challenge of bookselling, and much-desired distractions like sailing or trips to the mountains and ocean.

Raising organic food had always fascinated me, and it wasn't long before I left my own little patch and took over the responsibility of providing vegetables for the whole community. I enjoyed the farmwork. I liked the outdoors, nature, and the work was routine enough to allow me to think of other things simultaneously. I also loved to think.

Other chores, like delivering food baskets to the neighbors and to the medical doctors, who rarely charged the Center for their services, or sweeping the hallway, scrubbing the floor, or helping Brother Ambrose with the Christmas decorations, were not enjoyable in themselves. But like a good religious, I would quietly say ejaculations [short prayers] to gain merit in heaven, and I would offer up my work for the salvation of souls. (On top of the list was my own soul, and that of Sister Mary Kristine.) At Christmastime I would say the ejaculation: "Divine Babe of Bethlehem, come and take birth in my heart." Sister Catherine had asked us as children, to say it 5,199 times during the four-week span of Advent, because we were told Christ was born 5,199 years after the creation of the world.

As adult members of the community, we shared in all their festivities as well as their work. There were some talented actors and actresses among the Big Brothers and Sisters, and at times the whole community rocked in uproarious laughter as otherwise pious religious became transformed into a bungling toreador, an Italian barber, a Laurel and Hardy, an Irish band leader, a Jewish merchant, or a boasting cowboy, to name but a few. The skits were generally held together with clever verses, often put to inappropriate tunes whose humor only the adults would get.

After the Connor case, movies had replaced the homemade entertainment, and skits had become rare (maybe only twice a year). So movies were welcome, yet one could feel through the infrequent skits the tremendous unifying spirit the community must have had in the early days. While the rest of the world scorned them, and while they told off the world, among themselves they could laugh at the worst of their enemies caricatured in their skits.

I felt that spirit occasionally when I saw the skits depicting typical but comical bookselling skirmishes in the world of Pious Frauds. I felt their spirit of unity strongest when a lecture ended with the whole community singing the rousing song of "No Salvation" (to the tune of "Barney Google"):

> No salvation outside the Catholic Church.
> No salvation, it will leave you in the lurch.
> You've got to take the whole of it,
> You can't belong to the soul of it.
> No salvation outside the Catholic Church.
>
> No salvation outside the Catholic Church.
> No salvation outside the Catholic Church.
> Without that personal submission to the Pope
> You'll lose your charity, faith and hope.
> No salvation outside the Catholic Church.
>
> No salvation outside the Catholic Church.
> No salvation outside the Catholic Church.
> That crazy thing called Baptism of Desire
> Will lead you into everlasting fire.
> No salvation outside the Catholic,
> The Roman Catholic,
> Outside the Catholic Church.

It was finally my turn to feel some of the world's hatred for our little community at St. Benedict Center when I began to go bookselling at the age of seventeen. I quickly lost whatever surface attractions I felt for the world as person after person snarled at me for "sponging off society by begging." That we were selling, not begging, was of no interest to them. Religion was nothing to them; all they cared about were their worldly pleasures, pleasures that would one day damn them to everlasting flames. How foolish they were, I thought. Nonetheless, we had to support our community, so I learned the skills that were needed to produce anywhere from one hundred to three hundred dollars a day all by myself. I was a very apt pupil.

And my teacher was none other than Brother Giles, who had been my childhood model for something far removed from commerce.

When it came to personal devotion and holiness, Brother Giles was my hero. To me, he seemed the holiest of all the

Big Brothers by far. He would kneel in chapel, his head looking up toward the altar, faint sighs of "divine love" coming from his lips. His hands were folded, barely touching, his eyes closed, and his face noticeably red. I wondered how Brother Giles could do it without being embarrassed, but he appeared to be oblivious of anyone else (which made me conclude at the time that he was surely a saint). When Brother Matthias, who had the place next to Brother Giles in chapel, would come along, he would have to tap him on the shoulder in order to get by.

Brother Giles prayed continuously, all day every day. I would watch him as he walked down the hill toward the barn. It was his assignment to milk the cows. He wore a pair of blue overalls and big heavy rubber galoshes that were caked with dried cow dung. He limped down the hill calling for the cows to come to the barn, yelling something that sounded to me like "sherbert." Whatever it was, the cows understood it, and they would follow him as he limped across the field. (We were told that he had been injured in a battle in World War II, and that a piece of shrapnel was lodged in his leg. I'd also heard that before that he had been a football star.) The few times we were allowed in the barn, I'd watch him as he put the suction cups for the milking machine on the cows' udders. All the while his eyes looked as if he were half-dazed, and his mouth would move slowly with prayers to God.

I was pleased to learn, shortly after I became a professed religious, that Brother Giles was the one assigned to teach me bookselling. I was pleased, but in another way, to learn that he was an entirely different person when he was out in the world.

The first bookselling trip was a one-day venture into the countryside of New Hampshire, which was what we called "highway stuff" (as opposed to "street stuff," which meant selling in the commercial areas of cities). The Center always had code words for everything. We had to protect ourselves from our enemies.

With our little black bags full of books, we would jump out of the car at every area that had a few gas stations, or shops, or small hotels and motels. I watched as Brother Giles showed me how to go door-to-door, asking each manager of a business if he or she would care to contribute something to help the Brothers. We sold the books for one dollar each, but on stops like that it was better to ask them to buy what we called the "multiple," that is, five books at one time. Several times I saw Brother Giles convince a gentleman that he should give him five or ten dollars, and that he would send the books. If the gentleman didn't want them, we would send the books to a hospital.

For week-long trips there would be an assigned prior, or superior, on each trip. He was in charge. It would take us one or two days on the road to get to our city. The length of time on the road depended upon the distance of the city. Chicago or Detroit, for example, was a two-day trip. We would then sell for four days in the business areas, and generally we would try to sell individually to the people in each business as well as to the manager of the store.

I learned fast that the small businesses that were totally owned by one or a few individuals were much more apt to buy ("sponsor") a large number of books to be sent to hospitals. Chain stores were always a problem, because the manager said that he had to get approval from headquarters. We would usually work in pairs, but sometimes we separated and each one took a side of the street.

I learned how to "crack" factories, by going in the back past the security systems, which were supposed to keep out solicitors. And then, after cleaning up in the back trying to sell as many books there as we could, we would enter the front office and try to sell to the manager. Sometimes he would buy a whole box of books for the employees without realizing that they already had our books because we had just been in the back.

In the heavily Catholic areas, we generally ran into the problem of people discovering that we were with Father Feeney and therefore, as they said, "excommunicated." On learning this, they would try to get their dollars back. Sometimes we'd have to escape and slide out side doors in order not to confront them as they waited for us in the lobby downstairs.

In the Protestant areas we would change our lines to suit their interests. Generally, since they didn't care about religious books on the Catholic Faith, we would emphasize our campaign against the filth and rotten books on the newsstands, the "smut," as I would call it.

Occasionally we encountered people who claimed they liked the filth and rot in newspapers and magazines on the newsstands. In those cases, I would go on about the harm it did to children, and generally they would agree.

In areas where there was a monastery nearby, people thought we were from there, and we did nothing to change that impression. Sometimes we created it. I would say, "Hello, I'm Brother Luke from the monastery," and then continue my pitch. If they questioned further, I would say, "Well, the motherhouse is back in Massachusetts," indicating, of course, or trying to give the impression that we had a local monastery even though we were actually staying in a motel.

As we continued making these trips, I learned a lot of the history of past bookselling. I found out that times had been much more difficult: when the Brothers were very poor, they couldn't afford to stay in a hotel or a motel, but would stay in seedy areas, often sleeping on the floor with people walking by them or over them and with stockings passing over their heads. Down South, one of them once slept with his head in a refrigerator. At night they could hear the rats gnawing nearby.

I also learned about the violence and that they were often thrown in jail. Sometimes people would actually chase them. There was the story of the time the butcher got mad and chased one of the Brothers with a knife. Another time one of the Brothers got angry and knocked a man out, but then he returned the man's dollar by putting it on top of his chest as he lay there.

Then there were the comical stories about the Brothers who would get wound up in their work. One day Brother Louis Maria rushed up to a cab and said, "Quick, take me to some good stuff, to some good street stuff." The cabdriver didn't know that all he meant was "Take me to an area where there are a lot of little stores where I can sell to people in the stores and to the store managers."

I learned about the time Brother Albert, a very intellectual Brother, went from floor to floor in the garment area in New York City using the outside fire escapes. He would climb down from floor to floor, come in the window, sell in that area, and then go back out on the fire escape.

I also heard about a very hot summer before they had black suit coats to make them look like religious. They had worn heavy black overcoats. Everybody thought they were odd, but sales went up.

It didn't take long for me to develop into a very good

bookseller. One week Brother Giles and I broke all records by averaging eight hundred dollars a day as a team. Typically, on a week's trip we would leave the Center in the early morning, Father Feeney having given us two hundred dollars. During the day as we drove, we would be in silence. Occasionally, we would have to say the rosary, or some other prayers, and there'd be a quiet meditation and then maybe a few minutes of talking, and then silence again. It would go on like that all day, or for two days if the trip were a long trip. There would be six Brothers in the car, and it would also be packed with food and books, though some of the books would have been mailed out ahead of time.

I was usually the cook on these trips, so it was my responsibility (in addition to the regular bookselling) to make sure that the right food got packed, and then to help pack and unpack, so I'd know where everything was, including dishes and silverware and sandwiches and lunches and whatever.

If it were a long trip, we would stay overnight in a little motel where often they would only charge us about twelve dollars a night. The six of us would all crowd in; sometimes we would have to pull in extra cots.

If we were in New York City, we might stay in the Margaret, which had an excellent view across the East River and looked directly down on Wall Street. We were told that at one time it had been a very nice place to stay. As the cook, I quickly cleaned out the shelves and chased away the cockroaches, set out the dishes, and put the food in the refrigerator.

We'd get up early in the morning, put on our disguises, and oftentimes be out of the street and on our way to some nearby church while it was still dark. We would break up throughout the church so that the priest wouldn't recognize us as being Father Feeney's boys. That way we were able to get Holy Communion without any trouble. Our disguises generally consisted of old civilian clothes. I often wondered if the priest was surprised to see his congregation suddenly increase by six men, because these churches were always relatively empty.

During the day we would work in pairs, and sometimes we had to rent two extra cars. When I was with Brother Giles, we generally got the good stuff, because everyone knew Brother Giles would "cream it," meaning that he would take for his team the best bookselling areas. We would generally work independently of each other, though we would rendezvous every few hours, or at least for lunch. The first thing I would do when I walked into a place of business or an office building was to size up the situation and determine how much I should ask them for. I would generally ask to see the manager first, and if he were busy, then I would start selling to the secretaries in the office. If it were a self-owned business, it would be very important to get to see the manager because he usually had the authority to give us a large contribution. Sometimes I would walk in a stranger, and five minutes later I'd walk out forty or fifty dollars richer because the manager had agreed to "sponsor" a box of our books. Often I could go through a day with no more than forty books in my bag and be three hundred dollars richer by the end of the day.

In the Catholic areas of New York City there were often Italians, or Puerto Ricans, who generally didn't speak English too well. We had learned expressions in Italian or whatever language was needed, asking them "to help the Brothers for charity." In some areas the women seemed excited about what they thought was my similarity to the late President Kennedy, and I would take full advantage of it, smiling all the way and collecting the dollars as I moved down long tables of the garment workers.

Often, the manager wouldn't allow us to solicit. He would say, "Well, we have hundreds of these people every day, and why should we discriminate and allow just you." Other managers were friendly and said, "Sure, Brother, go in, but I don't think they'll buy anything. They're all sinners." Even when they agreed to let us go around, I would try to get the manager at least to pretend to take a book and smile at us; even if he didn't want it, I could take it back afterward, but it helped sell books among the employees.

I developed my line so that I could anticipate practically any question people would ask. The most common one involved proper identification. I was a stranger, and they didn't know who I was. We didn't have any real IDs, so I explained to them that IDs could easily be made up. The important thing was that I, as a person, was a religious Brother and had all the knowledge and wisdom that came from studying in a religious institution. Since I knew the names of at least three saints for every day of the year, and in many cases knew what year they had died, I'd ask the potential customer to open the book about the saints at random and ask me any question. Usually they didn't even bother. Other times, if they were foreign, I took the chance that they were named after a saint on whose day they were born, and I would tell them their birthdays or the birthday of their wife or husband. This always amazed them. People were often superstitious, and they figured out that if they gave to the Brothers they would have better luck with the horses or the numbers that week.

Secretaries in the offices sometimes engaged me in conversation, and I stayed to chat, even though I was really supposed to keep moving. Oftentimes they were pretty and would ask me questions, such as: had I really taken a vow of celibacy at so young an age. I would always explain to them that it was a question of higher priorities. I was not abnormal, but I had chosen freely; and I had chosen this life as a form of sacrifice for God (which, for the most part, I truly believed: but I also liked talking to the young women). To them, it must have seemed insane.

I thought the people I met in big cities were absolutely foolish to be slaving their lives away in these huge, noisy towns, living in skyscrapers. After a whole life of misery they would all end up in hell anyway.

In some of the factories where I sold books I noticed that the workers had wicked pictures of totally naked women, and I was absolutely shocked. I never really looked at them. But out of the corner of my eye I could see the flesh-colored tones, and I knew I shouldn't look. One crude sinner who laughed when I tried to sell him a book, asked me if I would like to look at *his* holy pictures.

Even after I got to be pretty good at pressuring people and getting them to buy the books, I still had one problem: how to leave. Sometimes I would bow out several times, thanking them profusely, until they would begin to wonder if they had been duped by this overpolite salesman.

When we worked the skyscrapers in the big cities, we generally used the stairs. We were afraid of meeting people in the elevators who had changed their minds and now wanted their money back. But using the stairs was risky, because in many buildings, for security reasons, the stairway doors will not open *to* a floor but only *from* a floor. More than once we found ourselves having to traipse all the way down to the bottom floor to start all over again.

At the end of the fourth day we would always report our

take to the Center, but the actual figures were always transmitted by code. (The Center, and especially Sister Catherine, firmly believed our phones were tapped.) The different years in which particular saints died were used as part of the number, usually preceded by the date of an important religious event. For example, if we took in $4,430 that week, we would call in and say, "Four times the conversion of Greenland, plus St. Augustine." As Greenland was converted in the year 1000, and St. Augustine died in A.D. 430, that meant 4 × 1,000 + 430, or $4,430. Only a very knowledgeable Catholic with an incredible memory could have broken our code.

Christmas season, not too surprisingly, was always our best time, and I remember that in my second year of bookselling we had a Christmas week in which we took in six thousand dollars in our regular four days of selling.

We all knew what would happen after we left a city. Some faithful parishioners would take the books they'd bought to their parish priest, and he in turn would see that the volumes were from "Father Feeney's outfit." He would then tell his congregation that the Brothers from St. Benedict Center were in town, and he would warn them not to buy the books. Of course, by that time we were already out of the area. In a year's time, or so, when we returned, the warnings would have been long forgotten.

Eventually, the novelty of the bookselling wore off for me. In its place I found a growing discontent. Soon I came to hate the physical fatigue, the huckstering, and the almost constant pressure. I realized that we were not really fighting in God's name; we were cheating people.

After two years as a fully professed Brother, a Slave of the Immaculate Heart of Mary, I decided that it was just all too much for me. I longed to leave, but I could not. My guilt before the eyes of God was becoming unbearable.

He had chosen me to help defend the Faith in what was most likely the last age of the world, the time of the Great Apostasy. Yet, I—because of my petty selfishness in trying to satisfy my lustful desires—wanted to reject that divine calling. If I left, I could certainly not expect the grace of God to protect me, and it was certain that I would fall by the wayside and be damned to hell.

Besides my fear of hell, there was the overpowering disgrace among the only people in the world whom I knew.

They would guess my cowardly motives, the pleasures of the flesh, and be disgusted with me. I assured myself that I really loved Sister Mary Kristine, that it was not lust. I would be supremely happy, even if I could never see or touch her body, but could just know that we loved each other. I didn't expect her to leave, but I reasoned that there would be other girls in the world about whom I would feel the same way. If only I could leave without disgrace and guilt!

My frustration turned into anger, which I directed at Sister Catherine. It had been her scheme to trap me into the religious life, to keep me so fear-ridden through a life of strict and harsh punishments that my conscience could not function freely. I had told her that I didn't have a vocation, and if she, the sole pillar of my conscience, had agreed, I would have been able to leave without remorse. I reviewed in my mind the strategies Sister Catherine had used to ensure that our free choice of a vocation was the one she wanted.

In the world, boys and girls were allowed to talk to each other, but this was not allowed us after the age of nine or ten. Information about family life, parents, children, and the love and happiness that could exist was never even hinted at.

Selfishness was the word used to describe a parent's love for a child. Our parents were not selfish, they had given us up to God. The concept of romance I had picked up during my seven months in the world was completely hidden from us. Books and movies that had anything slightly related to it were edited "clean." Brother Philip, the movie censor, was so skilled at his job that he could edit out a major actress from a film and still preserve an interesting remnant of the original plot. (I often wondered if the movie distributor ever observed a pattern to the new splices of the returned film.)

Censorship for the sake of purity so pervaded our entire lives that I concluded that the delights of the sins of impurity must be overwhelmingly enjoyable. Seeing the card block out the movie projector's beam—just as a beautiful but scantily dressed girl walked in—only increased my desires. Once I saw a woman guest tap the Brother showing the movie and politely ask him to read his cards using another light as it tended to block out the picture on the screen. Once informed of his purpose, she quickly learned to put up with the annoyance.

Even Father Feeney's sermons were censored. The interesting point was that we always knew where. He could be telling us that Jesus passed from the womb of Mary without violating the virginal character of her body, when his eye would catch that of someone in the Big Sisters' pews. Without any subtle cover-up, which Sister Catherine would use, he would abruptly change the subject, making it all embarrassingly obvious.

The farm life was a continual problem. Baby lambs or donkeys or calves weren't born, but were suddenly "bought." When a cow gave birth in the field, the children had to be rushed into the house until the crisis was cleared up.

The New Testament was forbidden reading until we were about sixteen and older, and children as old as twenty had to leave a Thursday-night lecture when the subject of abortion came up. Stories in the Roman martyrology read during dinner covered gruesome tortures of saints, yet one day they were purified of the parts where virgins had their breasts cut off.

Nothing had made Sister Catherine angrier than sins of impurity. The worst descriptions of hell were read to us children after someone had been caught doing something against Holy Purity. Sister Catherine's face would become inflamed with rage, and for days we would shake in mortal fear of being tortured in hell with pitchfork demons whose stench was almost worse than the excruciatingly painful flames. I knew I could never hold my hand over the gas flame of the stove for even a mere minute. The realization of being totally immersed in much hotter flames for all eternity, and never burning up, was overwhelming.

Though I had managed to escape most of the horrible punishments the other children received, I vividly recalled the constant fear in which I lived. It seemed that someone was being punished everyday. Their screams were a constant reminder of what could happen to you if for any reason you incurred the wrath of the Angels or Sister Catherine.

Some children were so nervous that they could never eat their breakfast, and an Angel threatening punishment if the white-faced child with bulging cheeks and panic-stricken eyes dared to vomit was a common occurrence. Breakfast *had* to be eaten, and sometimes a child who had vomited it up would eat the vomit rather than get caught.

The Friday-night horrors of badges, followed by the "sentencing" and the inevitable "execution" on Saturday, kept stomachs churning and nervous hands shredding paper napkins under the table. The suspense of the ceremonies surrounding a flogging with the rubber hose was almost worse than the beating of twenty or thirty lashes across your naked back and legs. Saturday morning meant the sound of reveille with the raising of Our Lady's Army flag and the sight of Sister Catherine at attention saluting; you only hoped that somehow she would forget the punishments due later that morning. But first you had to sit through Mass, and then try to stomach a breakfast that might include slimy, slithery soft-boiled eggs. The suspense of waiting outside the corridor as one by one the Little Brothers were called in and you heard their pleading and screaming will never be forgotten. Some beatings were given to a child in the bathtub, because it hurt more if your skin was wet.

In addition to the strap and the rubber hose, there were the unusual punishments. It was well-known to all of us that J.M., who wet his bed up to the age of fourteen, was often treated brutally. He would be tied down to the four corners of the bed for a beating that sometimes could go up to a hundred or more lashes, and other times for confinement during the day so he wouldn't eat. He would be put on bread and water for as long as a week, and once he was given no food for eight consecutive days. One punishment involved the use of a jar in a brown paper bag; it was rumored that the Angel was allowing biting insects to sting his body. Whatever it was, it caused him to scream at the top of his voice. Some of the other punishments used on J.M. included very hot water, and the flame of a match applied to his bare bottom, so he could get a sense of the pain of hell.

I clearly recall one episode when I was to receive a new punishment. I could be very stubborn, despite the threat of punishment, if I were convinced that I was right and that Sister Catherine would ultimately overrule the Angel. But on this occasion Sister Catherine had agreed that absolute obedience required blind submission. She had told me that St. Ignatius once said that a subject should agree with his superior who said the sky was red even if it were obviously blue. I had told Sister Catherine that I could never do that, and she had ordered the hairbrush treatment for my defiance.

Sister Julia, my Angel, was by far the most kind, and I almost felt sorry for her when she complained to me that she didn't know how to go about it. I was bending over the bed and she was holding a hairbrush with plastic bristles. She had finally called to another Angel, who informed her how to do

it. "Yes, you hit with the bristles down on his bare bottom."
With the curtain tucked under her chin, she smiled as she
pronounced the word "bottom." The punishment was quickly
completed, and I was relieved to discover that (at least the
way Sister Julia delivered it) it was painless compared to the
strap or the Big Punisher.

But the most terrifying punishment occurred when a certain Angel would sit on your head while she beat you. It had happened only once to me, when I was about ten. On the first blow I tried to gasp with the shock of the pain and found that I couldn't breathe. My face was completely buried in the pillow under the weight of the Angel. I panicked and struggled frantically to get out. Finally, I begged her to get off, promising not to jump around, and I ground my teeth together trying not to move as the blows burned my thighs and legs. When I would hear other children's muffled groans and then hear them break loose for a moment, screaming that they couldn't breathe, I wanted to tell the Angel that *any* punishment was more tolerable than the desperate feeling of being smothered.

As I worked up my resentment toward Sister Catherine, I convinced myself that she had definitely been wrong. The punishments were completely out of proportion to the offense. When I was younger, I had justified the extremeties of the punishment by thinking of the alternative: hellfire. Even our Lord had said that it would be better to cut off a hand than to let the whole body burn. But now I looked back at such offenses as breaking silence, wetting your bed, or talking back to the Angel as not deserving of eternal damnation in hell. The idea that God gave boys bottoms for punishment (as one Angel put it) seemed ridiculous to me now.

Armed with my indignation toward Sister Catherine, I went to Sister Mary Agnes to prepare her, by various excuses, for the announcement that I did not want to continue my religious life.

I told her that I had been trapped by Sister Catherine, who had used a regime of great fear on all the children. Sister Mary Agnes was surprised that I criticized Sister Catherine. She asked me to show more gratitude in return for everything Sister Catherine had done for us. I didn't (because I couldn't) describe our punishments except to say that they were excessive. Then I brought up the delicate subject of censorship. I thought we were old enough to know the facts of life, and old enough to read good books about romances. That, I said, should have been part of our education in order for us to make a free choice. I did not dare mention my interest in Sister Mary Kristine, for I was afraid it would shock Sister Mary Agnes.

I got my first hint at the facts of life by accident. I was on a bookselling trip to Atlanta, Georgia, and had to purchase an electric plug. The salesman asked me what kind of a plug and held up two of them. "Do you want a male or female plug?"

I looked at the prongs on one plug and the holes in the other, and I was disgusted. Why couldn't God come up with a more decent way for procreation, I thought.

I finally went to my spiritual adviser to find out about the facts of life when I was about nineteen. He said, "Well, you know that a woman's body was made by God to receive a man's body."

"What?" I said, and he repeated it. Then I said, "You mean a *part* of a man's body?"

He smiled at me as though I was being fresh. I told him that I didn't have a vocation and that I wanted to leave so that I could get married someday. He asked me if I could remain continent. I didn't understand, and he said I should wait for another year.

The lure of the world was growing stronger. I remembered my life with the Souers family on the lake in the summer of 1965. I remembered the girls in their bikinis, the sailing, and the water-skiing. I imagined how happy I would be if I could be there again, but this time with Sister Mary Kristine. I knew she would look sensational in a bikini; for one thing, she had the largest bust of any girl at the Center.

I watched her every chance I could. I had permission to make home movies of the Center's mountain trips, the ponies and horses, and the life on the farm, but whenever I could, I used to zoom in on Sister Mary Kristine harvesting potatoes or running with her horse. At Christmastime, I got some close-ups of her face as the children received their presents. Later, in the quiet of my room I would replay the films and freeze the projector when she was smiling and looking right at me.

At one time I wondered if Sister Mary Kristine could get pregnant if we secretly loved each other, even though our paths never crossed. But that seemed foolish to my scientific and logical mind: how could anyone be sure who the father was? Then I concluded that pregnancy was caused by the fluid in my wet dreams. Sister Catherine had asked Brother Simon to talk to us about it when I was fourteen. He had come in and told us not to worry about it, to ignore it, and to forget the dreams we had. He told us never to touch ourselves except when we were washing. I was careful not to commit sins of impurity, mainly because I hated to tell it in Confession. Father would always ask probing questions and details, and then scold in anger.

My spiritual adviser told me that marriage was not a bed of roses, that I would still have to practice restraint. He said that in the world husbands and wives commit sins of impurity all the time, and that they are sent to hell because of it. I now wondered once again if it was impure for a husband and wife to undress in front of each other. The next time I spoke to Sister Mary Agnes, I asked her. She said that it was all right for them in marriage, that God had intended a husband and wife to be "united in one body." I was so pleased to think that perhaps someday I could enjoy the pleasure of a woman's body without committing sin. I imagined how much fun it would be if I were married to Sister Mary Kristine.

The Center life became more and more difficult for me. The assignments I was given were no longer exciting. Everything seemed to bore me. During the long prayers, I continued to think of other things like the snowmobile we got one Christmas, or the motorcycle. We made occasional trips to the mountains or to Canada or to Washington, D.C., and I lived for those events.

I started pulling pranks. One time I taped-recorded the Angelus bell, and then I played it throughout the house so that everybody would say the Angelus at the wrong time. When the Brother who had rung the bell at the proper time came back, he was accused of ringing it twice. Nobody could resolve the problem.

I grew to hate the tension of bookselling. I preferred to stay at home, in the peace of the country and the farm.

Conflicts grew in my mind. I wanted to leave, but I felt terribly guilty about the scandal I knew it would cause. Other people might lose their vocations because of my actions. Also, God wouldn't give me the grace to save my own soul if I were rejecting a true vocation. I believed that I was doing it for my own selfish pleasures, perhaps even my own sexual desires. If that were the case, then surely God would punish me with hell, the horror of which was still quite vivid in my mind.

When I would stand up to sing the Epistle in chapel, I was convinced that everyone could read my mind and could see how terribly wicked I was. Waves of fear would rush through me, softening my muscles and even my bones. I would begin to tremble from head to foot. My voice would falter, and I would be deeply humiliated. They couldn't help but notice; my performance was atrocious.

Somehow, stoically, I continued my life at the Center. I was waiting for the right opportunity to leave. At least that's what I kept telling myself.

Chapter Eight

Life at the Center had become quite painful for me. At times the conflicts in my mind were too much for rationalization. All I could do was cry in the quiet of my cubicle at night. On the one hand there was my love of a girl, Sister Mary Kristine, and on the other the fear of damnation if I abandoned my religious vows.

Years of daily instruction had impressed upon me that I had only one life to live—one opportunity to earn the salvation of my soul. If I failed, it would be the greatest tragedy; no second chances were given. I would be in hell for all eternity—not one day or week or year or century, but forever. Never again would I see or talk to my fellow religious who had remained faithful to their calling from God. I would be alone among the wicked in a fiery world of the worst torments, gnashing my teeth with a despair beyond human comprehension.

I also realized that as a religious brother I would never have the love of a woman. Never would I be hugged or kissed, never would she see me cry, nor hear me tell her how much I loved her and how happy she made me. Occasionally I was able to listen to some of the more somber music of Tchaikovsky, and I would feel that the whole world had seen my tragedy and was crying with me—he has only one life and he will never have a woman like Sister Mary Kristine to love.

But the power the Center held over me finally weakened irrevocably when many of the Big Brothers and Sisters whom I respected became transformed by internal dissension at the Center into petty, vindictive beings. It was the violent events during my last months there that made me seriously doubt God's supposed will for me. It was the strife between factions that caused Sister Mary Kristine, one of the Jones sisters, to depart into the world. And it was the ensuing relaxation of the strict rules that gave me my first chance to chat with her after six years of silent watching.

The memory of her smile and the lilt of her voice was one of the things that finally overpowered my guilt and drove me out of the Center.

Brother Martin was whispering to someone in the speak place. "She would like to cut the Brothers up into little pieces and fry them," he said.

I looked up from the study table and smiled, even though it wasn't funny. I guess it sounded ridiculous. But it wasn't just that. I had a habit of smiling when I feared that unpleasant feelings were about to come to the surface. I was trying to deny my feelings of disgust for the Big Brothers and Sisters. Sister Sylvia, I heard, had encouraged the Little Sisters to throw rotten eggs at Brother Simon, the Big Brothers' prior. The Big Sisters were trying to turn the Little Sisters against the Big Brothers, and the hostilities between both sides were getting worse. Would the Center fall apart from interal dissensions? I wondered.

I put my pen down and sat back against the hard metal chair. It was so difficult to concentrate on philosophy. I was studying act and potency as they related to God and creature, which I normally would have enjoyed, but my attention was elsewhere. There was a meeting upstairs, and occasionally I could hear the voices of the Big Brothers and Sisters. Shouts of anger would burst out and then subside.

I got up and went to my room. I had a stomachache. I lay down and smoothed out the folds of my cassock. I wished I could learn to relax more. In a little while I would feel better. I stared at the ceiling and tied and untied knots in the cloth sash about my waist.

If only they would let us in on all the issues, I thought, certainly I could help to find a solution. The Sisters did not want to attend the Brothers' lectures. The Brothers did not value what the Sisters had to say (except for Sister Mary Salome, who taught church history). The Brothers wanted to introduce more of the holy hours like Compline and Terse. The Sisters needed the time for other things. It seemed to me that they would disagree merely to prove who was in control.

Both sides claimed Father Feeney's authority when it was to their advantage, though Father was only the figurehead and spokesman. Sister Catherine had run the Center. Since her death, both sides had managed to work things out quietly for over a year. Now things seemed out of control.

One of the reasons that the split in the adult members of the Center was causing me so much tension was that I could not understand it. Or rather, that it all seemed to be blown up out of proportion. Years later, there would be serious theological grounds for difference (with a liberal and a conservative faction, and eventually a third group), but now it seemed to be as much simply personal as anything else. One of the biggest differences seemed to me to be between the men and the women, the Big Brothers and the Big Sisters, but there was no *issue* of great difference to argue about other than gender. At least that's the way it looked to me, and fearing that it could not be that simple, I was getting sick over it.

Noises were getting louder upstairs. I could make out angry voices, and I could hear the sound of footsteps shuffling into the room above. It seemed to be getting crowded. A door slammed and rattled the windows in the house.

"God is going to punish you," screamed Sister Julia, her voice rising above those of all the other Sisters and Brothers who were shouting at one another.

"Jesus, Mary, and Joseph," I prayed as I jumped out of bed. Sister Julia sounded almost desperate. Oh, my God, they're going to do something really violent, I thought.

"Don't let 'em! Don't," said a Big Sister whose strained voice was not recognizable.

I had to see what was happening. I ran to the bakery-room door and peeked out. Big Sisters were all over the outside stairs going up to the front room. The Brothers must have kicked them out, I thought. Others were hurrying from St. Anne's and joining those surrounding the stairs. Their eyes were flashing with horror. Some prayed aloud and looked upward. At the top of the stairs Sisters were peering into the windows of the front room.

"Don't hurt him! We're out here! Unlock the doors!" They made it sound as though Father Feeney was struggling to get free of the Brothers.

Sister Maria Imelda grabbed a broom and rushed up the stairs. "We're coming in," she yelled as she pushed the broom like a battering ram toward the window of the door. "Should we break in?" She turned to Sister Mary John, who stood calmly near the steps and signaled no. She was the Sisters' strategist, it was rumored. They continued to shout through the windows. Then, like a flock of blackbirds scared by an unseen signal, they took off and retreated back to St. Anne's. It was over.

I was disgusted. Were these the same Brothers and Sisters who so peacefully chanted the psalms and prayers in the chapel just this morning? I felt like I was discovering a new kind of personality behind the religious garb and holy prayers of my superiors, the elder Brothers and Sisters. They no longer seemed like peaceful and quiet religious. I saw them now as rebels, fighters. It is part of their makeup. The vehemence and anger they turned on family and the world for the defense of the Faith in the earliest years of the Center they are now using on one another. It seemed so unnecessary. One thing was clear: the situation was a mess.

Nine of the eleven remaining families were split over the Center's growing internal dissension. The parents could not agree on their responsibilities to their own children who wanted to leave. The Brothers thought that they should set up homes in the world. The Sisters felt that the children should fend for themselves if they forsook their religious vocation. The youngest child was seventeen and therefore, they argued, old enough.

I was about to return to my room when the Angelus bell rang. I stopped, blessed myself, and looked around. There was nobody watching, so I sat down on a bench instead of praying the Angelus as was required. My stomachache was still there. It was lunchtime and often the food would lessen the pain in my stomach. I continued thinking as the bell counted out its pattern of three—three—three, and then nine rings.

I wondered if, deep down, the Brothers wanted to go back to a normal family life. I didn't want to be a Brother, but unfortunately God had given me a vocation to be a religious. It was depressing. I would never have the love of a wife or children unless I left. I didn't want to see the Center fall apart, but then, the more members who went, the less I would be disgraced if I decided to leave.

The bell had stopped, and noises in the house resumed. But I remained seated. Using my fingernail, I half-consciously scraped at a white food stain on the hem of my black cassock. What would it all come to, I thought. Brother-husbands begged Sister-wives to be sensible, but they were insulted and ridiculed instead. The children were caught up in a confusion of loyalties. For years they had looked up to their elder Brothers and Sisters, who now openly rankled with one another in bitter verbal disputes. At first, the children tended to side with their immediate superiors. The Little Brothers were now under the care of the Big Brothers. The Big Sisters took charge of the Little Sisters. Thus Little Brothers and Little Sisters treated one another with a disdain reserved for "those on the other side." The split ignored all family relations. Blood brothers and sisters vied with one another and were trapped in the internal strife.

The Jones family was an exception. They were united from the start. Much of the trouble had originated with four Little Sisters, the Jones sisters. They were bitterly against their superiors. Among other things, they disliked the fact that certain Big Sisters degraded the Big Brothers, and especially their father, Brother Isidore. They found support in their mother, Sister Marcelle Marie, and together they were a formidable group that was causing a lot of trouble over at St. Anne's.

"They've gone, they've all left," Brother Martin said before Mass one morning. "The Jones sisters, Sister Marcelle Marie, and most of the other Little Sisters—they left St. Anne's last night."

"Where? How?" I asked.

"They left in a van driven by two of the Big Brothers. They're hiding someplace a good distance from here. The other side is furious. They're upstairs right now, demanding to know where they are. They've made Father command the Brothers under holy obedience to tell him where they went. But, of course, none of them knows."

"Brother Simon must know," I said. I wondered what the Big Brothers were planning. "How long are they going to be gone? They're only trying to put pressure on the other side. Right?"

"Yes, of course," Brother Martin replied. "When Sister Sylvia and her group realize that they're going to lose everyone, then they'll come around." Brother Martin's lean face was flushed, and a white streak crossed his cheek. It always appeared when he was excited. There was a look of devious triumph in his eyes. I knew what this controversy meant to him. He had finally succeeded in bringing his sister, Sister Susan, and some others over to our side. However, I doubted that this latest show of force would make the Big Sisters surrender.

"But they still control the money," I said. "Sister Sylvia took over all the bank accounts when Sister Catherine died. She thinks she has replaced Sister Catherine. I think the Brothers resent having to go to her for approval of the money they need. It will just—"

"Yes, I agree," Brother Martin said. "Women should be subject to the men."

"But they would never listen to that," I said.

Brother Martin went on. "Even convents are always subject to a bishop. The Church never allowed women to have the final say in an order without the permission of a male superior."

Later that day, I noticed Sister Mary Agnes in the kitchen. She saw me and looked away. The expression on her face was severe, and she concentrated on the pans she was scrubbing. I went over and asked her if she had a minute, but she didn't want to speak to me. I had given her a letter explaining that my uncontrollable trembling fits were the result of a mental state produced by an upbringing of constant fear under Sister Catherine's regime. She had torn it up. Perhaps she would listen if she thought I might leave.

"Sister Mary Agnes! Please! Forget this stuff about the Brothers and Sister Catherine. I'm concerned about my own vocation."

She looked up. There were soapsuds on her veil and perspiration on her forehead. She stared keenly at me. "I don't understand how you can keep supporting Jim Williams and Alexander Zahedi, and all those wicked men who openly defy Father's authority."

She must be furious, I thought if she calls the Big Brothers by their worldly names. But I wasn't going to let her rile me. She went on.

"They are not even religious. This morning they refused to obey Father when he commanded them under holy obedience to tell him where they took the Little Sisters. It is just unspeakable."

I resented her claim of Father's authority. "Why don't you obey Father when he tells you to go to the lectures given by Sister Mary Salome, Brother Basil, and Brother Albert?"

I could see her taking a deep breath. Her face was tightening up and she looked at me as though I were part of the intrigue. I had accused her of disobeying Father, and she could not deny it.

"Listen, Brother Luke, if you think for one moment that we can be fooled by that, you are wrong. Poor Father, he is so innocent. He is so confused by the whole situation and the pressure the Brothers put on him. They have fooled you."

Here she goes, I thought, with all that emotional junk and the Brothers' scheming plots that the Sisters have concocted over at St. Anne's. I stood back and listened.

"Brother Isidore and Brother Simon have studied all the brainwashing techniques used by the communists and they are using them on the rest of the Brothers. Brother Isidore! Is God going to punish him! I know what he really wants. He plans to go back and live with his wife. If his children leave, then he and Sister Marcelle Marie will go and set up a home in the world. That is why they are attacking Sister Catherine's memory and Father. They want you to believe that they were forced into separating and taking the vow of chastity. Brother Isidore stood up before the whole community and told such vicious lies. It was unbelievable. Father never forced us to separate. Each of us did it on our own. We took—"

"Well, I don't know what went on at the meeting," I interrupted, "but I do think that parents have a duty to take care of the children who leave."

We argued some more about parents' obligations to their marital vows and their duties to their children. I left feeling worse than ever. This was a sensitive subject for Sister Mary Agnes, and I thought I understood why. She had already made some irrevocable decisions at a time when the whole Center believed, at least on the surface, that a Sister's religious vows to God superseded her marriage vows. Now the same Brothers who had supported her in court, the same ones who had encouraged her throughout the long arduous years of the Connor case, in which she had lost her husband and three of her children, these same people now were saying that she was wrong in God's eyes. How could she accept that?

The issues were becoming clearer and increasingly painful to me and others. It was no longer just a rational question of right and wrong. Intense emotions were involved. I saw Brothers pleading with their wives. I saw them ridiculed before other members of the community. No Brother or Sister deserved this treatment. I thought the blame fell on Sister Catherine. I felt very bitter toward the old Center regime.

Sister Mary Agnes still believed in it, and yet I admired her courage and strength. I decided that I would no longer try to convince her that the Brothers were right. She deserved her peace of mind. There was nothing she could do now. She had nowhere to go. Brother Michael or I could leave; we were old enough to go our own way. Our younger brothers in Ohio were well-established in their own life-styles in the world. No, she had to live her life under Sister Catherine's principles.

Several days later the van returned. The Little Sisters moved into the Brothers' guesthouse. St. Anne's tried in vain to get the Brothers to send them back. Gradually, some of the Little Sisters left the guesthouse for the world as their parents agreed to help them out.

The adults continued with their meetings, but things just got worse. Bitter quarrels always broke out. At times the Sisters would pray the rosary aloud in unison and drown out the voices of the Brothers. The situation became hopeless. They called in a lawyer to monitor the meetings, but to no avail.

I argued that the Brothers should go their own way and separate themselves from the Sisters. I had given up on Sister Mary Agnes. For weeks our eyes never met as we passed each other in the yard, the halls, and the chapel.

"Brother Luke."

I turned around. It was Brother Michael, the oldest of my four younger brothers.

"Did you know that the Big Brothers—"

"Listen, we'd better go over to a speak place," I said as I saw Brother Hilary, our superior, coming through the door.

As we entered the hallway, Brother Michael went on, "Did you know that the Big Brothers had no idea that the Big Sisters used to punish us with the Big Punisher?"

"I'm sure they did—certainly Brother Simon and Brother Isidore knew."

"They didn't, and I told them all about it. Wait until the news gets out." Brother Michael spoke with intense satisfaction. He had a gleam in his eyes, as though he had done something mischievous. "I told them that Sister Catherine punished the children with a rubber hose called the B.P. for Big Punisher. I described the whole process, the black bag she carried it in, and some of the trivial reasons why we were flogged. They couldn't believe that the Little Sisters also got it."

"When did you tell them all this?" I asked. I was surprised. It had never occurred to me that all this would be news to Big Brothers.

"Oh, and I told 'em about J.M. and the matches and all," Brother Michael went on.

"When, when?" I asked.

"Well, let's see. Thursday, yes, it was Thursday, but this morning I met Brother William Mary. He believes now. He checked it out with his children. He and Brother Matthias said the same thing—they never understood why the Peterson children freely chose to live in a small house in the city with their mother, instead of out here in the country with the horses and fields. They're mad, really mad, at the Angels and Sister Catherine."

"I just had an idea," I said. "Let's tell Sister Mary Agnes. What do you think she'll say? You know, I doubt she'll believe us. She thinks Sister Catherine is a saint."

"Yes." Brother Michael laughed. "Saint Catherine holding a rubber hose in her hand."

"Have Sister Mary Judith paint a picture and hang it in the chapel," I said.

We laughed at the thought.

"But seriously," I went on, "I think we should tell Sister Mary Agnes everything, especially the cruel stuff. I don't know why I never thought of it before."

I knew it was an excellent idea. I always felt that Sister Mary Agnes loved us because we were her children. When she would visit us in Ohio, she would cook breakfast for each of us just the way we liked it. When Benedict and later Brother Michael had their operations in Akron, she was so concerned about every detail of their recovery. Certainly the thought of her children being beaten so often under the command of Sister Catherine would make her angry.

After dinner, Brother Michael and I walked down to the Big Sisters' dining room, where they were doing dishes.

"Sister Mary Agnes," I asked, "may we see you for a moment?"

She seemed curious to know what Brother Michael and I were up to. We stepped into another room and she started right off.

"If you think you're going to convince me how wonderful those wicked, wicked men are—"

"Oh, no," I replied with assurance, "I just wanted to know

if you were aware how we were brought up under Sister Catherine. The fear of the children who were punished because they couldn't eat their breakfast, how Sister Catherine would—"

"I don't want to hear your condemnation of our beautiful Sister Catherine. After all she did for you! The one thing she couldn't tolerate was ingratitude. She was a mother to—"

"Wait a minute, I didn't finish," I said.

"I've already heard all about your criticisms of Sister Catherine."

"How did she punish us? Do you know?" I snapped back.

"She tried her utmost to bring up good holy children who would love God and be loyal to His Blessed Mother and to have enough courage to stand up to her vicious enemies with whom you have so ungratefully conspired. Those to whom God has given the most, when they betray Him and His Dearest Mother, oh, are they going to get it. I just can't believe the injustice that—"

"Do you think it is all right to flog a child with a rubber hose because he wets his bed?"

"What do you mean?" She was fingering the corner of her apron and she seemed apprehensive, as though she were expecting something horrible. There was anger in my eyes and I hoped she could see it. I felt sorry for her, but I intended to tell her exactly what had happened, no matter how much it hurt.

"Do you think it right to tie a child down on his bed with ropes and whip him, to feed him only bread and water, to burn him with matches and with hot water. Do you think that is right? That it is holy?"

I went on with a stiff voice. "Sister Catherine and her Angels were absolutely wrong in the way they raised us. It was a system of fear. Did you know that such things happened?"

"No, I did not, and I don't believe it," she replied. She paused and stared in bewilderment.

Brother Michael was watching her intently. "It is true, Sister Mary Agnes. It happened to us; it is true," Brother Michael said. "Ask Paul, Matthew, and Benedict the next time you visit them in Ohio."

She drew back and crossed her arms. "I don't believe it; no, I don't believe it." She said this with a confidence that showed she knew Sister Catherine too well. She could not have been capable of such a thing. "I remember I once asked

Sister Catherine about Matthew's screaming when he was being spanked. I could hear him from our wing of the house. But Sister Catherine assured me that it wasn't as bad as it sounded. For every time she hit Matthew, she hit the wall ten times."

"That's ridiculous," Michael said indignantly.

"Burning with matches, I can't believe it," she repeated.

"I've an idea," I said enthusiastically. "Suppose the Angels told you to your face that what we just said is true, but that it was done for our own good, would you believe them?"

She looked at me with amazement. I had suggested undeniable proof, the word of the Angels.

"I guess I would," she finally said.

"Would you agree that it was the proper way to raise a child?"

"I think Sister Catherine did her very best to raise you as holy children," she replied. But she was obviously confused. Her hand was resting now on the table beside her. She kept shifting her attention between me and Brother Michael, as though one of us would suddenly deny it.

"But you still don't believe what we said?" Brother Michael asked.

"No, I don't," she said firmly.

"Then why don't we all meet with some of the Angels, like Sister Mary Judith, and we can discuss it? Would you be willing to set up a meeting between you, myself, Brother Michael, and Sister Mary Judith?" I asked.

"Okay, if you want I'll ask her."

I was surprised that she agreed so readily. But I feared that Sister Mary Judith would refuse to come.

"Don't tell her what we're going to discuss. Just say it is about our upbringing. I want it to be a spontaneous discussion, so you can learn what really happened. Please, for your own sake. You are our mother and you ought to know how we were brought up."

The next day, Sister Mary Agnes told us that she had arranged for us to meet with her and Sister Mary Judith in one of the classrooms at St. Anne's after dinner. As Brother Michael and I walked across the yard that night, we wondered what Sister Mary Judith would say.

"I doubt she'll deny it," I said. "She couldn't possibly look me in the eye and deny that these things happened. Why don't you do the talking, though? I was one of the good ones, but you got it all the time. You mixed with the bad Little Brothers. You experienced all of this more than I." I tried to ease my nervousness by giving Brother Michael the dirty work. I had not even considered what Sister Mary Agnes might do if our meeting were successful.

We rang the bell and Sister Mary Agnes opened the door. Her manner was serious, her face deeply perplexed. Brother Giles, the only Big Brother who had joined the Sisters' side, was talking to Sister Mary Judith in one of the classrooms. Sister Mary Agnes showed us into an adjacent room. As she left, Brother Michael said in a whisper, "Sister Mary Judith has her husband nearby to defend her if necessary."

I laughed nervously.

"Excuse me, Sister Mary Judith, Brother Luke and Brother Michael have arrived," Sister Mary Agnes said in a gentle voice.

"Oh, thank you. I'll be right there."

We waited. I wished they would hurry up. Was Brother Giles going to come also? I hoped not. I wiped my sweaty hands on my cassock very slowly so Brother Michael wouldn't notice. I started thinking about the beatings, and just the thought made me mad.

Sometimes the Angels seemed out to get us. No matter what we did, we somehow ended up in trouble, and that fear was what kept me in line. I remembered Matthew getting punished. I could hear his muffled scream, "I can't breathe," as one of the Angels sat on his head and whipped his struggling, naked body. I had a terror of suffocating ever since I almost smothered under the weight of a pile of branches in the old apple orchard. The Angels were cruel and they kept us in constant fear. I snapped out of my reverie when I heard them coming.

Sister Mary Agnes entered, followed by Sister Mary Judith, whose eyes were smiling in her usual perceptive way. She closed the door.

"Good evening," I said. I grinned as I walked across the room and pulled up a chair for Sister Mary Judith. "I feel like I've jumped five years into the past, sitting in this classroom with you in the teacher's seat."

Sister Mary Judith laughed her three staccato hisses, a most familiar sound.

We were all seated. Looking directly at Sister Mary Judith,

I adopted the cold serious manner I had come to use when fighting for control in an emotional situation.

"Things are rather confusing now. We are over at St. Therese's and you at St. Anne's. Disputes have been going on for over a year. There is distortion in what we hear about you and I'm sure it happens in reverse. But we wanted Sister Mary Agnes to hear directly from you some of the facts about our upbringing. This way, we can avoid confusion over what really happened."

I stopped to catch my breath, then continued.

"I feel that Sister Catherine's regime was too severe. Certainly it limited the children's freedom of choice of a vocation. But I know that others think differently."

I paused. The room was still with anticipation. Everybody was looking at me. Sister Mary Judith was serious. She remained at ease and watched me attentively. I could see fine lines radiating from the corners of her squinting eyes. I had talked very rapidly. It had come out okay, I thought. I continued twisting and unraveling the black sash on my lap. I must get on with it and get to the point.

"There has been some discussion recently about the punishments the children received. Rather than have fantastic stories going around, I thought it would be better to hear it from you."

Now, Sister Mary Judith knew what we were going to discuss, yet she showed no surprise. Maybe she was going to spring across the room and slap my face. She had a lightning stroke always accompanied by a slow determined voice, "Put—your—hands—down." But she remained seated.

Sister Mary Agnes and Brother Michael were now watching Sister Mary Judith. I went on. "I realize that some of the Little Brothers like J.M. were unbelievably stubborn and that you tried your hardest to do what was necessary for the salvation of their souls. Some of the punishments that were used—well, of course, there was the strap, a barber's razor strap." Sister Mary Judith, her lips drawn tightly together, nodded yes. "I was rather good, so I rarely got it." I laughed. "Then, of course, there was the Big Punisher—the B.P., we children called it." I turned to Sister Mary Agnes. "It was a rubber hose, oh, about three feet long."

Sister Mary Judith spoke up. "Sister Catherine was the only one who used that, and she only used it when one of the children was very bad. It was like a last resort."

"It was used very often," Brother Michael said, interrupting suddenly. "I received it myself many, many times for trivial things and often from you." Brother Michael was indignant and Sister Mary Judith seemed a bit defensive.

Brother Michael drew his weapons. "And if the child were even worse, you would put him on bread and water or burn him with matches or hot water, or you would—"

"I did not burn any child with matches," Sister Mary Judith answered firmly. "Sister Catherine was the one who did that. You must realize, Sister Mary Agnes, that Sister Catherine wanted someone like Jerome Mary (J.M.) to have a fear of hell. She would hold a lighted match near his skin just long enough for him to feel the heat. It was more to frighten him into the fear of God's punishments than to actually burn him."

Sister Mary Agnes' hands were clutched together on the top of the desk. Her eyes kept growing wider and her mouth was partly open as the argument continued.

"How about the hot-water treatment? I know *you* did that to J.M." Brother Michael was out to expose the cruelty of Sister Mary Judith so that Sister Mary Agnes, our mother, could see it for herself.

"What do you mean?"

"You know, using a hose to spray J.M. with boiling hot water while he was undressed in the bathtub."

Sister Mary Agnes let out a faint gasp. Brother Michael leaned forward with a look in his eye that seemed totally convincing in righteous anger.

"Oh, I think I know what you're referring to. I did spray him with water, but as soon as I felt it get hot, I turned it off."

"In the meantime, J.M. was screaming at the top of his lungs. And it never occurred to you that the water was hot? Not until you felt the heat through the hose? I would say that was a bit late."

"I did not intend to spray him with hot water," Sister Mary Judith said. She was unruffled by Brother Michael's accusations and looked at him as though he deserved the strap.

"Then why spray him with water at all? What was the point? Being sprayed with lukewarm water is like a shower—rather enjoyable—certainly no reason to scream." Sister Mary Agnes' expression kept changing as she followed the arguments back and forth. She seemed to understand

Brother Michael's feelings. Her face would imitate his emotions when he spoke.

"Now, Brother Michael, as I said before, we did not intend to burn any of the children. We only wanted them to be afraid, frightened, so they would be obedient. That was all that was ever intended."

"That is ridiculous." Brother Michael was angry now. To my surprise, I realized I wanted to stop it. I hated to see emotions flare up. Sister Mary Agnes had heard enough. I could see moisture in her eyes and she was staring at the floor. I wondered if she was thinking of her other three children, who had refused to return to the Center. I felt guilty. But Brother Michael was still arguing, so I interrupted.

"Never mind, Brother Michael, I think Sister has made it quite clear that all these punishments were not done to cause pain, but rather to make the stubborn child good. Often mere fear was sufficient. I don't think we have to go on about this. I just wanted Sister Mary Agnes to hear Sister Mary Judith explain what actually happened before any rumors develop."

I got up. "Thank you for your time." I nodded to Sister Mary Judith, who remained composed. She looked at Sister Mary Agnes and said nothing. I opened the door and beckoned to Brother Michael. Sister Mary Agnes followed.

We stepped into another room, and Sister Mary Agnes asked, "Why didn't you ever tell me this before?"

"Quite frankly," I said, "I thought that you knew or would approve of it. Sister Catherine and the Angels thought there was nothing wrong with it. They were trying to save us from an eternity of everlasting flames. It never crossed my mind to tell you. You were just another Big Sister we would visit occasionally at community meetings. Any personal problems or fears I had I took to my Angel or to Sister Catherine—certainly not you."

Sister Mary Agnes looked as though she couldn't believe what I was saying. She was crying.

"Didn't you know you could always come to me?"

I realized then that she had presumed over the years that we were attached to her in some unique way. I felt I should stop, but I couldn't.

"No, not at all," I said. "You were not anybody special we thought would protect us. Why should I have gone to you? Sister Julia was the person I knew best, I trusted her the most."

"Why?" She asked. She turned to Brother Michael to see if he would give a different answer. I noticed a slight trembling in her hand as she touched a tissue to her eyes. I was right, she really did love us even above the religious ideals that prompted such punishments. I felt that I had been ruthless.

"Brother Luke can say that," Brother Michael replied. "His Angel, Sister Julia, was the easiest and nicest of them all. I had Sister Mary Judith, so I would always go to Sister Catherine if I could possibly reach her."

"Well, actually, I usually went to Sister Catherine," I said, "because I knew that she could cancel any punishments if I got to her in time."

We put on our coats and walked to the door.

"It's getting late," I said. "I hope we haven't hurt you. I just thought that you should know some of the details of our upbringing. Perhaps when you visit our brothers in Ohio they can tell you more. I know Matthew had a very rough time here. Can we discuss this some more with you sometime, maybe tomorrow?"

With the door ajar, we chatted a bit about Brother Michael's horse, which had escaped from its paddock that morning. Still holding a tissue, Sister Mary Agnes described how fresh the horse had been. I was pleased. She looked happier. I wanted to leave quickly because I never knew how to say good-bye when emotions were involved. It would be too embarrassing for me to hug her. I did not know why. I remembered that she had hugged me on the day I was professed. I had felt very awkward.

Brother Michael was still talking, so I interrupted him to say that it was late and that we'd better run. We finally said good night, waved good-bye, and agreed to meet again the next day.

I was jubilant. Now at last she would not believe that Sister Catherine did everything perfectly. She would admit that mistakes had been made in the upbringing of the children. She was on our side.

The following day we met Sister Mary Agnes as she came from the kitchen. I knew that she must have had time to talk it over with the Angels at St. Anne's. As she approached, I saw her face. Something was wrong. She looked steadfastly ahead, her lips pressed thin, and her white-knuckled fingers clenched the hem of her long black sleeves. Even her walk displayed a frightening stoical determination.

"Listen, Brother Luke and Brother Michael, I don't think we have anything to talk about," she said with a quaver in her voice. "Don't think for one moment that you fooled me with your scheming smiling way of trying to trick poor Sister Mary Judith into admitting to the truth of those preposterous stories. This is just another one of the Brothers' tricks to defame Sister Catherine. You're trying to make a big thing out of a few minor incidents in order to disguise the real issues. Sister Catherine will not be disgraced, and that's that." She avoided our eyes and started to turn as though she would walk by us.

I couldn't believe her words and tone. What could have happened? Was she afraid of them? What could they do to her? She had given up her husband, her children, and her relatives for the crusade. She had nowhere to turn for support. But certainly that was a minor consideration for her. Sister Mary Agnes had unbelievable courage when it came to standing up alone for what she believed was right in God's eyes. How did they change her? I was flabbergasted.

"I can do no more," I said in utter dismay. "You heard it from Sister Mary Judith's own mouth. For your own sake, for your own peace of mind, please speak to Paul, Matthew, and Benedict when you go to Ohio on your next visit. They can tell you whatever you want to know. Please do that. That's all I can say." A sickening feeling went through me. I didn't know what I was dealing with. Her loyalty to the other side seemed mysterious, unnatural.

Brother Michael was dumbfounded. He said nothing and we left.

"What could have happened to her?" Brother Michael asked.

"I don't know."

I got in touch with Paul, Matthew, and Benedict, and told them briefly what had happened. They promised to tell Sister Mary Agnes exactly how they were treated while at the Center. But when she visited them several weeks later, she refused to discuss anything about the punishments they had received.

I spoke with Brother Simon, hoping he might be able to explain Sister Mary Agnes' behavior. All he said was that my mother's loyalty to the cause was most important; her children came second. He remembered how she had preferred to remain at the Center rather than live with us out in the world. He mentioned how Sister Catherine expressed her amazement that my mother refused to set up a home. But I didn't believe that at all. In my opinion, Sister Mary Agnes always did exactly what Sister Catherine wanted.

Sister Catherine had told us, both directly and through Father Feeney, what she considered to be proper religious behavior. Our calling by God was first; selfish family affections should never interfere with the crusade. How often we had listened to the scriptural quotation, "Unless a man hate his mother, father, wife, children, and his own life also he cannot be my disciple." I had always felt that Sister Mary Agnes loved her children, that she loved us dearly. I had heard that she cried when we became two or three years of age and had to be taken away from her. She had given us up because she was a perfect slave to Our Lady, a perfect disciple of Sister Catherine. She knew her true calling from God. Twenty years of daily religious instruction had given her a rigid conscience that shunned the selfishness of motherly affection for her children. She had read stories about holy women, like Mother Connell, who had chosen God rather than her children. The choices for her were exclusive. Either life for God at the Center or life with her children in the wicked world which despised God. The two were incompatible. She could not work out her salvation as a mother in the world. But perhaps Brother Simon was right. Sister Catherine may have preferred that Sister Mary Agnes set up a home for us in the world. No, it was inconsistent with everything I had ever heard Sister Catherine say.

I had given up trying to convince Sister Mary Agnes of the Brothers' ideas. When they finally let us participate in their private meetings, I argued that we should plan our own future independently of what the Sisters would like.

At one meeting I presented those ideas that we as professed Little Brothers had agreed upon. We were against any policies that pressured the children into the religious life. We disapproved of the fraud of the bookselling operation, and we questioned the logic of the Center remaining outside the visible authority of the Church.

I wanted the Center to survive. The Big Brothers and Sisters had dedicated their lives to the defense of the Faith and their work was needed now more than ever. The Church, I thought, was decaying because of the subversive idea that one religion was as good as another. I no longer believed in the Center's rigid interpretation of the Church's doctrine of no salvation outside the Catholic Church. Instead, I, as well as other Brothers, thought that it was a doctrine that allowed limited latitude for theological disagreements without involving heresy.

My main concern was still my own vocation. I hoped that God had *not* chosen me for the religious life, and even if He had, I thought I should go into the world and test it. I wanted to get out at a time that would cause the least scandal to my Brothers and Sisters. I planned to leave after classes were over in June. I hoped I would be one of several.

Already, many of the adults and children had left for the world. I felt they were unholy and selfish by deserting the Center, but I envied their new life outside. The Doyle family—mother, father, and four of the five children—was gone. The Lucases left. Brother Albert and Sister Mary Beatrice were planning to quit, to set up a home for their youngest daughter. Sister Susanna wanted her husband, Brother Saturninus, to join her and two of their daughters outside the Center. One of the O'Toole sisters had gone. Most of the Jones family had left, including their daughter Sister Mary Kristine. She was now living in the world. She could dress up in attractive dresses, as girls do in the world. The clothes would surely accentuate her beauty, and I wanted very much to see what she looked like now. I wondered how she would react when she saw the shocking impurity in the world. Would she wear the skimpy bathing suits girls wore?

Her father, like most of the Brothers who had left to take care of their families, continued to work days at the Center. As I was twenty-one years old, I decided to speak my thoughts, and I went to him and told all about my interest in his daughter. To my great relief, he was not shocked; he agreed to speak to her about it. Later he told me that she denied ever being aware of my paying any attention to her; however, arrangements were made for us to meet at the Center one Saturday.

The meeting took place on a sunny and unusually warm day in May. I was to see her late in the afternoon inside the red bus parked near the garage. All day I had been recollecting past moments when our eyes had met in the chapel, in the fields, or in the dining rooms. For nearly six years I had watched her praying the Office, working on the farm, or doing the dishes. And I never could talk to her. It was against the Rule. One day I actually broke the Rule, and she reported me. I never understood why. When our eyes met, I thought she was saying that she loved me, but that God wanted her for a higher life. Sometimes I could feel the passion in her eyes, and I imagined that she would steal away one night and quietly call my name outside my window. But it never happened. I kept hoping for another day, another chance to talk to her.

Now I had my chance, and I didn't know what to say. She would be only a few feet away. I would look into her beautiful face and try to find out if she really loved me as I hoped. It bothered me that she had turned me in only six months ago, and that she denied any awareness of my interest in her. Perhaps she didn't want to admit her affection for me to others. It was something too special to be disgraced in public.

When the time came, I walked over to the garage. My blue work shirt was dark with perspiration under my arms. I started to go back to put on my cassock, but just then I saw her and she saw me. She paused, then disappeared into the bus. It was the first time I'd seen her without her veil and long black habit. Her golden brown hair was cut short, and she looked very attractive in her knee-length light-blue dress. When I thought no one was watching, I entered the bus.

"Hi, Brother Luke," she said. Her voice had a lilt to it. I loved it. "Brother Isidore told me that you wanted to speak to me."

"Yes, I am very grateful he could arrange it," I replied as I sat down across the aisle from her. I couldn't believe it. There she was, less than three feet away, and we were alone. I didn't dare look down at her dress or legs. She might be offended.

She spoke up, "I wasn't aware of, you know . . . I had no idea that . . ."

"He told me. Well, I have been fascinated by you for years." I had said it to her, I thought to myself. She didn't appear to be surprised, so I went on. "I realized that I could not go on dreaming about you and being a good religious. That is why I accosted you in the hallway. I wanted to find out how you felt about me." I was getting out of breath, but

I didn't stop. "Then, of course, you reported the incident to your superiors, which was the right thing to do. I was only—"

"Yes," she said, "you frightened me. I didn't know what you were saying. I didn't know what was going on."

"Oh, I see. I understand."

She held her head upright and her shoulders back, as though she were proud of her breasts. I loved her arrogant manner.

"I think it might be easier for you now that I have left. You should pray to Our Lady to give you the strength to resist temptations. Just try to forget about me."

"That's not easy," I replied. I was annoyed. "I've been watching you for the last six years. I can't forget you just like that." I wondered why she said temptation. There was nothing bad about my interests. It could lead to Holy Matrimony, if only my religious vocation weren't in the way.

"Anyway," I went on, "I'm not sure I have a vocation to the religious life, especially since I'm so attracted to someone like you. I mean, I think about you all the time; I pray for you day and night. I know what you've been through. I hope everything is okay now. Are you happy out in the world?"

She looked at me and smiled. Maybe she was hoping I would leave, I thought. She was so beautiful.

"I left the Center because I couldn't stand Sister Sylvia and others at St. Anne's. I don't know what we're going to do, but right now I'm happy that I'm out of there."

I thought to myself that soon I would be out and we could get together again. My hands were sweaty. Suppose someone saw me here. I had better say good-bye.

"Well, I'm so happy, I'm so delighted that I could speak to you," I said, getting up. "I have many difficult decisions to make, but I hope to see you again."

She got up. "It will be interesting to see what happens."

I was hoping she would say something about wanting to see me again, but she didn't. I paused for a moment, then backed out of the bus as I waved good-bye. I felt dejected. I had nothing working for me, nothing to impress her with. If only I knew what she admired most.

For weeks afterward, I reconstructed our conversation. We talked back and forth in the chapel, at meals, in the classrooms, and in bed. At times I was convinced by the memory of her smile that she wanted me to leave the Center. Other times I feared that she had no interest in me—it was all my own imagining. I had to go out and prove myself. I was determined to leave when classes were over in June.

Several days before I planned to leave, I told Brother Simon and Brother Basil of my intentions. They tried to dissuade me at first, but soon they saw that my decision was firm. I asked them not to mention my plans to anyone. I couldn't stand the tension of facing the community at Mass and feeling that they all knew I was going to leave.

They would be thinking of my reasons, my selfish interests, my worldly desires for the pleasures of the flesh. No, I had enough anxiety just coming to grips with my own conscience. It could be that God indeed had given me a vocation and I was deserting Him. I was abandoning my Brothers and Sisters. Worst of all, I was giving bad example to the other Brothers. Many of them would probably leave after me. I had taken the final vows to live my life in poverty, chastity, and obedience. Now I was forsaking those vows, an act that was despicable in the eyes of God. I told myself that I really wasn't forsaking them. I was just taking a leave of absence. I was trying to decide if my religious vocation was true or if I had just joined under great pressures put on me. If I really had a vocation, I would return and Sister Mary Agnes and the rest of the community would understand.

The day before I planned to go, I went to Brother Michael's room. He was seated at his desk, reading.

"Brother Michael," I said.

He came over to the doorway.

"This may surprise you, but I'm planning to leave."

"Really." He paused. "Why?" He was searching my eyes carefully.

"Well, I do not believe I am called to the religious life. But I don't want my departure to affect your life. A vocation is an individual thing given by God. Some have it, others don't."

He laughed. "What a hypocrite you are!"

"What do you mean?" I asked. "What's so funny?"

"I saw you yesterday with Father—so sincere." He glanced out the window.

"Oh, yes, you saw that," I said. "Well, what did you expect me to do?"

"I know. I would have done the same thing," he continued, "but just the sight of you there. Father came up to you and said, 'Forever, you'll be a Slave of Our Lady forever,' and you answered, 'Forever, Father,' and he said, 'I'm not forcing you, dear, am I?' 'Oh, no,' you replied. Then, of course, he finished with 'I'm your father forever,' and you bowed your head for his blessing, saying, 'Yes, you are my father forever.' "

"Yes," I said, "and then he looked at me as though he were going to cry, you know the way he does it. He started flattering me with his spiel about how holy he sensed I was when he gave me Holy Communion. He's been doing that to everyone these days. He's really worried about all the children leaving. I wonder what he'll say when he finds out about me. I'm going to tell him tonight. I'll leave early tomorrow morning."

"Tomorrow?" Brother Michael looked directly at me. "Whom have you told?"

"Just Brother Simon, Brother Basil, and a few others. Sister Mary Agnes doesn't know," I said. "But don't you tell anyone. If Brother Martin or any others ask why I left, just say that I did not think I had a vocation."

"Brother Luke, I'm planning to leave also." Brother Michael waited for my reaction.

"You're leaving also?" The thought crossed my mind that he had decided just then. "What do you think Sister Mary Agnes is going to do with both of us gone?" We stared at each other for a moment. "I'm going to write her as soon as I can after I'm gone. I'll be staying with the Doyle family in Cambridge; Brother Simon arranged it for me. But that must be kept secret. I don't want her to know where I'm living. When do you plan to leave?" I asked.

"I'll wait until they get over your leaving."

It was Wednesday, June 16, 1971. At about nine o'clock, after all was quiet, I went down to Brother Simon's office, where he and Brother Basil were talking. They gave me last-minute advice. Father Feeney was in his office at the other end of the building. If he saw that I was truly determined to leave, he would absolve me of my vows. I planned to ask for one hundred and fifty dollars so I could buy myself some regular clothes, shoes, and whatever else I might need.

As I went through the hallways and rooms toward his office, I tried to overcome the feeling that I was damning myself by abandoning my vows. The thrill of life in the world had lost its glamour. During the day, I had been thinking about Sister Mary Kristine living out there happily free of her habit, the religious rules, and her superiors. Time after time, I had pictured myself with her: swimming in lakes, bathing in the sun, sailing, possibly even driving my own car. I would be free to go to the movies, watch television, go skating, skiing, or hiking. But now these images seemed to fade away. I couldn't conjure them up to boost my determination. The reality of what I was about to do was awesome.

God gave each of us one life to live and do His will. He had chosen me for Himself. If I failed, I would get the everlasting flames of hell. It was foolish to buy even a hundred years of earthly pleasures for an eternity of torments. I reassured myself that I wanted to live a saintly life, but not as a religious. I was called to the married state, and God would give me the grace to work out my salvation. Yet, the words I had heard Father repeat for so many years kept going through my head: "To whom much is given, of him much will be expected."

The door to Father's office was open. He was seated in his armchair, reading. I hesitated to enter. I hoped he wouldn't go into one of his rages and begin to rub his hands together. I wasn't afraid of him, but when he got angry, I felt that God was looking into my soul, and it always made me feel guilty. Once a week for more than fourteen years I had confessed my sins to Father, and he had absolved me because I was repentant. Now I was rebellious, and I would refuse to obey him.

"Good evening, Father."

"Who's that?" He slowly turned his head, looking over his glasses. Some white hair had fallen across his forehead.

"It's Brother Luke, I've just come to . . . I just wanted . . . I've decided I don't have a vocation and I'm going to leave." I waited for his reaction, but to my surprise, he didn't explode in anger. I entered the room.

"You don't want to stay? You're going to leave?" His voice grew louder. I felt ashamed, as though the whole community could hear him say it.

"Yes, Father."

He got up out of his chair and came toward me. His face was growing redder and his left hand was shaking.

"You don't think you have a vocation?" he asked. His eyes seemed to expect me to change my mind.

"No, Father. I've given a lot of thought to it, and I've decided to leave. I came to be absolved from my vows."

"Right now?" he asked. A fear came over me. Was there some reason it couldn't be done tonight?

"Yes, tonight. I'm leaving very early tomorrow morning," I said firmly.

"Wait until tomorrow. You should give it more thought." There was a finality in his voice, as though further arguments were useless.

"No," I replied, "I've already thought about it and—"

"Have you told your mother?"

"She knows that I don't think I have a vocation." I was afraid that he would phone her at St. Anne's and get her to come over and beg me to stay. I hoped it was too late in the evening.

"You don't think, you're not sure," he bore down with a severe voice.

"I'm sure I want to leave. I'm going to leave early tomorrow morning just before Mass, so I just—"

"Well, I'm telling you to wait until tomorrow." He came right up to me. I could feel his breath. Instinctively, I raised my hands as though he were going to slap my face. He wouldn't dare, I thought.

"No, Father, my mind is made up. I'll be leaving before Mass—early, tomorrow." I tried to show my determination.

"Your mind is made up. You don't have a vocation. You want to forsake Our Lady and go into the wicked world where it is worse than hell!" His face grew red and he was rubbing his hands together and wheezing through his upper teeth. "I'm telling you as your poor unworthy father,"—he suddenly looked as though he were about to cry, then recovered and went on—"that you do have a vocation and God will punish you."

"I know, Father, but I chose—"

"You want to go into the wicked world? Do you want to get married?"

"I'm not sure, Father, it is too soon to tell, but—"

Father left his office in a hurry. I followed at a distance.

237

He walked past Brother Simon's office and went upstairs. Brother Simon and Brother Basil came around the corner.

"What happened?" they asked. "Did it go all right?"

"No, he refused to absolve me and left. He wants me to wait until tomorrow, but I'm determined to go anyway."

"He'll be back," they said.

A short while later I could hear him coming. He had his purple stole and a book. I knew he was going to absolve me. He told Brother Simon and Brother Basil about my desire to leave, and they, of course, showed their disappointment. At least he would not blame them for it, I thought.

I knelt down beside the fireplace. He held his hands over my head and spoke a short formula that, in essence, removed my obligation to follow the vows of poverty, chastity, and obedience as a Slave of the Immaculate Heart of Mary. As he pronounced the words, I eased my guilt by thinking that I would probably come back someday and be forgiven. It was over. I was no longer a member and was free to leave St. Benedict Center, where I had lived the first twenty-one years of my life.

I told him I needed some money to get started.

"How much?" he asked as he walked back to his office. He seemed resigned to my departure.

"A hundred and fifty should be enough," I answered. "I have to buy clothes and things."

"Is that all you need?"

I was surprised at his question. Should I ask for more? No, I better not push it, I thought.

"Yes, Father. That should be enough."

He unlocked a file drawer, counted out one hundred and fifty dollars, closed it, and left.

I waited in the room. I felt sinister holding the money, my own "filthy lucre." Brother Simon and Brother Basil found me. I told them how easily it had gone. I was lucky.

Early the next morning, I put on a yellow shirt and brown pants, an outfit one of the Brothers had found in the attic. I looked at myself. It was degrading—just another sinful worldly boy. I slipped my cassock over my clothes to hide them from the rest of the community. Once the car was out of sight, I took off my black garb.

Brother Hilary drove me to the bus station in Ayer, a small town nearby. My mind was blank. I refused to consider the gravity of my decision. Carrying a small suitcase with my few belongings, I boarded the bus. It was no time to have second thoughts. I waved good-bye to Brother's black-robed figure standing on the sidewalk. At least *he* would have the joys of heaven, I thought.

Chapter Nine

I had one very strong opinion about the world I entered in June 1971: it was thoroughly corrupt. Just as in the decadent world before the fall of the Roman Empire, people were lusting after the pleasures of this life with no concern for the hereafter. They had no strength of character and were incapable of suffering for a goal that rose above crass hedonism and materialism. I intended to live in the world, but not absorb its principles. "To be in it, but not of it" was my motto, a carry-over from my religious training.

I was very fortunate to be able to live with the Doyles, one of the former Center families. They could teach me those things of the world that I had to learn in order to function in it. Equally important, they wouldn't laugh at my ignorance, and with them I wouldn't be embarrassed to ask questions.

My first objective was to get a job so I could earn money to pay the Doyles for my support and lodging, and to be able to buy some of the things of the world that I did not consider wicked. Most of all, I wanted to take out Mary Kristine and show her a good time, sailing, ice skating, playing tennis, or going to the beach. The freedom I had seemed too good to be true, and I knew I could do all these things as soon as I had money.

The job market in and around Boston that summer was typically dreary, what with thousands and thousands of students all looking for work. But I was not planning to return to any school in the fall, so my chances were better. I was lucky enough to find a job as a teller in a bank in Belmont, a Boston suburb. I thought it was ironic that my mother's last job in the world had been in a bank.

One of the chief advantages of the job was that the regular income made it possible for me to buy a car. Unlike some of the other boys who had left the Center, I did not want anything fancy or flashy or even very fast. I wanted transportation—mainly for dates with Mary Kristine and so that I could travel back to the Center whenever I felt the urge for its familiar surroundings.

Mr. Doyle, with whose family I was living, worked as a car salesman, and I'd asked him to keep his eye out for something for me. One evening he came home to say that he had an extremely clean and dependable car, two and a half years old, with low mileage, but that it was rather plain. I told him that part didn't bother me at all, and shortly after seeing it and trying it out, I negotiated the first bank loan of my life and became the owner of a 1969 Rambler station wagon, gray. I loved it from the first day, and I guess it says something about my lack of materialism that I still own that same car today, six years and fifty thousand miles later.

On the job, I rapidly learned about checking and saving accounts, loan payments, Christmas-club payments, stop payments, and other banking matters. In the evening I took a course in commercial banking offered in Boston by the American Institute of Banking. (I got an A.) From my teller's window, I saw a good cross section of humanity. The poor old lady with her pension check, the young couple with their savings, and the rough truck driver with his huge weekly paycheck. I began to realize how tough this life could be, especially just trying to make a living. I was depressed. Too quickly, I saw that living in the world would not be all freedom and glory.

But it wasn't the suffering that bothered me, as much as it was the smallness of the reward. People were pouring out their healthy young lives just to be able to have a house, to eat, and to educate their children. I felt that was a poor recompense for their labors. All my life, when the going was rough, I would boost my spirits with the prospect of an eternal reward of infinite happiness. Now, striving for finite goals, yet tolerating similar suffering, was demoralizing. I was slaving away to make only ninety-three dollars per week, and to take home even less. And for what? To pay my bills. What's more, it was a waste of my talents, I thought. I remembered the times when I took in three times my weekly salary in one day by bookselling. I began to realize that people in the world also had it rough.

There were other things that made me unhappy, and the most depressing was my social life. My dates with Mary Kristine (now called "Kris") were disastrous. The harder I tried to please her, the less she seemed to like me. I joined a sailing club and took her sailing. We played tennis, went skiing in winter, went out to dinner and movies. I didn't know how to tell her how much I cared about her. Saying it was too embarrassing—she might think I was "after her body" (a phrase I had soon learned). I certainly couldn't touch her in any way, for fear she would become frightened. When, after a date I tried to kiss her, she turned her head so our lips wouldn't meet. Dating was frustrating, exhausting, frightening, and depressing. I tried to compensate for my awkwardness by spending a lot of money on her, but it did no good. She would thank me, but never express the slightest bit of affection. (Years later, I realized that she probably had just as many emotional hang-ups as I had.)

During my futile attempts to have the one thing I valued most—the love of a beautiful girl—I began to despise myself. There was something wrong with me. I wasn't good enough, I thought, but at the same time I felt I could achieve anything I really wanted. I decided I had to prove myself: to become successful by the world's standards, to be rich. I started going to night school, taking courses to become a real-estate agent.

The world was a strange place, and I was very uncomfortable. I was alone. I felt I was inferior in the eyes of everyone I knew at the Center (which I returned to almost every weekend for years) because I didn't have the strength to be a religious. I felt I was inferior by the world's standards, which I despised. It would laugh at me, I thought, if it ever knew how ignorant I was of its ways. So I turned into myself and became very bitter. I was determined to conquer, to show everyone I wasn't inferior. I would be admired and loved when my talents were known; I intended to succeed. Life became one big battle, and no matter how many times I fell flat on my face, I was determined to get up and push on.

The struggle was made worse by the constant feeling of uncertainty, as I tried to pretend I knew what was going on. Everything in the world seemed different. Its language was coarse and demeaning. If people weren't profaning the Holy Name of Jesus in such words as "Christ" or "jeez," they used offensive language like "goddammit" or "shit." Expressions like "that's cool" or "man" or "right on" irked me. I hated doing anything because it was "the thing to do." When I expressed enthusiasm by saying, "Oh, boy," I was laughed at. "You sound like my grandmother."

Then there was the ordeal of trivia. I disliked being forced to have conversations about nothing. Instead of talking about some philosophical subject like the difference between nature and person, people gossiped about things like some football team I never heard of, or something call Peanuts, which meant nothing more than a food to me, or their favorite childhood TV show whose name was as strange to me as all the new four-letter words I was beginning to hear. When I pretended I knew what they were talking about, I usually made a fool of myself. Even major political or historical events covered in the past by the news media (such as what prompted the major campus riots of the late 1960s) were topics I didn't dare to discuss.

I didn't really want to read the papers either. The headlines were generally unintelligible, much like the road signs were when I first saw them as a child, and the subject matter was of little interest to me. I'd be willing to read the papers if there were important topics like "NEW INSIGHTS INTO WHY EACH ANGEL IS A DIFFERENT SPECIES" or "HOW THE MULTIPLICITY OF CREATED BEING IS THE BASIS OF MATHEMATICS." But no such headlines ever appeared. People in the world seemed to be cramming their heads with so much useless information that they didn't have time to think on their own. One could function without a paper, I reasoned. If there were a major war, I knew I'd hear about it anyway. Often I stayed clear of new things, not so much because they were objectionable, but because they were different, strange—another reminder of an unfamiliar world.

People in the world let emotions gush out in all their disgusting nakedness. They could not control themselves and maintain their respectability. Blame was always placed on something other than oneself, and impatience led to verbal outbursts. A spilled drink was not your own fault, but that of the rug on which you tripped. When a lady was complimented on her hairdo, instead of pretending she didn't think it was so stunning (which is how the Center taught us to deal with personal praise), she openly soaked up the praise by saying, "Thank you."

The styles and fads often appeared ugly rather than beautiful. Hair built up into towering domes or kinky curls seemed comical if not downright repulsive. Bras seemed to be designed to emphasize the embarrassing bulges of breasts rather than hiding them. Sometimes, in a flash, I would picture a woman with her skinny heels, pointed breasts, plastic red lips, and outlandish hairdo suddenly thrown into the fires of hell. All her concern about such trivialities of dress would vaporize, I was sure, when she was faced with the experience of roaring flames.

Bathroom scenes were different. No longer was there bitter-tasting white tooth powder, but colored and flavored worms of toothpaste. Scented multicolored soap bars replaced the pure ivory-white bars. Bath towels were softer, more sensuous, worldly—red, green, yellow. The toilet was not an embarrassing chair to get out of as soon as possible, but a relaxing opportunity for newspaper reading. To me, that seemed typical of the wordly outlook. For people raised in the world, the practicality of reading the paper when you had nothing else occupying your brain was more important than toilet decency.

But by far the most disquieting aspect of the world was its preoccupation with sex. Everything—advertisements, TV, movies, comedies—seemed to be hinting at, if not outright screaming about, the lure of sex. I suspected that there had to be something quite enjoyable about sex, but I had decided to put it aside for a while. I feared it would be too deliriously exciting for me to handle right away. The obvious problem for me was that I would be torn between pleasure and the most terrible guilt. So, I put sex on the shelf for later consideration when I would have everything else under control. I didn't want it to interfere with my road to success. Once I had some money, once I understood the world, then I could indulge in that dessert.

However, there were other moral questions I needed answers to immediately. Was it a mortal sin to see women in bikinis either on the beach or on TV or in movies? Where was the demarcation line on a female leg above which mortal sin was the consequence of exposure? I was told that morality was not a rigid rule. It depended on the intentions to evoke the lower desires of man. That sounded ridiculous to me. Could the ugly go naked and not sin, yet the beautiful barely expose a leg and turn souls black with sins of impurity? If six inches above the knee excited me because of my sensitivity to the subject, yet total nakedness left others cold, how could I keep from sinning in this world unless I became like others—so accustomed to exposed flesh that it was boring. It seemed that sin was the key to not sinning. Would I have to indulge in scenes that "turned me on" before I became immune so that they didn't? I was very confused.

On the positive side, I became intoxicated by the scientific progress of the world. The idea that I could sit before a TV in a living room in Cambridge, Massachusetts (a room that was air-conditioned to a perverse temperature, one that nature outside was trying to undo), and while chewing on a fig from Egypt, watch a man driving his jeep around a boulder on the moon fascinated me to no end. But others took it for granted, complained that it was boring—"all rocks and sand"—and indignantly switched to a football game taking place thousands of miles away.

I hadn't been out in the world for even six months when I resolved to delve into the secrets of modern technology. Electronics seemed to be at the core of most major scientific marvels. I was told that MIT was the top school in the country for engineers. Having an ambition developed religiously to an uncontrolled degree by the expectations of infinite eternal rewards, I found it impossible to limit my desires and accept a school less than the best. I was a perfectionist, which I later learned could often be more of a hardship than a blessing. Impossible dreams lead to continual striving, continual discontent, and a very unhappy life.

There were problems to overcome in getting into MIT. I hadn't taken all the necessary college boards, and my marks were lower than those of the budding mathematical wizards that MIT attracts from around the world. Moreover, I wanted to get credit for some of my humanities courses so I could graduate in less than four years. The Center would have to make up a college catalog and transcript. When they balked and reaffirmed their disapproval of my applying to a secular university, I pointed out the benefits to them. I would be the first of the Center children to have Center courses accepted by any secular university, much less one as prestigious as MIT. The Center was skeptical, but I insisted, and my perseverance paid off.

When the time came for a personal meeting with an MIT official, I was more than ready. In a short interview with one of the admissions counselors, I told him that my background and upbringing shouldn't be held against me. It was innate talent and determination that mattered. When my time was up, he said that although I hadn't let him get a word in edgewise, I had said what *he* normally would say to the applicant.

He said he was convinced I had the drive needed to get through. One month later, in November 1971, I received the letter of admission; two months later I began.

I was awarded some scholarships based on financial need. I argued that though my father was a judge he could not help me because he had a second family to take care of, plus the education of the three youngest sons from his first marriage.

"But what about your mother?" the financial-aid counselor asked. "Can't she help with the tuition?"

"My mother is a nun."

If I had been shown the future that same November, I would have been a bit surprised. I would have seen that I would advance in two and a half years from freshman calculus and physics to a senior thesis in electrical engineering, that I would enter all the honor societies available to my discipline, that I would be elected President of the MIT chapter of Eta Kappa Nu (the Electrical Engineering Honor Society), that I would be admitted as an associate member to Sigma Xi, win a full-study graduate fellowship, and get my master's degree from Stanford University one year later.

If I had known that, I would have been more able to boast during the rare dates I had during those arduous years. But social life was secondary, for it could only interfere with my career. I was convinced that my worth as an individual was in what I accomplished, and so my self-esteem was directly related to my performance. I worked seven days a week, doing homework all day on weekends and often into the early morning hours. I had a tremendous amount of energy—and frustration—and I threw it all into my career. MIT would launch me into success, I hoped, and success would bring me love and esteem.

I paid for my education through scholarships, loans, and by working odd jobs—the best one was as a salesman for a coffee-service company. In the first year, when money was very tight, I would save quarters by hitchhiking to MIT rather than taking the bus. I could no longer afford my car, so I let the Center "lease" it for the cost of the monthly payments. They never used it. Later I took it back for my summer job as a salesman. As my final year came to an end, I began to relax a bit and take satisfaction in my improved situation in a thoroughly modern world.

Nothing impressed me more, that final year, than technological efficiency; and now I was part of it. I felt good, taking it all in when I drove my car to MIT—each cylinder and valve doing its proper thing, my left hand adjusting the heat, my right on the wheel, my feet using the pedals of clutch, brake, and gas, my ears tuned to the news on the radio, my eyes on the road, and my mind solving a second-order differential equation for the class: Solid State Circuits II. That was maximization of the performance of technological and human resources at its best. It was beautiful. And our modern society and economics made it all possible—the Middle East with its oil, the Midwest with its minerals, Detroit with its car production, and before me the police handling the traffic, the snow plow clearing the road, and the buses transporting the carless masses. My snobbish disdain for the modern world was changing into admiration. I was no longer just using it to achieve my goals, but I was really believing in it.

I have had a craving for efficiency for as long as I can remember. I hated waste and misused potential. Unfortunately, my Angel, Sister Julia, happened to be less than efficient, and other Angels laughed to themselves when I took over telling her how things should be done. In later years, I would tell fantastic stories of how I could improve the religious spirit in the community. My sermons, I claimed, would not be boring repetitious ramblings. Using the false (but convenient) argument that holiness invariably led to levitation, I said that each seat in the pews should have a weight indicator. As I preached, I would note what exhortations caused most of the needles on the read-out meters to deflect wildly, indicating levitation was at hand. Then I would know which of my words were producing a truly spiritual uplifting of hearts to God. That would be just one way to give efficient sermons, I concluded. The Brothers would laugh. "What a crazy imagination you've got!"

Efficiency dominated my everyday life. Whether it was shaving, brushing my teeth, toweling off after a shower, cooking breakfast, or whatever, invariably I had analyzed and experimented with all the options and variables in each case and had come up with what I thought was the optimum sequence of movements. From then on, my behavior in that task was identical each time—after every full stroke of the razor, three sharp raps on the edge of the drain cleaned it better than two—and the habits thus established freed my mind for thinking about more important things.

What I didn't like about my education in the world was the

pace, backed by the pressure to get good grades. Canned units of learning seemed designed to turn out technicians with the practical skills needed by society, but I wanted to probe into the fundamental premises of what I was being taught. In physics, I spent hours after class trying to relate the laws of Newton to some more basic principles of ontology and cosmology. I felt uncomfortable memorizing formulas unless I could derive them from Step 1. But the pace and the amount of work was so great that I had to succumb to the practical compromise of memorizing formulas and partial derivations I wasn't fully satisfied with. My reluctance stemmed from my realization that new discoveries are constantly wiping out old formulas, and I didn't want to waste my time learning some complex theory that would be rejected in a few years. But I knew the pragmatic value of the education I was getting, and I worked very hard, right up to my last day of classes.

To celebrate my graduation from MIT, there was a big dinner at the Center, and many of the Center children-alumni attended. I had survived the education of a secular university, without becoming an atheist or a member of some hippie religion.

They presented me with an official graduation card signed by all present, including the six Center children who were still religious. Enclosed was a fifty-dollar check so I could buy a class ring. I was touched and very grateful. When the religious members had stepped out of the room, I started getting the more worldly remarks. They wanted to know when I'd start chasing girls again, and they handed me a card signed by "The Whole Gang," which read: "It's been a lot of work but look what you've got to show for it—(inside) Now you can unhook a bra with one hand!" But the last line had been altered to read: "You *still* can't unhook a bra with *one* hand."

My party was not the first gathering of the children-alumni. We had gathered together on several other occasions in the last few years. Most of us lived within an hour's drive of one another, so it was easy to call a party. The first big occasion was the Connor brothers' reunion in January 1972.

The five of us had not been together since our days in Ohio nearly six years earlier. We decided to have a big party at the home of one of the original Center couples, the Doyles' house, where I was living. The Center children were now young adults, ranging in age from eighteen to twenty-five, but we all told stories about how cleverly we had outwitted the Angels. Some talked about old memories just to be able to discuss things that they would not tell their friends in the world. I showed the old movies I had taken inside the Center, and they were a hit.

The next important occasion was terribly sad: the funeral of one of the Center boys. He had been one of the five Little Brothers at my table until one of his parents left the Center and he had to go into the world. I remembered him as always being so full of enthusiasm; he used to put screaming life into our tank battles in Slaves' Field. I still have a vivid mental picture of him hurling cans of dry sand into the air, his face red and sweat-streaked, totally involved in the excitement. He died suddenly in August 1972 when he fell off a cliff while hiking in Colorado. He was eighteen years old. He left one brother and two sisters. At the wake, some Center children seemed almost despairing in their grief. Even those who had previously claimed they had never loved someone enough to cry, shed many tears. I did not cry in public, but I hoped that he had died in the state of grace and was already enjoying the happiness of heaven.

Another occasion when most of us gathered together was Angela's wedding. She was the first of the former Center children to get married. At the reception the bolder children were able to demonstrate the dances they had learned in the world. However, most were like me—too shy. We sat there instead and watched. I thought about how happy Angie would be. She had a husband, and maybe someday she would have children. Having your own family seemed so exciting.

Family life had become increasingly appealing to me over the years, though it was definitely a gradual process, and one I had really just begun. I remembered the early days of the Connor case when we took a quick course on relatives. We learned that we had four grandparents, not three or five. Each of our parents had two parents, so that meant four grandparents. Now family relations were discussed all the time. The idea of having a mother, a father, brothers, and sisters who were especially close was no longer repugnant to me. Family relations no longer appeared to be selfish or wickedly worldly. At times I became very bitter that I had not had that experience. Though it was difficult, I tried to establish close relations with my parents. My mother had refused to talk to me for over a year because I agreed with the

Center faction that she despised. I knew it would be some time before I could really think of her as a mother. But my father seemed willing to be friendly. I had written him on several occasions, and he replied in the same tone that I used: he expressed no more emotion or attachment than I had shown. Somehow I felt guilty calling him Dad or being affectionate in any way.

About a year after I left the Center, and each year after that, I went out to Ohio for a couple of days to visit my father. He expressed no resentment for all the trouble I had caused, and he let me eat and sleep in his house. Over the years I grew much more comfortable with him and could even joke about his graying hairs. He returned the kidding, noting that I had more than he. My hair had begun turning gray when I was sixteen. Though none of my other brothers had it, I knew it was hereditary (my mother had turned gray early), and it didn't bother me. In fact, I learned that some girls found it attractive.

My father now had a new family by 1974; he and Conchita had four sons of their own—Jimmy, Georgy, Joey, and Tommy. I got real satisfaction seeing the young boys run up to me and jump up and down with excitement, shouting, "Bob is here." And when the little children would run out and grab me by the arm or leg and tell me about their latest toy, I tried to talk back to them and be as excited. Still, for a long time, I felt very awkward, especially when picking up the youngest ones, tickling them, and saying little nonsensical things. But I did my best. Someday, I hoped to have the satisfaction of my own children jumping up and down excitedly, saying, "Daddy is here." Eventually I came to view it as part of my adjustment, and I enjoyed it.

My father expressed the most real warmth to me the time I wrote the following birthday card for his newest arrival. He said he would save it for him.

> Dear Tom,
> Happy Birthday!
> I apologize for writing this late but I only heard about your coming today.
> I wish to welcome you to this world of ours. It can be made to the beholder according to his wishes—all beauty with love and peace or smeared in hatred and strife.

As you become intoxicated with its riches you must remember that all that is good in bringing joy in possession must someday take leave with pain. If happiness is to be yours, and life not a sequence of deaths, you will have to consider the meaning and purpose of your existence. For your sake I hope you will take heed, and I wish you the best that life can give.

Your loving companion,

/s/ Bob

The greatest feelings of family closeness came, however, on those occasions when I got together with my four brothers. I discovered that we all had the same kind of mischievous attitude toward life and that we shared the same kind of sense of humor. In a rather perverse twist, we loved to laugh at whatever society took most seriously. If society considered it sacrosanct, to us it was suspect.

Sometimes we just went to a neighborhood bar and told funny stories about the old days—at least *now* we thought they were funny. Although not much of a drinker, on these occasions I would join in the beer-drinking because the mood was contagious. But the things that made us laugh the most were seeing someone caught in an incongruous situation, much like those presented on the television program *Candid Camera*.

Though I may have felt we were being too childish at times, we also all enjoyed being different from what we were supposed to be. Each of us had his own career, which he pursued seriously.

Michael, who had left the Center less than a month after I did, decided to work for a few years, first as a car salesman, then a salesman for auto parts, and lastly as a purchasing agent for a company that made road signs. Subsequently, he entered Princeton University, where he founded the Princeton Equestrian Team, became its captain, and led it through many competitions with other East Coast schools like West Point. Majoring in Middle East studies, he spent one summer in Lebanon and Iran getting a firsthand picture of some of their problems. He had his own troubles there— severe sickness, weeks on a crowded insect-infested train that was held up twice by armed terrorists, destruction of some of his belongings by a bomb blast, as well as the constant fear that as an American he was a possible target of Iranian terrorists. Michael now hopes to go into law and eventually into politics.

Paul, my next-oldest brother, graduated from the College of the Holy Cross in Worcester, Massachusetts, entered medical school at the University of Cincinnati, and will be working as an intern for the navy.

Matthew, who had been bounced around among broken homes until he graduated from high school, decided to enter the navy. After four years of service, most of it in Virginia, he entered the College of William and Mary, where he now majors in business.

Benedict followed his brother's footsteps a year later, served four years in the navy, and later entered college. He hopes to be a veterinarian.

All five of us met most recently with Dad in September 1976, to have our photos taken for his campaign. A judge since 1971, he was running for a higher judgeship. Though he lost in November, he must have felt good that September, when his five oldest sons came to Akron to give him support. It was the first time we had all gathered together in eleven years.

On that occasion, we decided to loosen Dad up a bit by giving him an eight-inch-tall glass filled with wine. Though he objected to the amount, our plan worked fairly well. We then started telling old-time stories, such as how we sabotaged his efforts by throwing up in the car and by refusing to eat for two weeks. He didn't seem to enjoy talking about *that*, said he had forgotten about those times, and then he told stories about the very early days of the Center.

He remembered Michael and me the best, he said, because we were not taken away from home until we were three and four. He said I was a very determined child, and that on my way to a Christmas play in which I was to act, at the age of three, I insisted on going barefoot so I could keep my new shoes shiny for the play. Michael, he said, would always bubble over, showing all his feelings. Once when the Center members were singing a song about how great the legendary St. Michael was in defeating the devil, Michael Connor beamed with satisfaction, thinking everyone was singing about him.

When the conversation grew more serious again, we asked

Dad why he had given up his family, wife, and children for his monk's existence in the Center. He said we could never really understand the situation. There was so much excitement in those days. All the young Center members felt they could get killed. "A mad angry crowd is terrifying. You don't know what it is if you've never witnessed it." Their windows were shattered by rocks, and once he was hit over the head with a lead weight. Every day there was some crisis, some battle. They needed one another and couldn't fight among themselves; they were too busy just surviving. They were young people, highly idealistic and easily impressed by their own importance. The world was against them, and they were against the world. *Time, Life, Newsweek,* were carrying the story. The Center was one of the stops on the Gray Line tours.

"We were young people getting a lot of attention. You know, Eisenstat, one of the greatest photographers in the world, came with a whole crew from *Life* Magazine. . . . We thought we were mighty important people—we, Churchill, and a few others."

It wasn't until he had reached the quiet of the country in Still River that he fully realized what had happened to his own family, Dad said. Before that, they were too busy attacking the outside world. However, Dad never really explained the reasons why families were separated. The most he would say was that everyone had to do it or they would have to leave the Center. He said that they were very idealistic, that they had to be strong to resist the world, and that they wanted to be saints.

He was attracted to the Center by its strong preaching. After the war everything was chaos, and all the boys were returning to college. But the secular teachings were equally confusing to these idealistic young Catholics. The Center offered certitude amid all the confusion. Father Feeney was an excellent speaker, and there were many very talented, intelligent, and energetic people there. There was a great spirit of unity among the Center members. It was "a very warm place, in the beginning," Dad said.

We talked at length for two evenings. During the day, we visited Dad's court. He sat in his black robes, in his judge's chair, while the attorneys argued their cases. I made some fresh remark, afterward, that Dad was reliving his deep desire to be a monk, but he'd only gotten as far as the black robes.

He laughed, and I was pleased. He told me that while he is cutting the grass or weeding the garden around the house, he finds himself singing some of the rousing songs of the early Center days. It was my turn to laugh.

The five of us were very happy that we could show Dad that we cared enough to fly from all over the country to help his campaign, even though it was a last-minute contribution: just a photo for his newspaper advertisements. Later, he sent all of us special color prints of the whole family. It must have looked impressive in the papers—nine boys ranging in age from two to twenty-six, and the father, fifty years of age, seated in the middle with his beautiful wife.

Unfortunately, he lost the election, but he would run again the next year when his own judgeship came up for election. He had won top awards for running one of the most efficient courts in Ohio, and it seemed improper that he should lose because of insufficient funds or because he was a better judge than politician.

After I left the Center, I had contacted most of the other relatives and friends in Ohio. They were pleased that I was out and happy. The Souers welcomed me very warmly, even though I'd once run away from their lake cottage, and thanked God that all had turned out well. Everyone had forgiven (and I hoped, forgotten) my insolence and ingratitude. Even Grandmother, who had to put up with so much from me, talked as though I were just as much her family as were her eighteen other grandchildren.

The five boys also had a happy reunion with our mother, at the Center, during the Christmas vacation in 1975. She then joined us for New Year's dinner at her brother's house. Jim, his wife, Dorothy, and their daughter, Gail, prepared a scrumptious meal—roast beef, baked potatoes, and homemade apple pie with ice cream. Michael showed slides of his summer's trip in the Middle East. When midnight approached, we watched Arthur Fiedler and the Boston Pops usher in the New Year on TV, and I tried to waltz with Gail, my cousin, and show off to my mother that I had learned some ballroom-dancing steps. She seemed very happy and relaxed.

But it had taken many painful years to get to that point. After I left the Center in 1971, Sister Mary Agnes spent most of her time during our visitations lashing out verbally against the Brothers' side, in the Center's two-way split.

Then, in January 1972, six months after I had left, she cut off all communications with me. The reason given—I had held a party with my four brothers at the house of one of the ex-Center couples whom she considered wicked because they had given up their religious vows.

For the next year and a half, I returned to the Center every weekend. It was my escape from the noisy world. I needed the peace and quiet, the familiar surroundings, to help me study and pass my exams at MIT. But Sister Mary Agnes ignored my presence. When she'd see me walking down the corridor in the dining hall, she would turn her head and let me pass by as though I were not worthy to be looked at. On several occasions I tried to reestablish communications, but I failed. Once I called her up, saying I had some interesting photos of my brothers. She said she would look at them only if I left them on the desk for her; she didn't want to speak to me.

Michael and I spent many hours discussing her situation. We concluded that she was very bitter against the Brothers and the families that had left because they had repudiated the once-basic principles of the Center. They had influenced and supported her decision to give up her husband and children years earlier, and now they had changed their minds.

We tried to find out more about the Connor case. To my surprise, the Brothers gave us the entire Connor files kept by the Center. We read through the transcripts and were shocked and deeply embarrassed to find out how little Sister Mary Agnes knew about our upbringing.

She had testified under oath in court that she tucked us in bed, read stories to us, and made sure we were dressed in the morning. We remembered her getting special permission to do it *once* or *twice*, but she had given the impression that she took care of us all the time. I felt, though, that she would have loved to do it if only she had been allowed. I knew that she had cried when her children were taken away, and it made me furious that she had to testify to support the Center's cruel separation. They had used her affection for us to defend the Center's antifamily regime so that no other couples would get similar ideas and try to leave. Now it was the Center's idea to let families leave, and there she was left alone to bear the pain of her decision.

I began to detest Sister Catherine, whom I saw as the chief manipulator. I felt Sister Mary Agnes had always loved us, and it was only her sensitive religious conscience that kept her a nun and not a mother. But I had no proof that Sister Catherine had forced Sister Mary Agnes to give us up. Brother Simon, when I asked him, claimed just the opposite. He said he remembered hearing Sister Catherine say that if she were my mother she would leave and take care of the five of us. I knew it was very possible, and probably true, and that she'd made such a statement. The question was: had she meant it? Sister Catherine and Father Feeney had used the same strategy on us children in order to make us become religious members. In front of the adult community, they asked us if we were being forced to such a decision, and we all readily denied it. But, quietly, over the years and in the secrecy of the Office, they had laid barriers so insurmountable that none of us could have made any other choice.

One day, while looking through the Connor case files, Michael found a letter from our mother to Sister Catherine that really should have been in Sister Catherine's files—and in a secret file at that.

The full page, single-spaced, typewritten letter is undated, but it must have been written sometimes in the summer of 1966. I am sorely tempted to include the entire text of the letter, for it is the best proof I have ever seen, on paper, of Sister Catherine's total control over the minds of those who called her their religious leader and superior.

But I won't reproduce it, for it would make my mother look like a pawn in the game of her own life. Suffice it to say that in the letter she apologized to Sister Catherine for being too concerned about her own children. After my mother mentioned her own "terrible ingratitude" and told Sister Catherine how badly she felt to see her superior's "anger and distress," she wrote that she really did intend to detach herself from the children, both here and away, and to give her attention to being a good religious, which was all Sister Catherine had ever asked of her. She ended saying that she knew that Sister Catherine wanted actions, not words, and that she would try to prove it.

After seeing that letter, I was convinced that Sister Mary Agnes loved us deeply, that she had at one time struggled against the wishes of Sister Catherine, but that she had finally succumbed out of guilt. She honestly believed that God, Whose will had been made clear by Sister Catherine, wanted her to remain a religious.

At the time he discovered the letter, Michael and I were once again on talking terms with our mother. But it had taken a dramatic incident to break the impasse.

A year and a half after Sister Mary Agnes had ceased talking to us, I got her to agree to at least listen to some of the problems that were bothering me in the world. It was a warm spring Sunday afternoon in 1973. I tried to find out her reasons for not wanting to resume family life, but she interpreted every question as part of a scheme foisted by Brother Simon from the "other side." It was a frustrating afternoon, but I remained outwardly calm, no matter how much anger was churning inside. I finally switched topics. I told her how lonely I was: I refused to compromise with the world, never attended student parties at MIT, rarely watched TV, had no friends in the "wicked world." I gave other reasons for my loneliness. When I came to the Center on weekends, it wasn't much better. She made me feel guilty because I talked with the Brothers she despised. She didn't want to speak to me. Though I was treated well by the family where I lived, it wasn't my family. I still felt like an outsider.

"Now why can't I come and talk to you as a son to his mother, without our conversations revolving around your hatred toward the other side?" I said. "Leave it out of our conversation. If I choose to talk to them, that is my business—they are my friends."

Sister Mary Agnes accused me of conspiring with Brother Simon. She said she had seen the two of us chatting together the previous day. That made me instantly furious, for it wasn't true. Maybe another Sister had told her that to keep us from getting back together again. I didn't know. I flatly denied it.

"Then you're calling me a liar," she said defiantly, and walked away.

All my efforts had collapsed again, I thought in despair, as I watched her stride away. It might be another year before she would let me talk to her.

Suddenly, I felt a surge of anger race through me. What I did next probably shocked me more than Sister Mary Agnes. Fuming with rage, I ran after her, grabbed her by the arm, and wheeled her around. I could feel my lips curling back, but I couldn't control myself as I yelled at the top of my voice that I was sick and tired of her stubborn refusal to treat me decently.

"If I have to wipe out this whole place, I'm going to get through to you," I screamed. At that moment I saw the horror in Sister Mary Agnes' face, and behind her was another Sister also frozen in her tracks. But Sister Mary Agnes suddenly melted and came toward me almost apologetically; I was so ashamed of my anger that I broke into tears.

For the next ten minutes, she consoled me, saying it must be terribly lonely "out there in the world." I told her that all I wanted was to be able to talk to her when I came to the Center; that I stood a much better chance of saving my soul if I could open up with my problems, rather than forgetting about the Center, and trying to solve everything on my own. She promised me I could always come to her for help and that she would leave the Center's politics out of our conversation.

We took a short walk; I wanted to clear my head. As I walked, I mentioned that I would cry about her after I had dreams that she had died. I would feel great remorse that I had never tried hard enough to make her life easier. I thought all of her sons should let her feel free to be part of our little problems, our worries, our lives. She didn't answer, but continued walking. I said that I knew she loved all of us and was doing what she thought best for our salvation. But with love always comes suffering and sacrifices.

I asked her if before I left each Sunday night she could fix me a lunch for the following day at school. She readily agreed, and that night I took home a delicious roast-beef sandwich and several eclairs for dessert.

It seemed to me that she would feel more comfortable with our suddenly renewed relationship if it wasn't all pleasure but involved some sacrifice. She wouldn't talk to me, I thought, if she believed she was doing so just to satisfy some earthly or worldly motherly instinct that gave pleasure. Rather, it would be justified in her mind only if it required a sacrifice and was for the good of my soul. I wasn't sure how, but I hoped the lunches would serve that purpose.

Our relationship has remained on good solid terms ever since that day. A year later, when I was getting ready to go to California, where I had accepted a job, we spent a few long hours talking. At that time, I was very upset about what had happened to the one Little Brother who had been in my class from my earliest memories and until the day I left the Center.

The news had come to me through his mother. One Sunday after Mass at the Center she stopped me in the vestibule and poured out her heart. I was stunned. Last week, her only son, I'll call him John, age twenty-four, had gone berserk. She was awakened one night by crashing noises. When she came downstairs, she found him stark naked, hurling his heavy weights against the walls of the house. Before long, his two sisters and his father and mother were wrestling with him, but he was too powerful, and it took several police officers to subdue him. His mother said he was now in the state mental hospital under heavy sedation. It was rumored that he had been given LSD.

I suspected it was worse than that: that the pressure of adjusting to the world after all the Center-imposed guilt complexes had been too much. He had cracked.

My brother Paul and I went to visit him two weeks later. Paul had already seen him several days earlier, and his description of John's plight horrified me. He said John was in despair, didn't want to live, was tied down hands and feet, was vomiting and pouring out sweat like Paul had never dreamed humanly possible.

The cold green elevator opened onto an empty hallway. We knocked on the door and were led down a large room of white beds, all empty except for one. At the end was John. His situation had improved, but his condition was pitiful. I tried to hide my shock as I looked into his glazed eyes. He just moaned and gave no sign of recognizing me. All the while he kept flexing his muscles, doing a kind of sit-up, as though he were trying to get out. Several days' growth of beard covered his face.

Paul saw that I couldn't handle the situation, and moved in to talk to him. As Paul encouraged him, John responded well.

As we were walking back down the corridor, one of the white-coated doctors asked me if I had been "raised in the same place." I said I had. He stared at me as though expecting some abnormality, then nodded. We moved on. Outside, I heard John's relatives (who had visited him just before we arrived) talking very bitterly. One woman said that John had threatened, in his delirium, to go back and kill Father Feeney and Sister Catherine, who had been dead for six years. "I could put the gun in his hand right now," one woman exclaimed.

The last time I spoke to Sister Mary Agnes before leaving

for California I could only talk about John. Tears came to her eyes as she heard and watched me describe John's predicament, and she begged me not to go back and visit him again. I said that all John needed was a beautiful girl whom he could really love and who would really love him. I guess I said that because I remembered his mother asking Michael and me to double-date with John. She wanted us to help him get started. But we hadn't. At that time I wasn't dating, as MIT was my total preoccupation. Michael felt it would be better if each of the Center children would handle his or her own problems.

Now I regretted that I had been so insensitive. I recalled the frustrations and depressions I had gone through. My only escape had been the challenge of MIT. But John never had that, and it had gotten to him.

Sister Mary Agnes seemed deeply concerned, both for John and about my worries over John. I told her I thought that John's problem had begun during all the violent dissension inside the Center. (He had been advised to leave when the Brothers found out that he had spent a whole night rowing up and down the Nashua River, comtemplating suicide.) Now he was furious at the Center and had threatened revenge. Sister said that she had heard about it and that they were careful to keep all the doors locked. "Of course," she added, "he's not malicious, he just can't help it—the poor boy."

I did go to see John the day before I left for California. He had bounced back beautifully in only nine weeks. Though still very nervous, his muscles still tight from the drugs he used, he seemed almost his old self. He winked a smile to me when I made a joke about some dictum we'd learned in philosophy class. We ended our short visit with a game of Ping-Pong, at which he beat me easily. "You've been practicing," I kidded, and he nodded a mischievous yes. The visit was as pleasant as the first one was scary.

When I departed from the Center, from my mother, from my friends, I told them that I intended to enjoy life from now on. Really. I would work less, I vowed, and spend more time in recreation.

One ex-Center member warned me not to go to California because it would corrupt my morals. I assured her that I was quite capable of resisting. But, deep in my heart, I was hoping that I would be corrupted—at least for a while. I felt

I had to swing to the other extreme, even if just temporarily, in order to get rid of my hang-ups and my terrible attacks of guilt.

My corruption officially began, at the age of twenty-four, when I went so far as to look at a *Playboy* centerfold—and to find out by accident what it meant to masturbate. In California, I hoped to do much worse, or was it better? I wasn't quite sure. The way I looked at life was beginning to change, and for that I felt grateful.

Chapter Ten

Before I left the Center, the strongest lure of the world on the outside was the idea that someday I might meet a beautiful girl, fall in love, and get married. At times it had felt as if that lure were all but pulling me out of the Center. Yet, one month before I graduated from MIT, and three years after I'd left the Center, I realized that I had put such a low priority on dating that, with the exception of Mary Kristine, I'd had only one date in all that time.

The problem was that, though meeting beautiful women had impressed me as the most exciting thing I could think of, it was at the same time the most frightening thing. As a result, I always found more important things to do, like a hot time with a calculus textbook. My failure with Kris had made me certain that I would fail with others. At least Kris understood me because she had been raised in the same place, but another girl would never be able to relate to the way I thought.

The result was that I didn't even try for dates, and did not have my second date at MIT until a couple of weeks before graduation.

My first date at MIT was with an undergraduate with dark hair and a fondness for pants that hugged her shapely thighs. I was to meet her at her coed dormitory, but when I got there, I was afraid to go inside for fear that a Friday-night sex orgy would be in progress. So I waited outside. When she came out a half-hour later, she chided me for not coming up to her room. She said that she had been waiting. That comment began a physical reaction on my part, one that was enhanced by the familiar way she put her arm about my waist and occasionally farther down.

Everything went smoothly—at first. We had a nice dinner, then I bought her her favorite peppermint ice cream at Friendly's, and after that we went to a nightclub for drinks and dancing. It was while we were sitting in the nightclub that I first became really frightened.

She suggested that we go back to the dorm and relax a bit, maybe watch some television. That wasn't too bad, but then she said that she loved living in the dorm because there were so many guys around, but that she definitely did not like guys with cold hands. "Nothing turns me off more," she said quietly, "than having a guy put cold clammy hands on my body."

I groaned inwardly. What she was talking about was a mortal sin, and I thought she wanted me to do it with her. If I refused, I would make a fool of myself. And if I tried and didn't do it right, then the word would get around that I was odd, that there was something wrong with me.

I tried to use up time by dancing. I got out on the floor and jumped around, waving my arms, head, and shoulders in the crazy, humiliating way everyone else was doing it. She in turn wiggled and writhed in a most tantalyzing manner. Occasionally she gave me a look and smiled as though she believed I understood what was going on.

I wanted to let her know that I liked her dancing; so, after the dance, I kissed her. She parted her lips a bit, making it a rather messy kiss, and I promptly wiped my mouth. She gave me an insulted look. Quickly, I realized that wiping off the remnants of a juicy kiss was not the thing to do, but it was too late. After that, she became disinterested, said she was tired, and wanted to go back. The date ended when I walked her to the main entrance of the dorm and said good-bye. The next time I asked her for a date she refused, saying bluntly that I was too straight for her. Actually, I had been planning to be more daring, but I never got the chance.

Except for occasional dates with Kris, I didn't date again for well over a year, but I did pick up more information about sex.

I had come a long way from the first time I had heard the word "sex." That occurred in February 1965, when I was fifteen years old. It was my first month away from the Center, and I had to fill out an application form for St. Vincent's High School in Akron, Ohio. On the printed form the word "sex" was followed by two boxes marked M and F. I asked Grandpa what the boxes were for—was it applicable to me? He said I was a boy—a male—and should check the M box.

I didn't know the word "sex" because the Center had always said "gender."

After seven months in the world, I finally realized that it was natural for men to be attracted to women, and that there was a real biological difference—a tantalizing incentive, even. I knew women had bigger breasts, but I wondered what they had elsewhere. The backside seemed to be shaped like ours, but I suspected there might be something different up front. I found out years later that my brother Matthew beat me to that discovery. One of the neighbors' children at the Souers' cottage on the lake in Indiana offered to play doctor, and showed herself to him. He, aged eleven, was shocked at the revelation. His first thought, he told me, was: how does she tuck it in? He refused to play the game.

I never actually had visual knowledge of a woman's entire body until two years after I had left the Center. I was twenty-three. One night I went to an X-rated movie, paid the $3.50, looked around to make sure no one was watching me, and then entered the small theater. I could almost feel the angels in heaven trying to hold me back, but I was determined to learn about the secrets of a woman's body. I already had a rough idea from the electric-plug analogy, but I wanted to find out precisely just where the receptacle part was. I knew it was somewhere under the panties, but just where and how to get to it was what I hoped to see.

The first picture on the screen showed a woman wearing what I later learned was called a dildo. I could see it was artificial, but I was greatly confused, especially when a second woman came into the act. What horrified me even more was when they started using their mouths instead of doing it the proper way. Finally, one of the women strapped the mechanical penis on and they "did it right." I had learned what I needed to know, and literally shaking with guilt, I promptly left the theater. I couldn't have been there more than ten minutes. I went to Confession the next day.

However, that was only a picture, so six months later I decided I need to see it live. I went into a bar in the combat zone, where, I had been told, people made love on stage. Instead, a woman pranced around on the table, gradually removing her clothes, which I found exciting but at the same time frightening.

The bartender charged me *two* dollars, a fortune for one bottle of beer. (I hardly ever drank; I hated beer, which the rest of the world was crazy about and only drank it on the rare Connor brother reunions.) Apparently, he expected me to down the whole bottle immediately and order another. Then, just as the woman on the table started to undo her panties, a young woman sat down beside me and asked if I wanted company. "No, thank you, I'm fine," I said, and turned and stared at the bare buttocks walking above me. I noticed the woman wasn't totally naked, but had some stringlike covering that she never took off.

When a second woman wanted to give me her company, I became scared and left. I speculated that they would lead me into some dark corridor, promising the delights of sex. Someone behind a door could easily club me over the head and steal my money. Though I felt very guilty about that experience, I justified it as part of my education. I should know at least *something* about the real world of sin.

In May 1974, the last month before I left for California, I decided it was time to try dating again. Of course, no permanent relation could result, but it would be good practice for the millions of opportunities I envisioned were awaiting me out on the West Coast. It was a Friday-night dance at the Harvard Law School. As I stood watching the young people doing their thing, I noticed a pretty blonde who seemed bored. She was small, slim, and looked about eighteen. I later found out she was a sophomore at a local university. We hit it off well. We danced a few times . . . when I wasn't casually bragging about my stupendous achievements at MIT.

Within the next couple of weeks we saw each other several times for ice cream and the like. She was beautiful all over, at least from what her clothes revealed, and I was anxious to know more. But I couldn't figure out how to begin. Then, a week before my departure, she wrote me asking if we could get together some weekend night. I was convinced the time had come. I called her up and we decided to meet at her dorm on a Friday night. Friday night, the time when all the other students around the country have their good times! My turn had come at last. It had taken so long. Three years had elapsed since I left the Center, and I was now twenty-four.

But first I had to get a condom . . . probably several. I didn't know how many times she might want to do it. It would be very embarrassing buying them. I didn't know what kind or size to get. Maybe, I thought, they sold a standard size, like with stretch socks.

The lady at the drugstore counter seemed surprised at my casual request for condoms. I had hoped she would view it as my weekly refill order. Perhaps I didn't pronounce it right. I repeated it, regretting with each passing second that I had ever tried to purchase them. She said that I was really looking for "prophylactics." As her loud words rang through the store, I felt all eyes fall on me. Now everyone thought that I was planning to commit that terrible sin, and I turned red with embarrassment. Here was Brother Luke, caught in a store, making plans to fornicate. If I turned around and apologized, they would laugh at me. If I said that I might never get to use them after all or that I was using them for balloons and not for what they were thinking, they would never believe me.

I calmed myself by accepting the public image of sinner, and I quietly repeated my request. I don't know how I got through the rest of it. I do know that I was told there were several brands and types. I believe I asked for nothing fancy, just the regular kind. "A dozen would be fine, yes."

The next question was, would I get to use any of them that night? At one point I thought I was getting pretty close. We had been talking for some time, sitting on the edge of her bed in her room. The door was closed and her roommate gone. I was simply infatuated by the beauty of her face as well as the rest of her, so forbiddenly contained in her tight white sweater and green slacks. Suddenly she asked if I wanted to visit "the lower part of the campus." Could it be she was using sexual code words?

I thought she was getting impatient for me to make my move, so I placed my hand under her long blond hair and touched the warm smooth skin on the back of her neck. Then I moved in closer and kissed her. I did it again, and she did not object. As I continued, and my breathing increased quite noticeably, she gently pushed me back, saying I shouldn't go too far. I told her that I thought she was beautiful and that I wanted her to treat me like any other boyfriend. I wanted to be as intimate with her as she would like. I wanted to see more of her beautiful body.

She stiffened, paused, then looked toward the door. I was embarrassed by what I had said, but maybe that was the only way she would ever find out how far I was willing to go. I looked her over. What a beautiful sight, I thought, if she now undressed before me.

"Okay," she said. "What would you like to see?"

I gulped with surprise at her mind-reading ability and her casual readiness to show me what I wanted. In a flash I imagined her standing naked before me, hiding nothing and sharing and trusting herself to me. She spoke again before I could answer.

"Would you like to see the lower part?"

"Sure," I could barely say it.

She stood up, and I felt all the energy drain from me. I felt too weak to talk. Would she really take off her pants?

She pointed to the door. "Well, let's get our coats. It will be cold walking down to the lower campus."

One week later I was on the road to California. All my possessions were packed in my Rambler station wagon, but there was a lot of room left over. I didn't own much. My belongings consisted mainly of some old clothes, a pair of shoes I had worn every day for the last three years, a pair of skates, an eight-dollar pair of wooden skis, a nine-dollar tennis racket, and my little clock radio. I sent my books, notes, and other paper files to California by mail.

But the best part of the trip was that I wasn't alone. Because driving tired my eyes, I had asked around for someone to help with the driving and expenses. To my surprise, Kris offered to come, and I was thrilled. We kept it a secret, so Center people wouldn't be scandalized, but she did tell her parents, and in fact we stopped to visit them on the way.

We had eased off our relationship, or rather, I had given up on my pursuit of her. But suddenly she seemed to change her attitude toward me. The night she suggested going with me I had been parading around the room in mock sophistication, wearing a flashy white sports jacket with a light pattern of multicolored lines, which was a graduation present from the Doyles, with whom I had lived for three years. Perhaps she liked it, I thought. More probably she saw a different person in me, now that my studies were over and I was feeling good.

Usually I was tense and worried. But now I had a degree, a good job with a large electronics company, and a graduate fellowship to pay my way for a master's degree at Stanford University in glamorous sunny California. Though I owed over six thousand dollars to friends, the bank, and MIT, I wasn't concerned; I knew I could pay it off eventually with my new job. Also, I tended to live very simply. I had no need for TV, stereo, expensive cars or other items I considered more as fads than real needs. At the most, I might get a stereo someday. With my low expenses I would be able to save.

Now everything ahead looked good. Somehow I felt that all my hang-ups from my Center days would be dissolved by the California environment. I would be normal like others—dating and perhaps even sleeping with my girlfriends.

I wondered if there would be any pattern to the kind of women I was attracted to. Kris had been a nun, and there was a new Sister at the Center I found interesting. Maybe nuns would excite me the most. However, none of the ex-Little Sisters showed interest in dating any of the Little Brothers. The only pattern I could observe was their interest in uniformed men. Most of them either were dating policemen or servicemen or were interested in becoming officers or entering the army. This was true with five out of the eight I saw most often. Perhaps it was because the only non-Center men they saw in their early teens were the troops at Fort Devens, the firemen, or the men in the military parades and in scenes of the Center's movies.

In my case, I found the appearance of holy innocence and purity highly stimulating sexually. Worldly women ready to show it all did not appeal to me, but shy ones, afraid to expose anything, had just the opposite effect.

Leaving Massachusetts meant leaving everyone I had known all my life. I would be lonely, I was sure, but there was one ex-Center couple in California, and I could visit them. However there were good feelings about leaving the Center area. The Center people represented a pillar of moral uprightness, and what I wanted most was to loosen up my conscience, or to suspend its function temporarily. I wanted to put out of my mind for a time all the fears of God's punishments, and all the reminders of good moral behavior. I wasn't going to change my religious beliefs—that was the coward's way when he tried to justify his wicked actions. Rather, I would be a sinner for a while and hope that God would let me live through it.

Sin would make me a whole person so that I could find a wife and have a family and happiness. The sins I intended to commit as often as I could and as soon as I could were the sins of the flesh. I wanted to make love, develop the art of erotic play, and simply have a fantastic time. I wanted to make up for all the lost opportunities of the last ten years.

Kris and I left for California on June 1, 1974. We had a beautiful two-week vacation traveling across the country. We took the boat at Niagara Falls, went water-skiing in Indiana, spent a quiet evening by a fireplace at Mount Rushmore while looking out at the Presidents' faces glaring white in the dark night sky. We toured the Jewel Cave 380 feet below the ground, saw the geysers of Yellowstone Park, the Mormon choir (and Vice-President Ford) in Salt Lake City, the high sierras of California, the Golden Gate Bridge, the gaudy nightclubs of San Francisco, the beautiful wild coastline of California, the extravagant wealth of the Hearst Castle at San Simeon, and finally the vineyards and mountains around Cucamonga in Southern California, where we ended our trip.

Kris had indicated to me early in the trip that there would be no fooling around. Yet often, as I became absorbed in the beauty of a sunset or an early morning, I thought that a personal love and affection would make things perfect. A couple of times I tried to put my arm around her, but I could feel her freeze. I was sorry the friendship had to be platonic, but at least it was a friendship.

Kris decided to stay on in California for the summer. She got a job as a nurse and stayed with the ex-Center couple in Cucamonga, California. On weekends, we would occasionally get together for a day of sailing or relaxation at the beach. But my interest in her—which had lasted for nine years—finally dwindled. At last, I was convinced that both of us had difficulty expressing our feelings and that we would be better off looking to non-Center people for a close intimate relationship. I had troubles enough without compounding them with hers. I told her it was all my fault, and she wrote me a parting note at the end of the summer, saying we should still remain good friends. Although I hadn't asked for any, she gave me a few bits of advice about not trying so hard and being my natural self. At the time I was offended by this gratuitous advice, but later I saw that she was right.

That first summer in California, the summer of 1974, was the beginning of a more comfortable life-style. My main objective was to find and nurture the most fertile environment for indulging in the pleasures of the flesh. I got an apartment in Playa del Rey within easy biking distance of the beach. One of those big "swinging singles complexes" well-known in California, it had heated pools, lighted tennis courts, a recreation center with poolroom, lounges, TV room, and a bar for parties. There was a gym, saunas, and Jacuzzis that went coed on Friday night. The place was swarming with pilots and pretty airline stewardesses. Everything was there for the maximization of the pleasures of life. My interest was so single-minded that I initially read the "message center" to be the "massage center."

Then I involved myself with flashy hobbies. I started taking flying lessons, but had to give them up because of the expense. I entered a sailing club and passed all the tests so I could rent any of a fleet of twenty-five-foot yachts for the weekends. They were equipped with ship-to-shore radio, had stereo music, and could sleep up to six. In my mind they were the most impressive display of the affluent life.

Moreover, I loved sailing, and nothing thrilled me more than a close-hauled tack with main and jib trimmed just right, and the feel of high winds and high waves. The heavy boat would rise and dive through the swells, sending cold waves splashing across the deck and drenching my clothes. That was excitement and beauty all at once. I was battling nature at its own game. It was just wind, waves, the design of the boat, and my own skill.

When I wasn't sailing or flying, I was biking the miles of paved paths running along the beach from Santa Monica down to Torrance, on the ten-speed bicycle I had bought for one hundred dollars.

My job, unfortunately, was less glamorous. I worked as an engineer testing electronic flight parts for communication satellites, and when the challenge of the work wore off in a couple of months, I became bored. However, the pay was quite good, and I knew that at the end of the summer the company would be sending me to graduate school at Stanford University, which was four-hundred miles north of the Los Angeles area where I worked.

I was impressed by how considerate the company's management was. I expected that only company issues would be important to them, but they took a great interest in my extracurricular activities. In fact, the director of the fellowship office shared my enthusiasm for sailing, and occasionally he would take some of us sailing in the evening on his thirty-four-foot yacht.

My social life, however, didn't improve, no matter how hard I tried. The young stewardesses at the apartment complex seemed more interested in the older wealthy men tanning themselves in their chairs around the pool. I felt that there was a clique of the elite, and I was excluded because I was a stranger. Eventually, I spent most of my time looking elsewhere for possible girlfriends. In the day I met women in stores, at work, or on the beach. At night I hit most of the many chic nightspots in Marina del Rey, where dancing, drinks, and available single women abounded. But they were too unreal and stereotyped for me. I got sick of that scene and tried the more offbeat bars in beach towns like Manhattan Beach.

One night I hit it off well with a beautiful dark-haired young woman who was training to be a stewardess. Our conversation was just getting better when a blond young man a few years older than I with a deep tan and white teeth moved in and took over. His manners were smooth and familiar, and I could see her becoming enchanted with him. I held on, desperately pretending I was still part of the conversation. He offered to take her to a quieter place where they could sit down and listen to an excellent guitarist while they watched the moon over the Pacific. She turned to me and asked if I wanted to come along, and I readily agreed. She then found another girl, who turned out to be her companion that evening, and the four of us walked off to the bar on the hill.

I was furious at ending up with a woman I wasn't interested in. The blond guy walked ahead with his arm wrapped about the slim waist of the woman I wanted. Occasionally he would whisper something in her ear, and she would give him a fresh smile. In the bar, we sat at a table and talked for an hour or more. The blond demonstrated his suave manners, and, impulsively, I tried to talk all of them into a sail in my boat the following day, a Saturday.

They thought sailing sounded like fun, and I was convinced I had won back the interest of the dark-haired girl. But as we left the bar to go to our cars, the blond took her aside. When the two of them didn't show up at the street corner, I walked back and found them tightly embraced, kissing, looking into each other's eyes, chatting a bit, and then repeating the act. They finally joined our party and we dispersed. They never showed up for the sailing, and I wrote my first love letter, telling the beautiful black-haired woman (whose address I had managed to get) how much I admired her. She never replied.

Such failures were repeated again and again. Usually, I could get an initial interest, maybe even one date, but then it fell apart. I wasn't sure what went wrong, but invariably the women lost interest. I guess my inexperience showed.

I compensated for my loneliness by writing letters to my friends and my brothers. I told fantastic comical tales about my social ineptitude—and uncontrolled enthusiasm—stumbling over and falling on top of luscious bodies lying on the beach "funny side up," wrestling with secretaries under the desk, or thrashing in bed with a date after being so stoned that I saw double and therefore had to "contend with four breasts and four legs instead of two." Or I would imagine myself sitting by the surf as a beautiful female body strode by, and with the push of a button on my latest invention, I would cause radio-controlled snaps on her skimpy bikini to suddenly release, leaving her standing naked before me.

At times I wondered if I were just more horny than lonely. I remember one night going to a strip show on Sunset Boulevard in West Hollywood and staring in tantalized amazement as a slim beautiful female writhed on the little stage. Her pretty face was offering little puckering kisses as she seductively undressed. When she reached for the final lingering black panties, the suspense was almost unbearable. Even those came off. She was totally naked, right there, only ten feet away. I was twenty-four years old and I knew many males my age had women like her every night. The thought caused waves of depression and desperation to sweep through me, as I wondered why I couldn't have my own woman to share everything with me. I resolved to keep trying, but I kept failing. Yet I wouldn't give up. I finally became convinced the problems lay with me and not the world outside. I wanted to know how to change.

I thought my social life would be easier once I got to Stanford, but it wasn't. After two months of studying for my master's degree in electrical engineering, I decided I had had enough. I was the image of future success as far as job, fellowship, and future career were concerned, but as a person I was a flop. If I couldn't bring the one thing into my life that I wanted most—love—then nothing else mattered. To hell with my job, my fellowship, and all the "prestige" I had enjoyed. I resolved to quit, to become a dropout, to be a bum for a while in the hope that I could expand as a human being.

It was like MIT all over again. I was racing through a tough program in engineering, and I was again putting social life aside. As I biked back and forth to school in the warm sunlight and watched students embracing one another, my loneliness became almost unbearable. Though I took great pride in my scholastic accomplishments, I was actually ready to throw it all over. Besides, I argued with myself, I really didn't want to be an engineer; I found it too boring, I wanted to go into business, to work with people and not cold inanimate oscilloscopes. I decided to drop out of the fellowship program, take some time off, and then enter business school. I would get my master's in business administration, an M.B.A. I felt that the company would respect my decision and let me go. Or maybe they would sponsor me through business school. After all, I reasoned, they needed good managers as well as engineers.

The company was upset and a bit confused by my sudden change. I spent a whole day speaking to various executives. They seemed impressed by my determination. What they didn't know was that I had nothing to lose. I would be perfectly happy being dropped from my job and my fellowship. I wouldn't mind bumming around for a while. But one farsighted company executive decided to back me. I would have to finish my master's in electrical engineering first, but then they would give me a two-year fellowship for my M.B.A.

I was very grateful for his support, and I resolved to suppress my social problems for a while. I had a new and exciting challenge and I was going to show the company that their confidence in me was worth it.

At first my spirits improved, but then, while I was finishing my master's degree in electrical engineering, I became extremely lonely. Life had come down to a bitter internal struggle over how to open up and express my feelings, how to show that I could love, and how to receive the love that I wanted so much.

At times in my loneliness I burst into waves of silent tears as the extent of my desperation suddenly hit me. It could be triggered by the sight of young high-school lovers, their arms around each other. I would think of how much youthful joy in love I had missed. More often my tears came when I heard some plaintive love song on the radio. If only I could have some love in my life, I would think. My feelings would come to the surface, and if I were alone, I wouldn't try to control them. I would cry quietly to myself without fear of being laughed at for being so moved by trite sentimentality.

I wanted to change my way of life, to somehow find a woman I could love and who could really love me. I had gradually come to believe that my problem was psychological and emotional, that I somehow feared women without really knowing why.

I had finally thrown over my religion, at least temporarily, because I had to get rid of any rational guilt feelings about indulging in sex if the opportunity ever arose. But it never did. I think I disgusted or frightened my dates: I either was too aloof, barely shaking her hand, or too desperate, suddenly lunging for a good-night kiss. She must have thought I was weird, I would think afterward.

I became convinced that sexual intercourse was the key to releasing my inhibitions. If somehow I could get in bed with a woman and learn what it was all about, then I could be more relaxed just talking to them. There wouldn't be that terrible conflict every time I saw a beautiful woman, and I would wonder if I could ever really make love to her. I was so obsessed with that question that no matter how I tried to convince myself it was the last thing on my mind, I still knew that it was just the opposite. Even though it was also the most frightening, I had to do it. Otherwise, I thought, I would never stop sweating and trembling when I was face-to-face with a real, live, beautiful woman. It was embarrassing, seeing my sweaty handprints on everything I touched, or trying to control the trembling fork as I ate my meal across the restaurant table from my date.

My physical fear, I think, came from the emotional conflict between how exciting sex might be and the horror of actually doing something so forbidden and so gross. Many times I thought of overcoming this by going to prostitutes. But that seemed degrading. I really wanted sex with someone I could love. What I needed was the love and intimacy of a woman, not the indifferent and impersonal thrill of bought sex.

Oddly, though, I thought I could somehow buy love. If my behavior seemed awkward to a woman, certainly my generosity would more than compensate, I thought. So, even in my poorest days I would spend lavishly on a date. Later, at Stanford, I would take a first date to an expensive restaurant and casually dismiss the cost as a trifle. But it didn't work, I gradually learned, because the dates weren't interested in my money but in me as a person. They wanted to know my innermost feelings—and that was the last thing I wanted to expose.

All my life I had prided myself on my stoical determination to get ahead, to achieve the goals I set for myself. Nothing fazed me. I was cool and collected, though obviously very enthusiastic and motivated. I wore a facade as my defense against anyone who might want to hurt me, something I had done since early childhood. I had learned to manipulate my superiors through controlled emotions so I would be spared punishment and get what I wanted. Now, I discovered that love (which seemed to be the real key to my happiness) could only be achieved if I let down my defenses, if I exposed my weaknesses, if I let myself become vulnerable.

It was extremely difficult, and the first time I tried it, I recoiled when it backfired. At Stanford, I found a friend to whom I felt I could open up. I told him about my unusual upbringing, my longing for the love of a woman, my innocence, and the fact that I was still a virgin at the age of twenty-four. During the Christmas vacation of 1974, we rented a ski cabin along with some other Stanford students. It was a lonely but peaceful three-week vacation in the high sierras in California. The skiing was poor, so we often hiked into the mountains, sometimes in the middle of the night with the temperature below freezing, the moon shining over quiet Lake Tahoe. The air was deathly still, almost shocked by the crunch of our feet on the ridges at seven thousand feet.

One night, as we were sitting around the fireplace, the conversation of the all-male group turned to women. I pretended, as I always did, that I was as familiar with women as I presumed they were. But, for some reason, my friend told the others I was a virgin, and joined in when everyone laughed at me. I wasn't as hurt by their ridicule as I was by his betrayal. He probably never realized it was such a sensitive point for me, but I never forgot. That experience made me close up for a while.

Five months later, in May 1975, I let down my guard again. This time I opened up to a woman, and finally it was a rewarding experience. I had met her at a party, had asked her to join me for an afternoon at the beach, and even though she agreed to the date, I was expecting failure as usual. It would be a tense awkward afternoon, I presumed, and she would never want to see me again.

As I drove to the beach with our bread and wine packed in the back, I found myself surprisingly relaxed because this girl was so carefree. She didn't seem to care about my nervousness, and in fact she even joked about it in a way that made me laugh at myself without embarrassment. I began to open up, and talked and talked about what bothered me. I couldn't believe her reaction. She wanted to hear more. And she seemed to like me the more I revealed.

After a while, as we lay on an abandoned beach, fully clothed (it was a chilly day), she seemed less interested in my story and more in me. At one point she looked me right in the eyes and touched my head, saying nothing as she slid her fingers through my hair and stroked my neck. She seemed to be saying she saw something lovable in me. It was an overwhelming experience. In that instant, I felt that I really loved her. Before I knew it, we were caressing and kissing.

The beach stretched on for miles in both directions. Behind us were sharply rising cliffs that sent back the crashing sound of the waves. It was typical California coastline in the San Francisco area: hardly any trees, except a few beautifully stark and windswept pines clinging to the edges of the cliffs.

What happened next is vividly impressed on my mind . . . as is the strange thought I had at the time. I imagined Sister Catherine and the Angels would be watching by my car, which was parked on the edge of the hill. Sister Catherine would be carrying her black bag with the Big Punisher, ready to give me what I deserved. But in reality there wasn't a soul around, except the two of us lying on the blankets.

The sun had come out and the day had gotten warmer. When she had first looked at me so lovingly, I was ready to cry with relief and happiness. But soon passion overcame me. She didn't mind when I stripped to my briefs, and when I groped under her shirt to undo her bra, she obligingly rolled over. I had to study the clip for a while before I could disconnect it. It was certainly an awkward moment, but she was very understanding. She must have been amused as I sat straddled across her, looking at her naked breasts and fondling them in amazement. The very idea that I was touching the real naked breasts of a woman was almost impossible to comprehend. They were so much softer than I expected.

I wanted her to enjoy the experience. I wanted to show her I cared and could make her happy too. Remembering something I'd read, I tried to arouse her by licking her nipples, but she just giggled as though I were tickling her. When I reached down to undo her jeans, she sat up. "Oh, no, no, no. You're quite an aggressive little devil for all your shyness." That rebuke ended our session for the afternoon. But it was a wonderful day.

We remained close friends, visiting each other often until school was out. However, she managed to avoid any occasions that might lead to a repeat or further development of that delightful experience on the beach. After that, I was far less inhibited about seeing the naked female body.

The summer of 1975 was quite adventurous for me. I joined my company's ski club and spent weekends water-skiing or sailing. We water-skied on the Colorado River in Arizona, where the contrast of the cold water and the dry desert air was delightful. One weekend we chartered a ninety-foot yacht and sailed to Catalina Island, twenty-two miles off the coast of Southern California. Another time we took a three-day cruise on a sixty-foot catamaran. In the evening we drank and danced on the wide boat.

That same summer I crewed for several sailing-enthusiast friends of mine in the company who liked to race their boats. I spent two days running the rapids of the Colorado River through the Grand Canyon, traveling fifty-seven miles down the river. On my way to the launching point on the river I stopped at Las Vegas and enjoyed one of their fabulous dinner shows. Beautiful naked women danced all over the constantly changing stage. But I remember very clearly that nothing that summer impressed me more than the awesome beauty of Yosemite Valley. Its grandeur cannot be described. I may have been somewhat preoccupied with thoughts of sex those days, but I was not blind to the rest of life.

In September 1975, I was caught up once again in the pressure and the routine of studies, this time at the Stanford Graduate School of Business. The competition was tough, but I enjoyed the challenge (and the opportunity to forget about my personal problems for a while). By January, however, after five months of monkish living, I had to face the fact that

I was running away from the tension caused by attempting a normal social life.

I resolved to do better, but my good intentions were not enough. I slid through the rest of the school year without dating or making any close male friends. I maintained my contact with my brothers through letters and phone calls, and used the rigor of study as a shell to hide within. I was beginning to look upon my loneliness as a necessary predicament that would always be a part of my life.

That thought, when it truly hit home, scared me more than anything had in years. It was then, the summer of 1976, that I realized I had better take some time off and do whatever it took to pull my life together.

I decided that writing a book about my strange past, my unusual upbringing, might provide me with the best chance of finding out why it was so damnably hard for me to open up emotionally to another human being. I wanted to dig up all the buried thoughts and feelings and lay them bare; I vowed to confront my hang-ups . . . and to overcome them. But to do this, to even have a chance of doing this, I needed to be free of deadlines and schedules. And if I should be lucky enough to meet an interesting girl, I wanted to be able to drop *everything* else and pursue that relationship.

During the summer of my writing, my self-induced therapy, I passed one barrier that had come to seem all but insurmountable. I engaged in sexual intercourse for the first time. Perhaps it is significant that up until it happened I had always used the phrase "making love," but when it finally happened, it was more carnal that spiritual.

I was twenty-six years old and I had been out in the world for almost five years. I no longer thought, as I did in the fall of 1971, that an attractive woman seen on the street was a walking mortal sin. I had come to think of sex as the inevitable and ultimate expression of the deep emotion of love. But, that summer, I came to see that that view was not exactly right either, at least for me at that time. Finally, I came to the conclusion that sex represented a cure that I desperately needed.

I reasoned that once the trauma of the mystery of sex was over, then I could expand as a person and pay more attention to the personality of the woman, which I considered the most important factor in developing a deep relation. Though sex would be fun, love is what would make sex really ecstatic.

I had suspected, though, that sex was probably a pretty exciting experience even in its own right. Certainly the whole world seemed to be fascinated by it. It was hinted at or exploited as a come-on in a million different ways in our society. There *had* to be something to it. For centuries, religions had tried to suppress its pleasures as though sex was so deliriously overwhelming that it took the fears of horrifying eternal torments to keep it in check. I wanted that forbidden experience badly, and one summer night I abandoned myself to its iniquity.

I had always imagined that my first total sexual experience would be the culmination of an overpowering, passionate romance with a young and beautiful California woman. Her figure would be the Hollywood ideal: luring sexuality barely contained in revealing clothes. In part it came true and in part it didn't. She wasn't from California, though her beautifully proportioned body was wonderfully obvious beneath her skimpy clothes. I did not have any feelings of love toward her, but I certainly did want to make love to her.

There is something about a woman's face that holds the secret to my attraction. It isn't just beauty or prettiness. It may be sensuality, but certainly not anything artificial. One thing I'm sure of: it's the sensitivity of the personality I think I see in the face. When I love a woman, I see only her face. If later I discover something about her that really annoys me, then her face seems to change, and she no longer appears attractive. The woman I first made love to had a very pretty face, but she seemed emotionless. But then, reality rarely satisfied our dreams, and I had nurtured this dream a very long time.

I met her in a movie theater. She sat alone in the row in front of me, and looked to be about my age, twenty-six. Her hair was worn in tight curls, a style I've never found attractive, but her eyes were dark and her body exciting. She wore a tight pullover that revealed her nipples. She wore tight denim shorts, cutoff jeans. At the intermission I went out for a Coke. When I returned, she was sitting in the seat next to mine, apparently because someone was in her chair. I sat down and immediately engaged her in a conversation about the last movie.

Before long, I learned that she had come from Colorado, was just passing through Palo Alto, and had borrowed a van from the friends she was traveling with. The others had business in San Francisco, and she planned to spend the evening and the entire next day and night in the Palo Alto area by herself. After the movie we remained seated and just talked. I told her I was on vacation, doing nothing, and would be glad to show her around the area. Gathering up all my courage, I asked to see the van in which she slept. When she readily accepted, somehow I *knew* that my time had come. At first I feared some trouble, but then I decided it was worth the risk. I wasn't going to let this opportunity go. I was lucky.

We sat on the little bed in her van, lighted a candle, and talked for a while. I looked into her eyes for a few moments, saying nothing, and then kissed her. She responded so warmly that I reached up and caressed one of her breasts. She was wearing no bra. Fear flashed through me. Something was wrong, she was too willing.

"You know, I have no particular plans for this evening," I said. "I would really love to spend the night with you."

"Okay," she said.

"I would like to make love to you."

"Well, I hardly know you. Why don't we take things as they come. Right now I'm up for some ice cream."

The ice-cream store had just closed, so we turned into a bar for a drink. She didn't really want one, but I was already trembling all over and I had to calm down. I have no memory of what she ordered, but I know the tequila sunrise I had didn't affect me at all. I did learn that she had been married, but was presently unattached. Her traveling friends seemed to be close to her, but how close I couldn't tell. Suddenly I realized that I didn't need to imagine any deep love between us; it was more than enough that being together was pleasant and sexually appealing.

Back in the van we decided to drive to a parking lot in Rinconada Park, where it would be quieter. There we made preparations to sleep for the night. The van had a rooftop vent that let in light from a nearby streetlamp. I could clearly see her breasts when she took off her sweater and climbed under the blanket. I removed all my clothes except my briefs and joined her on the narrow bed. I was already trembling, but I was going to see this through to its conclusion.

I don't want to describe everything that went on, for it took many hours. However, it took so long not because of my sudden skill, but because of my inexperience and nervousness. Though we kissed and embraced, even changing position several times, I didn't dare reach for any part other than her breasts. She kept telling me to relax.

"Your muscles are so hard. I've never seen anything like it. Can't you relax a bit?"

I tried to, but one hour later it was no better. Two hours later I was getting exhausted, but still she said my muscles were as hard as rocks. The tension was almost unbearable, and my head started to pound and ache. Finally, I decided to tell her that I was a virgin, that this was my first time, and that for some reason I was really scared. At first she laughed in disbelief.

"Well, you sure didn't strike me that way in the beginning with your aggressive manner. I don't think I've ever gotten into bed with a man so quickly."

I told her more about my background and she reacted in a very sympathetic manner. She seemed to understand my great difficulty, and when she said that she would help me relax, I felt tears coming to my eyes. It all seemed too good to be true.

By the third hour she began to get drowsy, but she still insisted I hadn't even begun to loosen up. So we decided to try to catch some sleep. It was about 2:00 A.M., I guessed, but I couldn't sleep. I kept changing my position. She could feel it, because she kept one arm wrapped about me, sometimes on my chest or shoulders, other times farther down toward my stomach. At times I thought she had fallen asleep, but when I moved, I felt her hands feeling my skin. Then, sometime about 4:00 A.M. she got up, somewhat disgruntled, pulled out a bottle of wine, filled a cup, and drank it. As I watched her sitting upright, her naked breasts catching the light from the roof vent, I became aroused. When I caressed her, she said I seemed much more relaxed. She responded very warmly, kissing me and stroking my back with her hands.

I moved my hands lower down on her body and was surprised to find her jeans completely unbuttoned in front. I could feel my heart pounding in my ears and my breath quicken. I wasn't sure she really wanted me to move my hands all over her, but when she didn't hesitate but even obligingly lifted her weight so I could slip off her pants, I knew she was giving me a chance to make love. Before long her hands were removing my briefs and her delicate fingers were all over me. I was ecstatic. I never imagined it could get that exciting. It was really happening. I was so taut with intense desire to make love to her that I couldn't slow down. I knew that the woman would take longer, but she seemed to be encouraging me with her hands. I entered her, and exploded immediately. However, I was surprised that there wasn't as much pleasure as I had anticipated. It seemed to peak almost instantly, and then it was over.

Almost immediately, I fell asleep. A short while later I awoke as the sunlight started coming in. I lay there, trying to comprehend what had happened. I had the greatest feeling of accomplishment. I had actually done it. I had made love.

We spent that day at the beach, came back to my apartment, took showers, went out to dinner, then returned to my place for the evening. Again my desires got out of control, and I made love to her before she was really ready. She told me I had to be more patient, but I was surprised that it took a woman so long to be aroused. I had worked at it for at least twenty minutes, it seemed. She said it would be different for each woman.

She had to leave the next morning. I felt ashamed that I had made love to her when I really wasn't interested in developing a long-term relationship. But she didn't seem to care. She said her two days in Palo Alto had been "delightful."

I felt inordinately proud.

I had hoped that when I finally had a sexual experience, finally gained a personal knowledge of this most human act that seemed to play such a large part in our culture, it would have a positive effect on my personality. For once I was right. As trite as it may sound, it is the simple truth that afterward I became a different person. Social relations on all levels were suddenly so much easier. I even noticed a new ease when I was with men of my own age, as if the wall of our difference had been toppled, which I guess is pretty much what had happened.

Quite simply, I no longer considered myself such an "odd" person, such a social freak. And, being happier with myself, I could relax more easily and enjoy the company of others. Unfortunately, after a while I had a relapse, but the change was wonderful for as long as it lasted.

In retrospect, I think I went a little overboard. Within a month of that epochal first time, I had relations with two other young women. The sex was great with each of them, but I found myself unable to contain my exuberance, my joy at the fact that I was actually *doing* what I had spent so long thinking about.

My engineering background must have been apparent, for I was subtly advised to stop spending so much time trying to "perfect the art," and both women told me eventually that I should not ask so many questions. They said they were beginning to feel like guinea pigs instead of people.

One woman finally told me that I was a twenty-six-year-old with the sexual maturity of a sixteen-year-old boy. The remark stung, but I knew she was dead right. And, as a matter of fact, I enjoyed the role. It would pass, in time.

My relations with these two women became much more serious. Each time, when I began to see just how much emotional involvement could be at stake, I backed away from the situation. As far as I was concerned, emotionally, it was too much too soon. I was barely able to cope with the impact of the physical side; I could not manage it if someone were to get hurt emotionally on my account. I realized that I was not mature enough to handle a serious committment. It may sound terrible, but all I wanted was variety.

There was another problem: my religious outlook. Actually, I should not say that it was a problem, for it was far less so than my purely (impurely?) physical difficulties had been. Many months before I had met the girl in the camper-van, I had gone through some interesting spiritual-intellectual gymnastics in order to rationalize my new attitudes toward what I had previously looked upon as sinful acts.

I now regarded the act of making love as the most beautiful thing a human could do. I wondered why so many religions and cultures had tried to hide it as though it were something to be ashamed of. Schools all over the country should be teaching people the emotional and psychological aspects of lovemaking as well as the physical.

My idealism got even more extreme. Religion should not be working against God's creative masterpieces by spreading layer upon layer of guilt. We should use religion as a force to strengthen the desires to express love. The concept of original sin, the dignity of virginity, began to seem like warped gropings of human minds and not God's.

The violence, strife, hatreds, and cruelty of religious movements—my own experiences especially included—seemed to be indicators that they were based on man-made principles not on the immutable laws of God. The Center's attitude that the end justifies the means because the end is so important now looked very immoral. The fear of hellfire had turned the Center and other religious movements into un-Godlike regimes.

The idea that I would go to hell for all eternity if I died after bringing such happiness to another person by lovemaking sounded ridiculous. The fact that I would be committing two mortal sins instead of one, by using birth control while making love outside of wedlock, seemed contrary to my own sense of morality. To bring a child into the world who would not have the warmth and care of a family seemed far worse than wearing a condom or taking the pill. The Catholic Church seemed out of touch with reality, and I no longer considered it a divine institution, but one that was human and therefore fraught with human errors.

I started to lead my life according to my own principles of morality—a kind of universal golden rule. I would look at the consequence of my action and go for the greater good. If making love invariably led to unwanted children, I would consider that immoral; but if, through modern technology, there were no evil consequences, then I intended to have sex without feeling guilty. Institutions and beliefs that produced guilt that strangled a person's ability to express his emotions, to show his need for love, and to find happiness in love seemed immoral. For me, immorality no longer meant impurity; it meant antilove.

I ceased going to the sacraments. I left the Catholic Church. I spoke to others, some of whom thought my antireligious attitude was founded on a gross distortion of what Christianity was all about. But I argued to the contrary. The Center was technically correct. It was preaching traditional Catholicism (and the Center's teaching in this area, as well as others, was undeniably excellent). Any reputable scholar could look up the Papal pronouncements, could read the innumerable prayers of the Church and the writings of the saints, and see that the Center was correct and consistent. The Catholic Church had claimed it had divine truths, unchanging dogmas of faith; and now, in our modern era, it was quietly revoking its outdated teachings. If I threw out the Center's traditional version of Catholicism, I had to also throw out the entire Catholic Church, with its claim to unchanging divine truths.

The Center was not to blame; it was the victim of a changing ideology. It had predicted that the institution of the Catholic Church would start to crumble (loss of vocations, and so forth) when the beliefs on which it was based were discarded, and that is just what was happening. Similarly, it was no surprise, at least not to me, to see that the Center's own religious vocations were steadily increasing as conservative Catholics from the outside world became Center members. As long as there was harmony between the Center's beliefs and its structural institution, there would be people who felt justified in making the sacrifices of renouncing the wicked world and becoming a religious. Fear of hell was still the key to the motivation of its members, I felt. If they thought that there was no hell, most of them would leave.

There were times, however, when I realized I was overreacting. I was trying to simplify a most complex situation. Religion has always thrived and always will, because of man's fundamental need to compensate for his unsatisfied desires. Religion offers that escape. When, as a religious, I wanted the love of a woman and realized I couldn't get it, I compensated for my unsatisfied desires by a mental reward of a much better love to be attained after death. Religion was necessary, and I felt that someday I would return to it in one form or another when I needed it. I still feel that way.

I also realized that my idealization of a moral man pursuing his natural desires was naive. The world has evil in it. There are deformed and crippled people. They aren't evil, but their condition is certainly undesirable. There are accidents, mental illnesses, and even that poorly understood concept of "evil desires." Some people want to kill, to steal. Though the cause might be traced to some guiltless source, the fact remains that these desires exist.

The social good is not man's prime motivation. I might want a woman who is happily married. Raping, seducing, or even getting her to make love to me willingly would, if it destroyed her family's happiness, be an evil consequence of my pursuing a very natural impulse.

Therefore, I realized that we have to set up barriers to prevent immoral actions. And religion seems to achieve that end much better than any laws of society, because it enters into the very conscience of man and controls his behavior when there is no ostensible check. Obviously, society benefits from religion. However, a religion that comes from God and one that is needed by us are entirely different ideas.

I was very confused and unhappy that I couldn't find certitudes. I had, I finally admitted, become an agnostic. I still have a great respect for religion, yet I find it despairing to think that religion has to use fear and its consequences in order to ensure a healthy society. What is even more confusing is the question of the object of religious truth. If there is a God Who is interested in us, why has He made everything so ambiguous? Each religion has its answer, but few can claim consistency in its teachings from earliest times—in my mind, a necessary prerequisite for any divine law.

Rather than worry about these things, I ignored them. I led my life as I chose. I decided I would strive after the goodness and beauty of this world, but I would use common sense. Once I'd made that decision, I began to enjoy life much more.

Not long ago, I was sitting in a fine restaurant in Palo Alto. It was evening. Across from me sat an unusually pretty young woman whose personality was every bit as attractive as her face.

She was laughing delightfully as I went through my "baked-potato routine." As an object lesson in maximizing the enjoyment of all natural pleasures, I would provide a running commentary as I ate the potato more skillfully than anyone had ever done before—and with greater enjoyment. After an elaborate ritual of preparation, I began the actual eating process, commenting, "Hmm, even the temperature differential of the sour cream and hot potato is right."

My date knew that I was exaggerating, but she also knew—because we were friends—that even the simple act of eating a good meal was now far more pleasurable for me than it had ever been.

I had gradually exorcised many of those terrible fears of my childhood, those guilt-bearing devils that plagued my first quarter-century of life. I had begun to enjoy the good things in life with the explicit intention of finding pleasure and yet not feel guilty.

And if the rest of the evening that stretched ahead of us concluded the way that I hoped it would, I could definitely enjoy that with no qualms at all. However, and this is the im-

portant change, if the evening did no_
well, that would be all right too.

My growing-up process had reached the poin_
actual act of sexual intercourse was no longer necessary
date to be, on my terms, "successful." I was slowly beginning
to appreciate the greater values of love and friendship, and I
was working to achieve both. I felt that I had come a long
way.

Only a few short years ago, if an attractive woman had
walked up to me at work, or in the school library, just to ask
an impersonal question, within seconds I would begin to
tremble. My stomach would churn and I would feel the sweat
begin. Now, I could relax because of certain changes I had
undergone.

In the past, when I wanted the admiration and love of a
woman, I used to feel that I had to prove something to her.
The fact that I might be lovable just as I was and not because of something I had done was difficult for me to accept.
At the Center, every satisfying reward I received had been
granted because my behavior met the required standards.
Now, I realized I did not have to perform to win love.

I began to feel much more comfortable giving and receiving physical affection. From the time we left our parents'
apartments to be raised as Center children, the Little Brothers
and the Little Sisters were deprived of normal gestures of affection—physical gestures such as hugging, hand-holding, and
kissing.

When I had first attempted to make love to women, or
even to get at all close to them physically, I found that the
slightest touch would be so pleasurable that I could almost
have stopped right there. (The only experience in my youth
that was even comparable was the odd but almost ecstatic
feeling I would have while getting a haircut, a feeling that
would last for several minutes afterward. Being touched, even
though incidentally, was so unusual as to be very special.)

But the change that has had the greatest impact on my
day-to-day life was learning to be more open. I was now beginning to make friends, friends of both sexes, and I was no
longer worried about telling a friend my worries or fears. I'm
sure what I am talking about will sound strange to many
people because they have never had any difficulty being open
and direct with others. But for me, and for many other Cen-

children, that basic human experience was a long time in coming.

I don't kid myself that I have solved all my problems. But for years I had viewed other people in either one of two ways—as those who might punish me (the ironically named Angels) or as those who might turn me in (my fellow Little Brothers and Sisters). I no longer feel that way about people. And that change, I know, is healthy.

Epilogue

Writing this story, my "life story," was every bit as hard as I thought it would be. There were many moments when it was painful to continue, most often those times when I was trying to get at my deepest emotions. During such moments, the tension and the stomach pains of my youth returned, and it was as if the intervening years had never been. Soon my clothes would be soaked with perspiration, and I would have to take a walk to distract myself, to calm myself.

Near the end of the writing I realized that it wasn't just the reliving that was bothering me. I was worrying about the final visit that I would soon be making to St. Benedict Center for my last bits of information. Because I knew that the Center would resent it, I had kept my work secret, but the suspense of awaiting the reactions of the people I'd grown up with increased every day. Horrible dreams, which I hadn't had in years, began to plague me at night; during the day, I assured myself that the Center had changed.

And it certainly *had* changed, particularly in the last few years. To the great surprise of many who remembered him from Sunday afternoons on the Boston Common, Father Feeney was restored to good standing within the Catholic Church. And, of great importance to the Center's future, two of the Brothers were ordained as Catholic priests by the bishop of Worcester. Soon the local and Catholic press contained detailed accounts of the "homecoming."

Briefly, what had happened was that the Catholic Church had finally concluded it was being inconsistent in its treatment of Father Feeney and his followers. The ultimately successful argument was that if liberals whose beliefs bordered on what everyone in the Church once considered heresy were allowed to belong and to flourish, which was obviously the case, what point was there in keeping out a small band of ultratraditionalists.

It should have been a happy moment for all concerned, but it wasn't, for the simple reason that once again there was internal dissension at the Center. Ever since the death of Sister Catherine there had been highly charged factionalism, and arguments sprung up over even small decisions that had to be made. Clearly, the opportunity to rejoin the Church would be no exception, and when the time came, it was not.

Since 1970, about two years after Sister Catherine died, the Center had been split into two, and later three, and for a while even four distinct groups. The rivalries and the suspicions were so intense that these groups often treated one another in worse fashion than they had ever treated outsiders. One group—the most recently formed—even resorted to occasional violence (pushing, shoving, and shouting of phrases filled with hatred) to accomplish its ends. It could be said, and not unfairly, that with most of the children now gone, some of the Center's adults were beginning to act like children.

Saint Therese's House, the largest group, was the section of the Center most respected by the outside world. Its superior or head, the newly ordained Father Simon, had led his group away from the practices that had caused so much trouble in the past. Dictatorial decision-making was replaced by a more democratic process; the pressure on children to remain in the order against their will had been slackened; and married couples were no longer considered to be full religious members. Moreover, St. Therese's group was providing jobs for some of the husbands who had left to take care of their families. (I heard this cost the Center forty to fifty thousand dollars per year.)

St. Therese's group had joined the Church and was now being gradually incorporated into the Benedictine Order. The other two groups refused to join because they wanted a clear declaration from the Church that they were correct in their doctrinal teaching that there is no salvation outside the Catholic Church. Ironically that question was not settled—or even addressed openly—by the parties involved in the reconciliation. The members of St. Therese's group were merely given the right to exist as part of the Catholic Church. Their beliefs in the doctrine of salvation have changed only in that they regard their original position as an opinion. They no longer consider those that fail to agree entirely with them as heretics.

Personally, I was heartened by the changes at the Center. For one thing, it would make my final interviews a lot easier to conduct. I had many, many questions to ask the adults of the original Center.

I wanted to search more deeply into the why of the parents' turning over the children for communal upbringing; the vows of celibacy; the dissolution, for all practical purposes, of their marriages. I hoped to gain a better understanding of the environment, the pressures, and the high ideals that motivated them. I wanted to know what they now thought of Father Feeney and Sister Catherine. (How, I wondered, did Father Simon's group now view Sister Catherine? Did they still approve of some of her earlier Center policies?)

I expected that few people would be candid with me. Even the married couples who had left would probably be guarded in their statements, for the Center still meant a lot to them. After all, it had been their home, their very life, for over twenty years. What's more, some of them were financially indebted to it by reason of employment or loans.

I particularly wanted to speak to the children with whom I'd grown up. I wanted to ask them how they now felt about their upbringing. What *did*—or did not, despite rumor—happen on this or that occasion? How had the Center affected their lives?

I knew that many of the children were very bitter about their past. Some couldn't bear to bring back memories. Others refused to visit the Center because to do so actually made them tremble. I hoped most of them could open up without fear of repression; however, I knew some had tried before and were quickly silenced. Recently, when reporters and TV cameras were allowed on the Center property, and the viewers in Boston were to get a first-time glimpse into life at the Center, some children had planned to "spoil" things. They wanted to tell the world what the Center had been like in the past, but at the last minute friends and relatives convinced them not to talk.

Most of all, I wanted to speak to my mother. I had on old letter promising that she would detach herself from us, as Sister Catherine had always asked. I wanted to find out what had caused her to write it. Had Sister Catherine or anyone else put pressure on her to give us up? I didn't know how willing, if at all, she would be to tell me. I was anticipating many problems, both from her and from St. Therese's House.

As it turned out, things went smoothly. No one tried to stop me, though there was obvious tension over the matter. The strongest objection was merely a hint of disapproval: their reasoning was that any book involving the Center should include everyone's input, collected over years of research, and there were many, I was told, who would never cooperate. I suppose I was expected to throw up my hands and give up.

However, overt pressure to desist in my work started two weeks after I returned to California. One of the original Center children told me over the phone that she had received very strong complaints from her family and the Center. She was adamant. "Nobody had objected while you were there because it happened so fast, and you appeared so determined anyway. Sure, you have a right to write your *own* story, but it should not be published for a hundred years." I knew I was about to lose a close friend, and I feared that loss was only the beginning.

The night I arrived at the Center I told Father Simon that I was writing the early memories of my life. His immediate response was "Why?"

"Because I think it is a story that should not go untold. I want to know if you will cooperate in answering some questions."

Father Simon and several others were anxious to straighten out some of my "wrong ideas." They were careful to point out that the mistakes of the early Center were not the fault of Father Feeney or Sister Catherine. The separation of the children from the parents was suggested by one of the Center couples. Only after two years of persuasion did Father Feeney and Sister Catherine make it the policy for the other couples. It was the same situation for the vows of celibacy. Two of the twelve young couples thought it would be a supreme sacrifice. Within two years, all the other couples had also "volunteered." The final separation of the couples—husbands and wives living in separate quarters—was required by Father and Sister Catherine when the Center moved to the country and had separate buildings for the men and women. Again the couples were free to comply or leave the Center, as one couple did. That couple, however, eventually had to take the Center to court before they could recover the money the Center made when it sold their house in Cambridge.

According to Father Simon, Father Feeney and Sister

Catherine would never force anything on the Center members. Rather, they acted more as a stabilizing influence, tempering the enthusiasm of the young members. However, most of the original Center couples I spoke to said that pressure *was* used. They believed in the cause of the Center, and it was made quite clear to them that if they didn't volunteer to do what all the others were volunteering to do, they would have to leave. My mother told me she cried each time she had to give up one of her children.

As I listened to the complimentary stories about Sister Catherine, I began to wonder if the people who told them really believed she had not manipulated them. They said she hadn't, yet they also gave all the evidence that she had.

Sister Catherine, I suspected, took advantage of the enthusiasm of youth, its strong desire to break away from the establishment and express its own ideas. One week these youths were students at Harvard, the next they were teaching courses at the Center. And it went further than that. The Center had its own publication, and the students' writings were suddenly being published alongside articles by the famous Jesuit literary figure Father Feeney, or Richard Cushing, the archbishop of Boston, or someone like Clare Boothe Luce.

The more information I collected about Sister Catherine, the more I became convinced of her manipulation. For one thing, she seemed to be an exception to her own rules. She broke silence whenever she chose. I learned that one of her pastimes at her home was watching TV, which was strictly forbidden for Center members. (Her favorite shows were cowboy movies, the *FBI*, and *Perry Mason*.) All the couples had to turn in their wedding rings, but she kept hers on, and when it wore out, she selected one of the Center couple's rings that happened to fit. I was told that she still wears it to this day in her coffin.

Father Avery Dulles, S.J., one of the cofounders of the Center and one of Sister Catherine's many godsons, said that she was one of the most extraordinary persons he had ever known. She was a very charismatic person who had an enormous power to attract people and incite enthusiasm. He said she had an uncanny ability to assess people and knew how to bring out their best qualities. (Avery Dulles left the Center in its earliest days to enter the Jesuit Order.)

The Center members noted that Sister Catherine was the first to recognize that liberals were destroying the true Faith from within the Church. The articles in the Center publication *From the Housetops* support this claim of her early concerns. While everyone else was writing about "Catholics and Communism," or "Oddity and Obscurity in Hopkins," or "The Real Largeness of Chesterton," Sister Catherine was sounding the warning in such articles as "The Failure of Inter-Faith, A Plea for No Appeasement" (why should we make terms with Christ's enemies), and "Disasters in Education" (the anti-Catholicism of secular universities like Harvard). It wasn't long before the Center school was flourishing with Harvard dropouts. Within a year or two, other student-writers from the Center joined in her attack against the liberals in the Church.

Almost two years before Father Feeney was silenced by the Church, Sister Catherine had written an article titled "A Bishop and His Queen," imagining a future clergyman who rises to become Pope. He is driven by his love of Our Lady and becomes another Saint Athanasius (*contra mundum*—against the world), thundering the Truth despite the suffering it brings on his people. "And they said of him that he bore the whole of the twentieth century on his shoulders, that he had saved the Faith in his age, as Athanasius had in his." I wonder if Father Feeney ever expected to be so glorified by his strong stance on behalf of the Faith.

Four months before Father Feeney was silenced, four years before he was excommunicated, and five years before *The Point* (the Center's second periodical) started exposing the conspiracies of the Masons and the Jews to overthrow the Church, Sister Catherine outlined the plots of the devils who were conspiring to seduce the Church. In an article titled "Rebuke Him, O God," Sister Catherine described devils in hell on the "Committee on Salvation Outside the Church" worrying about the "plague of a priest" who is spoiling their grand scheme to destroy the Catholic Faith through the inter-faith movement.

I was very grateful to the Brother at the Center who gave me copies of these publications, particularly *The Point*. It was a four-page monthly publication that started in 1952 and ran for about seven years. Reading it, I got the impression that its writers were having a very heady time. With total freedom, they used their sarcastic wit against the world. Clearly, no one restrained them. One wonders about the Center's editorial judgment when the martyrdom of the twelve-year-old St.

Agnes is described as flippantly as "The removal of a head by a sword is a process that varies little with individual performances. In this sense, Agnes' martyrdom was, if not routine, regular."

The Point apparently reechoed the Center's preaching on the Boston Common, but in somewhat more controlled language. It insulted Harvard University in every way possible. When commenting on the suicide leap of a famed professor of literature, F. O. Mattheissen, "probably the most representative of all Harvard teachers" (to use *The Point*'s words), the unsigned author wrote: "Harvard had considered Matthiessen's brains one of its most valuable assets, and it was upset to find them splashed vulgarly across a Boston pavement."

In February 1953, *The Point* published an open letter to President Eisenhower: "And here is what I have to tell you, Dwight Eisenhower, Mr. President, head of our great nation: Unless you become a Catholic . . . before you die . . . you will never save your soul." Toward the end of the letter, it said, "The end of some of our past Presidents has been sad, indeed. President Harding's, for instance, and President Wilson's, and very much indeed, President Roosevelt's. I do not want your end to be such a one. . . ." It was signed by Father Leonard Feeney.

Most of *The Point*'s eighty-four installments, however, were devoted to attacking the Masons and the Jews, who, the authors claimed, united to destroy the Church. "Thus was established the great alliance in the empire of Satan: the Masons and the Jews; the Masons with their power, controlling government and business, plotting and planning at the highest levels, the Jews with their influence controlling the press and entertainment, insinuating their nervous, impure, infidel values into all of society, and corrupting it to the core."

What struck me about the Center's attacks on the outside world was not who was attacked or how, but the apparent necessity for someone or something to be attacked. As one blunt ex-member put it, "We couldn't keep attacking people in the Church, so we got off on that anti-Semitic kick." It was during those seven or eight years of *The Point*'s publication that the married couples gradually turned into religious members. All the Center adults talk about the great unity they had in those early days when they were fighting the outside world.

But once the separations were complete, the Center ceased its ferocity; their books contained only harmless stories on the saints, and their bookselling operation boomed. It was also during those years of excitement that Father's and Sister Catherine's authority became strengthened. The democratic process would never have worked, I was told. Fast decisions had to be made in the midst of each crisis. Center members didn't question why so-and-so suddenly left their ranks. In a few years, all the older members (though they believed in the Center's crusade) were dismissed. Only the young healthy booksellers remained.

On the last of my three-day stay at the Center, Father Simon asked me if my book would hurt their work. I told him that as long as he admitted that grave mistakes had been made, that Sister Catherine was not saintly, and that the Center was no longer the same Center of the past, then no one could blame his present organization. He said that every saint made mistakes, and that Sister Catherine had the highest intentions though she tended to rule with her heart and could go to extremes. As far as the upbringing of the children was concerned, he said that Sister Catherine had been of the old school: she had believed in corporal punishment.

He surprised me by saying that the rubber hose she used was called "Miss Mason," because he, Father Simon, had once told her that he had been punished with one as a child by a lady of that name. (I had never heard that name before. We children always called it the Big Punisher.)

I also saw, and tried to talk with, Father Feeney several times. He just stared at me, saying nothing, and when asked by someone else, I declined to go to Confession to him. He was eighty years old and very ill with Parkinson's disease. The Sisters of St. Anne's House would spend many hours each day helping him go to and from his room downstairs to the car or upstairs to the chapel. I was told he recognized people, but had great difficulty in speaking. Father Feeney died about a year later.

That same week (and, subsequently, by phone) I spoke to several of the children who had left the Center. Only six of the original thirty-nine children are still at the Center. Their stories brought back sharp memories. When they were little, several said they tried to be holy by imitating the stories of the saints. Their stories of penances were amusing. One Little Sister ate saltines dipped in warm water, and another slept on a hard block of wood instead of a pillow. There were children who flogged themselves with ropes in their little hermitages, or who made crowns of thorns and pressed them on their heads.

The happiest memories of the youngest children involved nature—playing in Slaves' Field, riding the ponies in the woods, or running through the fields in spring. The older children who had not been taken away from their families until the age of four, five, six, or seven put a greater value on the community meetings. They viewed each one as an opportunity to be with someone special. But none of them felt they could open up and actually tell their parents about their fears and worries.

The worst memories of the children involved the fear of punishment, the horror of hell, and terrible guilt before the eyes of God. Each had his or her own vivid memory about the stories of devils burning the beds of saints or carrying off souls to hell. There were many sleepless nights for those scared children who believed the devils would get them.

But the children seemed most emotional when they talked about how the Center affected their present lives. The most prevalent theme was love—or rather the total lack of any conception of what love was about. They found they couldn't open up emotionally and form deep friendships. The result was extreme loneliness. Some found escape in alcohol or other drugs.

The Little Sisters (I spoke to seven of them) were very sensitive about the Center's way of denying the attractiveness of being feminine. They told me how inferior they felt; they thought they were ugly, or stupid, or unsociable. One remembered wishing she had no breasts when they started to show. The Little Sisters I spoke to said they never really believed they could be loved, and I knew just what they meant. After leaving the Center, when they were shown physical affection, they either were overwhelmed by the sweet novelty of it, or they were cynical, thinking that it was only sex that men were after. Many of the children saw their biggest problem as learning how to express their emotions, to somehow slip out of their shells and develop real friendships.

There were also several funny stories about the Center's efforts to hide anything to do with sex. Some of the children speculated that the dogs were boys, and cats were girls. Others searched the dictionaries only to find that every key word had been inked out. The older children tended to be so guilt-ridden from fear of hell in punishment for impure thoughts that they simply didn't *try* to figure out the facts of life. It wasn't until the children left the Center—at ages ranging from sixteen to twenty-four—that they heard or read what sex was about. At that time only eight of the thirty-two children who left the Center were married. The original Center children now ranged in age from twenty-three to thirty-two and half of them are twenty-six or older.

The Little Sisters had many interesting stories. They were not told anything about menstruation until they experienced their first period and had the courage—or fear—to ask what was happening. The Angel told each one "not to worry, all girls got it, even Our Lady had it." The Angels and the girls called it "Emy," and the boxes of Kotex were carefully hidden in the attic and covered with a blanket. The younger Little Sisters wondered why the older ones were rattling paper bags in the cubicles. (They eventually found out that they should give their Angel a paper bag with the used Kotex to be burned by a Big Sister in an incinerator.)

Many of the Little Sisters were scolded and even punished for "G.A.-ing" (Getting Attention). If they were caught smiling or looking toward the Little Brothers, Sister Catherine would get furious. It was then that she broke into her worst descriptions of hell, sending all the children trembling to bed. One Little Sister, age eleven, was punished by three different Angels in one day for G.A.-ing.

I learned that the punishments for the Little Sisters were similar to what happened to the Little Brothers. Just about every Little Sister got the rubber hose at some point in her life. Some of them also mentioned more than one hose. I was very surprised to hear that, as the old hose wore out, replacements appeared. There was a black hose, a red one, and a green one. The Little Sisters would be required to lie down on the bed and bury their heads in the pillow, looking away so they couldn't see the hose. One Little Sister told me she had her head wrapped in a blanket so her screams wouldn't be so loud. Sister Catherine would then pull up their dresses and lash at their bare backs, thighs, and legs. Often they had to remove the blue bloomers they wore, leaving just the white panties, and occasionally they had to take off even those. The number of lashes would run anywhere from five to thirty, except for the really bad ones, who got it up to one hundred times. The Little Sisters talked a lot about the welts, the bruises, the black-and-blues that covered their thighs and legs. Most were very bitter about the experience.

Then there were the unusual punishments. The Little Sister who wet her bed the most was kicked down the stairs in the morning as she went to the bathroom to wash the sheets. Later, she received the rubber hose. Twice she was confined to her cubicle all day, tied to the bed with ropes. Occasionally she had to sleep at night in an empty bathtub.

Another punishment was having to get up and go to the bathroom every time one of the nineteen other Little Sisters went during the night. Other punishments used included isolation, when no one talked to you for days; the bread-and-water diet; eating cold leftovers from a previous meal if you didn't finish everything on your plate; and sitting on the lawn in silence for one week during recreation periods. Many of the Little Sisters couldn't eat their meals, they were so nervous. As with the boys, vomiting was common.

I found it odd that one Little Sister often spent her playtime spanking her doll with the back of her crucifix.

I spoke to nine of the boys, spending the greatest amount of time with J.M. In general they all found it difficult to open up emotionally and form deep friendships. None of them had close friends during his entire life at the Center. The reason all gave was distrust. You lived in constant fear of being punished, and turning another in could save *your* skin.

Excess punishment for trivial offenses was common. One could be beaten for not polishing the lower rim of one's shoes, or eating with one's little finger sticking out, or because one's hat fell off the hook. Face slapping was so frequent that to this day some of the children are still head-shy.

Without question, J.M.'s punishments were the worst, and during the morning I spent with him he went on and on coolly describing them. The litany of punishments is too long to mention, but included among them are all-day beatings with the rubber hose, burning with hot water, burning with a match, wearing a girl's dress with a bow in his hair, isolation from everyone for days, bread and water for a week, no food for a week, no desserts, food mixed up into an unappetizing mush, being tied to a bed to prevent eating during a starvation punishment, being tied down for a beating (this was rare—only a dozen times at the most), no movies, and so on.

He said that the most horrible punishment was when the

Angel sat on your head, almost smothering you while she beat you. In a flash of humor he said that there were benefits to Center life. "I have no cavities because I never was allowed dessert, and we rarely had candy." (That is true; almost everyone raised at the Center has excellent teeth.)

J.M. told me that as far as he knew, biting insects were never actually used. The Angel only threatened it. She claimed that there were biting ants in the cold mash she was applying to his bare bottom. He screamed as though it hurt because he didn't want to be given something worse, like the hose.

At twenty-three, J.M. is a blond, stocky, powerful-looking man who is fiercely independent, yet talks in a gentle tone. As he described his memories, he kept leaning forward, his hands clenched, and occasionally folding his arms tightly against his chest. At other times he placed one of his powerful hands against his stomach as though suppressing some pain. Yet, in cold, calm, determined language he continued to describe his punishments. His wife (tall and beautiful with dark hair) sat coolly in a chair the whole time, looking back and forth between Shane, their eighteen-month-old son, and her husband.

In the conversation he casually referred to some scars on his hand from a motorcycle accident last summer. At forty mph, he was struck by a car on the freeway and sent sprawling on the pavement, his wife clinging onto him. His skin had been torn and bruised; he had had a huge hole in his elbow, a broken foot, a sorely twisted shoulder and hip; and he had looked very bloody. But he had continued his journey another eighty miles to his home. "The only difficulty was my broken foot," he said. "I couldn't shift the gears easily."

The main reason for J.M.'s defiance was his fierce independence. If he didn't care to obey, no amount of punishment would break him. The Angel would lock him outside the corridor in the rain and cold, and he would spend a whole afternoon shivering. Once he thought of escaping across the river to Fort Devens. As he put it, "Life had to be easier elsewhere, I figured."

When I asked if his life now was in any way affected by his upbringing, he readily dismissed it. He was, he said, perfectly normal. His wife thought so too, though she was surprised at what had happened to him. (J.M. had never told her before.) She knew that he had been beaten a lot, by "some vicious nuns," and that the dent on the side of his skull came from being hit with a metal dustpan brush, but that was all she knew.

That same weekend, I spoke with John, the Little Brother who had the breakdown. He is my age, twenty-seven. Everything considered, he was doing very well. He had lost weight, looked good, and was carrying a full-time job as a cabinet-maker, his favorite occupation. He seemed to find a certain peace and satisfaction coming back to the workshop of his boyhood days and doing his carpentry. The Sisters of St. Anne's House had agreed to pay him to do a shrine for a statue of the Infant of Prague. He told me that it was healthy for him to work on projects like that.

I was amazed at his strength of character. He told me that his emotional problems were hereditary; his uncle and aunt had had similar difficulties. He felt, though, that the resultant tensions from the contrast between the Center's upbringing and life in the world had set it off. When someone would remind him of something fearful, he said, he would look away, take a few deep breaths, and smoke a cigarette or two until the image passed.

He told me about his fears that he would not have enough money to pay for his room and board, and how he wished he could afford a private psychiatrist and a private hospital. He went on to say that he was really an entirely different person when he was out in the world. He looked huge, powerful, and no one dared to mess with him. He kept repeating, "No one knows where I'm from or where I'm going."

While admiring his amazing handiwork and his intricate carvings, I was struck by the remembrance that here was someone who only seven years earlier had studied Thomistic philosophy and integral calculus.

I spoke with his parents, who told me that they had just found an excellent private psychiatrist. They hoped that the Center might help with the expense, but so far it had not.

Their comment made me more aware of the predicament that the adult Center couples found themselves in. They had given up their whole lives, all their possessions, to the Center. Now they had no hope for retirement; they all expected to work to the day they died. The lucky ones had children who offered to send them on paid vacations and showed promise of possibly being able to help them financially in their later years. But in general most of the children were just as poor. (Only five of them have college degrees.)

And then there was my conversation with the Little Brother, now twenty-six, who had been beaten so severely right in front of all of us. He said those who had punished him had said they were sorry, and that was good enough for him. However, he was still very bitter against Sister Catherine's old regime. He had even seriously considered suing them.

He felt badly for his father, who kept begging his wife to take off her nun's habit and return to him. After years of trying to convince his mother of her duties as a married woman, this son cut off communication with her. His life had been very harsh all along; yet, by managing a Seven–Eleven store, he was proving his determination to make it on his own. However, it took him years of odd jobs to get there. After getting kicked out of the Center, he was put in military school; then he joined the army, did a two-and-a-half-year stint in Vietnam, where he saw the worst side of war, went AWOL for a while, got an honorable discharge, and then bummed around for several years. I was impressed by his ability to bounce back.

The only other Little Brother sent from the Center to that same military school rebelled against established authority. Real life wasn't satisfactory; he started living in an imaginary world, telling fantastic tales to his acquaintances about his near misses with underworld gangsters. Yet, it was quite real when he became involved in some unknown offenses and was arrested by the FBI, sent to federal prison, and released on parole a year later.

I was particularly interested in finding out about the other family that had left the Center shortly after my father first won his case in Massachusetts. I learned that Sister Catherine had used the identical procedures to turn the children against the worldly parent as she had done with the five Connor boys. This time "the villain" happened to be the mother. The children became convinced, for a while, that their mother was possessed by the devil. They called her "devil" and insulted her continually. One child suggested killing her. Another actually poisoned her coffee with iodine, but she smelled it in time.

The children finally adjusted to the world, but not immediately after being beaten up for their "Mary names" (there were two boys, but like me they have Mary in their names) and for their blue-and-white uniforms. It took three years for the two oldest to find friends. One of the girls rebelled against all authority, started drinking, and was in a reform school by the age of thirteen. All four children were on drugs for some time.

I had spoken to the children who I knew had it the worst. Their revelations strengthened my determination to see our story told.

The most arduous task of that weekend was getting myself to tell my mother that I was writing my memoirs. Because I wanted her to tell me about her past, I kept postponing my announcement, hoping she might catch on gradually and not suddenly refuse to talk to me. We talked for two nights, five or six hours each time, and ending usually around 1:00 A.M.

On the first night I asked her about old times: her family and our births. I was not prepared for the story that unfolded. When I went to bed that night, I cried as I realized what a great woman she was. I never before felt so proud being one of her sons.

Her troubles began when she was fourteen, and her mother was dying of tuberculosis. Three nights a week my mother slept in the same bed with her mother, to take care of her more easily. Her father, a fireman, was away on duty at the station. In the last stages, when hospitalization was required, my mother changed (Catholic) high schools so she could be close by and visit her mother every day after school. This continued for two years, to the bitter end, when her mother became delirious and no longer recognized even her own husband.

My mother would go from school to the hospital, and then home, where she cooked for the family: her father, sixty-seven years old; Fran, a half-brother, twenty-eight years old; her brothers Jim, twenty-one years old, and John, sixteen years old. Her only sister, Edna, then nineteen years old, was already married. The rest of the family would visit the hospital two or three times a week. After several operations, when ribs were removed and the bad lung perpetually collapsed, my mother's mother finally succumbed at the age of fifty-two.

My mother continued to cook for her father until eight months later, when it was discovered that *she* had T.B. She was hospitalized a few weeks after her seventeenth birthday.

For the next two years she lived in a bed, writing to her friends and trying to complete high school. Once a week, air would be injected into her chest, collapsing her bad lung. This process continued for six years, though she was released from the hospital when she was nineteen. Being chronically short of breath, she learned not to overexert herself.

For the next eight years, she worked at various jobs while living at home and taking care of her father, who was then in his seventies. She dated off and on, she told me, and usually redheads like my father.

The Center came into her life when she heard that a famous literary priest whose poetry she had read and admired was lecturing on Thrusday nights in nearby Cambridge. Eventually, she became one of his admiring followers and took poetry classes from him.

It was at the Center that she met my father in July 1948. He struck her then as very persistent, "a bit of a show-off, but endearing in his own way." Dad was a hard worker, though, she said; he could be quite fussy when he came home, complaining about "neatness." Sometimes, she said, she would take one of us "babies" and go for a walk until she cooled off. But she said repeatedly that Dad had treated her "very well."

Next I learned the story of my own birth. It was three in the morning of February 6, 1950, when my mother realized that something was happening.

Being quite poor and having no telephone or car, my father ran down the street and got another Center couple to drive them to the welfare hospital in Lawrence. There they discovered for the first time that it would be a breach birth. For hours the doctor tried to turn me around, but he couldn't. The labor dragged on all that morning, all that day (February 6), all that night, all the next day (February 7), and all that night. At 11:00 P.M. I was finally born by cesarean—a nine-pound baby.

My four brothers were born, a little over a year apart, for the next four years, all by cesarean. But my mother fought each one out, trying to convince the doctor that it could be a natural birth. By the time of the last birth (Benedict) the doctors were strongly scolding her for taking such risks. She remembers hearing two doctors who happened to be brothers arguing, "But she'll kill herself if she continues this way."

"Oh, no, this is only the fifth cesarean. Our mother had seven."

"Yes, and she's dead."

My mother didn't worry about it. God would take care of her. Birth control was out of the question, and they wanted a normal husband-wife relationship. But then along came the vow of celibacy. God, in a manner of speaking, had solved the problem.

Then came the separation of the children. One of the couples, after years of arguing, convinced Father Feeney and Sister Catherine that the children should not be raised disparately, by different parents, but together under a uniform, well-controlled program. My mother said it was a real sacrifice for her, and she cried and cried each time one of us had to go. She told me the story of the time Michael and I went. Michael (three years old) was jumping up and down with excitement. "Mom, did you see my new bed?" And then, after all his excitement wore off, he asked, "Will you still tuck me in?" Up until that point, she had been heroically smiling, if torn inside. Now it all came out. Michael couldn't understand why she was crying.

It was late, and I still hadn't told her why I was asking so many questions. Strangely, she never asked. I did say that I thought she had had a rough life. She laughed and told me about the latest trouble: it had to do with the third group that had split off from St. Anne's.

The Sisters of St. Anne's decided not to let Brother Giles and his group of Sisters and Brothers use their chapel for Mass. Father Tom, Father Feeney's brother, came to the door with Brother Giles' group assembled behind him. He insisted on coming in and saying Mass for all. The Sisters let him in, but tried to keep Brother Giles' group out by locking the door. It was useless. In a matter of seconds wrecking bars were tearing down their door. They called the police, but they would arrive too late. The Sisters blocked the entrance.

Brother Albert and the rest plowed through, sending the Sisters sprawling to the floor. My mother felt Sister Gemma's body fall on hers as she lay on the floor. One of the stampeding Brothers stepped on her ankle as he rushed forward on his way to the chapel. A Sister from Brother Giles' group pointed a finger at my mother lying on the floor and said disdainfully, "The grace of God has departed from you."

The police finally came in time to hear Father Tom preach

piously from the altar that "None of this would have happened if the doors had been left open."

I had always felt that my mother was under great pressure from the factions in the Center, and now I sensed in her a slight disgust for the whole mixed-up situation. I told her that I wanted her to know she had five loving sons, all in college, all capable within a few years of supporting her for the rest of her life. She laughed, as though it would never be needed, but added, "It's very sweet of you to think of that, darling." She said that years ago, when Judge Wahlstrom had asked her on the stand what she would do if the Center ever fell apart, she had dismissed it as an impossibility. But now it seemed possible, she said.

On the second night, after talking at length about our personalities as children, I got ready to tell her that I was writing my memoirs. But I couldn't, and so the conversation continued to ramble. Eventually, I even told her about the severity of some of the punishments. She readily agreed that Sister Mary Judith and the others were wrong in going to such excesses. But she maintained that Sister Catherine was not at fault.

I told her that the reason she was saying that was not that she believed it, but that it was now the policy to regard Sister Catherine as a saint. I said she wasn't speaking out of deep conviction, but blindly, because of pressure from her community. She had not believed me, years ago, about Sister Mary Judith. Now, she did so only because Sister Mary Judith was no longer one of her own group.

Angry, I asked her why she couldn't just believe me *as her son*. I was saying harsh things to her, and it hurt me terribly. I wasn't really sure what it was that made her stick by Sister Catherine. I suspected my mother was torn within over what to do. Suddenly, I burst out crying. But unlike years earlier, now I wasn't ashamed.

I kept crying for the next half-hour as I told her what I was really up to. She learned that I had dropped out of business school six months earlier, that I was trying to make sense out of my life and my behavior, that I was looking for love, that I was dating girls, that I had gotten more intimate than I would admit, that I was at last enjoying life and experiencing some real happiness and peace, that I was torn over the problems of my past and trying to understand why I couldn't express my emotions . . . and that I had decided to write my memoirs.

Suddenly I realized that she was caressing my head, all the while kissing me and saying how much she loved me. She said I had been "overworking" all these years. She said she was delighted that I had taken some time off so I could straighten things out. She went on and on, and though I do not remember everything she said, I remember feeling uncomfortable about her caressing me.

I loved the idea of a mother saying she loved me, of having her hug me, yet somehow it felt odd coming from Sister Mary Agnes. Did she really love me as I thought a mother should?

For a moment I wished she would act like a nun. If she wanted to show her affection she should just agree with me that what had been done to the children by the Center was very wrong, that we children had a right to a family life, and that Sister Catherine and Father Feeney were ultimately responsible for destroying it.

At the same time, I wanted to push out of my mind the idea that my mother was a nun. I wanted her to be a warm, compassionate woman who loved her son no matter what he did, even if his actions were contrary to her beliefs or to what Sister Catherine would want. Yet somehow, in my mind, Sister Mary Agnes had become the conscience of Sister Catherine. If only she would repudiate Sister Catherine, I thought.

Bluntly, I asked her if Sister Catherine had ever pressured her into staying at the Center. Had she worked on her to become less attached to us? When she denied it, I told her I had the old Connor files, which the Center had turned over to me, and that in those files I had read the letter in which she, my mother, had promised Sister Catherine that she would detach herself from her children and be a good religious.

She appeared surprised, but not upset, and she wanted to know how many other letters I had. She said she could not remember the incident that might have prompted such a letter and that she would have to see it first.

I started talking against Sister Catherine and the Angels. As the words came out I still hoped she would agree with me. But she was strangely quiet. I stared at her, dazed in silence, many tears falling slowly.

As she soothed me she spoke in equally loving terms (or so

I thought) of Sister Catherine. That angered me. She knew everything now about what had been done to the children. For a moment, I hated her, but that feeling terrified me.

I tried to understand her. In a sense, she was a victim of the Center's separation of families. It was not her fault. Her priorities in life had been gradually wrenched from her and replaced with those of the Center. Religion was all that mattered. Her family was quite secondary. This realization was horrible.

I buried my face in my hands and she stopped the kind words for her religious superiors. In a flash, I remembered my mother's description of how she wept when her children were taken away. Even she must remember those feelings when we meant so much to her that she cried. I remained silent. Perhaps she loved us more than any mother ever loved her children, perhaps she had endured the pain of separation because she loved our souls and was concerned about our ultimate salvation. But that wasn't the kind of mother I wanted now.

I loved the dream of the real mother I might have known had she never been separated from us.

I started to smile. I guess I realized that it was at once hopeless and a relief. Why couldn't I accept her as she chose to be? More than twenty years ago she had set her goals to be those of the Center's leaders. No one, not her husband, not the courts, not the knowledge of the harm done to the Center children, and not even her own sons could dissuade her. She was first and foremost a nun, not a mother.

The next day as I was leaving, Sister Mary Agnes happened to mention that she was deaf in one ear. I was surprised. Her partial deafness was something I had never known, never even suspected. And then it hit me. I hardly knew her.

As the jet carried me back to the West Coast I thought about mothers and fathers, brothers and sisters. I wondered what it would have been like had I been part of a family.

Someday, I hope, I will know.

SIGNET and MENTOR Books of Special Interest

- [ ] **THE WORLD'S WEIRDEST CULTS edited by Martin Ebon.** From around the world, from the earliest dealings with the forces of evil to the terrible tragedy of the Jonestown death cult, here is a shocking but true look at the various strange beliefs which have flourished in the past and the bizarre groups which are still actively recruiting members today. (#J8767—$1.95)*

- [ ] **HOW THE GREAT RELIGIONS BEGAN by Joseph Gaer.** Revised and enlarged edition. Inspiring stories about the spiritual leaders who founded the world's great religions: Buddha and Jesus, Zoroaster and Mohammed, Martin Luther, and many others. (#E7764—$1.75)

- [ ] **THE BRAIN CHANGERS: Scientists and the New Mind Control by Maya Pines.** Winner of the American Psychological Foundation 1974 National Media Award and chosen by the Book-of-the-Month Club, this book is "A fascinating and lucid account of our emerging capacities to modify both brain and behavior."—**New York Times Book Review** (#J7855—$1.95)

- [ ] **SOUL MURDER: Persecution in the Family by Dr. Morton Schatzman.** A bizarre and frightening case of mental illness in which a son was driven mad by his own father. A devastating indictment of the system of inhuman childrearing that shaped the society that produced Hitler... "An enthralling psychiatric detective story!"—**Newsweek** (#ME1499—$1.75)

- [ ] **THE VARIETIES OF RELIGIOUS EXPERIENCE: A Study in Human Nature by William James.** With a Foreword by Jacques Barzun. The famous classic on the psychology of religion. (#ME1603—$2.25)

* Price slightly higher in Canada.

SIGNET and MENTOR Books You'll Want to Read

☐ **THE WORLD ALMANAC BOOK OF THE STRANGE** edited by The World Almanac. The most comprehensive exploration of the world of the mysterious, the bizarre, and the undeniably extraordinary. Includes pyramid power, the Loch Ness Monster, experiments with ESP, UFOs, and much, much more. (#E7784—$2.50)

☐ **THE PSYCHOPATHIC GOD: ADOLF HITLER** by Robert G. L. Waite. The most complete and shockingly revealing portrait of Hitler ever written . . . "The one most worth reading!"—Alan Bullock, author of **Hitler: A Study in Tyranny** (#E8078—$2.95)

☐ **DISCOVERING YOUR HIDDEN SELF: Exercises in Re-Creative Psychology** by Dr. Ann Frisch and Dr. Paul Frisch. Your personal guide to getting in touch with your feelings for a more creative, fulfilled life. (#E6994—$1.75)

☐ **UNDERSTANDING MEDIA: The Extensions of Man** by Marshall McLuhan. Here is the new spokesman of the electronic age who declares that down through the ages the means by which man communicates have determined his thoughts, his actions, his life. The most influential book by the most debated man of the decade. (#MW1493—$1.50)

☐ **THE NEW MUCKRAKERS** by Leonard Downie, Jr. An inside look at the new American heroes—the star investigative reporters . . . "The best book on the subject!"—**The New York Times Book Review** (#ME1628—$2.50)

THE NEW AMERICAN LIBRARY, INC.,
P.O. Box 999, Bergenfield, New Jersey 07621

Please send me the SIGNET and MENTOR BOOKS I have checked above. I am enclosing $_____ (please add 50¢ to this order to cover postage and handling). Send check or money order—no cash or C.O.D.'s. Prices and numbers are subject to change without notice.

Name _____

Address _____

City_____ State_____ Zip Code_____

Allow at least 4 weeks for delivery
This offer is subject to withdrawal without notice.